Dedicated to

Our parents, who inspired us throughout civil services preparation journey.

Our teachers, who have shaped us intellectually

&

Our dear aspirants community who toil in silence to build their careers in civil service.

Foreword

It gives me great pleasure and pride to write the foreword for this insightful work on Indian Society. I have known the authors, Ms. Ayushi Singh and Mr. Nityanand Jha, for several years and have witnessed their journey as officers. Both are deeply sincere and passionate about public service, and I have personally seen their relentless commitment to the welfare of people during our posting in Palghar district, Maharashtra. Their dedication has always been inspiring.

The authors bring with them rich first-hand experience of engaging with critical social issues such as inequality, poverty, women's empowerment, and tribal welfare. They have not only studied these challenges but also taken meaningful initiatives to address them in the field. This unique practical perspective has been woven into the book, making it especially valuable for aspirants, since real-life examples and applied insights carry immense weight in the Civil Services Examination. Truly, this book is a repository of such knowledge.

What further strengthens this work is the fact that both authors have themselves successfully navigated the Civil Services Examination. They understand its demands and the right approach needed to succeed. Their ability to present multiple dimensions of contested social issues, while encouraging aspirants to form balanced and informed opinions, is particularly commendable.

The book stands out for its comprehensive coverage of social issues, allowing aspirants to rely on a single source rather than dispersing their efforts across multiple references. It is, therefore, a highly recommended guide for all serious aspirants.

I congratulate the authors on bringing out this **second edition** of the book and wish them great success in its journey ahead. I am confident it will serve as a valuable resource for aspirants. My best wishes to all readers as they prepare with this book.

Ashima Mittal, IAS
AIR 12, CSE 2017
District Collector and Magistrate
Jalna, Maharashtra

August 2025

COUNTER THE COUNTERFEIT & BUILD A STRONG FOUNDATION FOR SUCCESS

Books are our best friends, is the adage we have grown up with. However, the pirates of piracy are continuously forging 'our best friends'. Our books and their supplementary online resources are copyrighted, and we don't lend any right-to-copy. Piracy is synonymous to stealing books.

Knowledge comes real, let's not encourage its counterfeit. Therefore, we appeal all our readers to discourage pirated books and **choose authentic ones**.

HOW TO IDENTIFY THE PIRATED BOOKS?

1 COVER AND SPINE

- Look and feel (new or used book)
- Blurred images on the cover
- Hologram pasted on front
- Defective spine (wrinkles) or air pocket at its bottom
- Unclear ISBN/bar codes
- Missing/non-operational Unique Coupon Code for exclusive access to McGraw Hill Edge

2 TEXT/PRINTING/BINDING

- Uneven inking of pages
- Poor quality or blurred photographs/images/charts
- Substandard paper quality and opacity
- Misaligned pages
- Missing pages
- Inferior binding quality

You can further watch this video on How to identify a pirated book

For more information about identifying piracy, visit https://www.mheducation.co.in/piracy

To report a pirated book, send 'Hi' on WhatsApp code given on the back cover or write to us at **support.india@mheducation.com.**

Reported pirated books are examined to combat their piracy.

Let's fight the Pirates of Piracy and resolve to go for original!

About the Authors

Ayushi Singh, a native of Uttar Pradesh, completed her undergraduate degree in Political Science (Hons) from Miranda House college, University of Delhi. She secured an impressive All India Rank of 86 in the Civil Services Examination (CSE) 2018, earning her selection into the Indian Administrative Service (IAS). During her training at the Lal Bahadur Shastri National Academy of Administration (LBSNAA), she simultaneously pursued a postgraduate degree. Her professional journey began as a Project Officer with the Integrated Tribal Development Project (ITDP) in Jawhar, Palghar, where she served for two years. Subsequently, she was appointed as the Chief Executive Officer (CEO) of the Zila Parishad in Gadchiroli, Maharashtra. She currently serves as the Additional Tribal Commissioner (ATC) in Nagpur.

Nityanand Jha hails from Madhubani district in Bihar and was raised in Guwahati, Assam. He is a graduate of the Indian Institute of Technology Kanpur (IITK), where he completed his B.Tech in 2014. During his undergraduate years, he also served as a Visiting Research Scholar at the National University of Singapore (NUS).

After graduation, he dedicated himself to mentoring civil services aspirants in New Delhi while preparing for the Civil Services Examination. His efforts bore fruit in CSE 2018, where he secured an All India Rank (AIR) of 128, earning him a place in the Indian Police Service (IPS), Maharashtra Cadre.

Following his training at the Sardar Vallabhbhai Patel National Police Academy (SVPNPA), he began his field career in September 2021 as Assistant Superintendent of Police (ASP), Palghar district. In November 2023, he was posted as Additional Superintendent of Police, Gondia district. He is currently serving as the Deputy Commissioner of Police (DCP), Nagpur City.

2

INDIAN SOCIETY

For Civil Services and State Services Examinations

AYUSHI SINGH, IAS | NITYANAND JHA, IPS

McGraw Hill Education (India) Private Limited

Published by McGraw Hill Education (India) Private Limited,
Registered Office: Anjana Complex No: 5/90A, Butt Road, St. Thomas Mount, Chennai - 600016

Indian Society, 2e

Print Edition:
ISBN (13) : 978-93-6444-303-6
ISBN (10) : 93-6444-303-9

E-Book Edition:
ISBN (13) : 978-93-6444-057-8
ISBN (10) : 93-6444-057-9

1 2 3 4 5 6 7 8 9 7101348 29 28 27 26 25

Printed and bound in India

Typeset at Insight Publishing Solutions, C-3, West Vinod Nagar, Delhi-110092
and printed at Rajkamal Electric Press, Kundli, Haryna-131 028.

Cover Image Source: Shutterstock

Cover Designer: Anita Kanojia

Visit us at: www.mheducation.co.in

Write to us at: support.india@mheducation.com

CIN: U80302TN2010PTC111532

Toll Free Number: 1800 103 5875

Preface to the Second Edition

This book is designed as a comprehensive and structured guide to address questions on *Indian Society* for the Civil Services Examination (CSE). The content is thoroughly researched to not only support aspirants in answering society-related questions but also to help them build informed perspectives for the essay paper and the final interview.

While Indian society is vast and dynamic, the topics have been curated to closely align with the UPSC syllabus and frequently asked questions. The focus is on analyzing issues and trends rather than merely reproducing facts. To aid better understanding, the material is supplemented with data, diagrams, and flowcharts wherever relevant.

A key strength of this book lies in its integration of current affairs and contemporary issues, enabling aspirants to rely on this as a single resource. The technique of linking current events with syllabus themes and keywords - crucial for effective Mains answer writing - has been demonstrated through examples in the book.

Another unique feature is that the book has been written from an aspirant's perspective. As former aspirants and now serving civil servants, we have experienced diverse aspects of Indian society firsthand and sought to reflect that understanding here. In this edition, we have also introduced *Debate Corners* to encourage brainstorming and critical thinking.

We believe that the concepts and explanations presented here will help aspirants develop a balanced outlook - an essential quality for success in the Civil Services. We sincerely hope readers find the book useful and effective, and we warmly welcome feedback and suggestions for its further improvement.

Nityanand Jha, IPS

Ayushi Singh, IAS

Preface to the First Edition

This book is meant to be a comprehensive and well-structured guide for answering Indian Society and related questions in Civil Services Examination (CSE). The well-researched content will also help candidates in forming informed opinions for the essay paper and answer questions at the final interview. Indian Society is a diverse and dynamic subject, yet the topics have been curated in a manner such that core UPSC syllabus and frequently repeated questions have been addressed. Emphasis is on the analysis of issues and trends instead of mere reproduction of facts. The content has been duly supported with data, diagrams and flow charts wherever necessary.

Another strength of the book is its attention to current affairs and the addition of dynamic issues so that the candidates can prepare from this single source. Linking current affairs topics with syllabus and keywords is an important skill for Mains answer writing, and candidates can understand this technique from the use of examples in the book. In addition, the most unique feature of the book is that it has been written from the perspective of aspirants. As former aspirants and now serving civil servants, we have seen diverse aspects of Indian society and tried to incorporate this in the book. We expect that the concepts and explanations given in the book can help sincere aspirants in developing a well-balanced approach, which is a much-needed quality in aspirants. We look forward to feedback and input on further improving this work.

Nityanand Jha, IPS

Ayushi Singh, IAS

Contents

1 Salient Features of Indian Society: Diversity of India

A. Features of Indian Society

1. Diversity of Indian Society

'India is a garden of all kind of flowers, and they know how to live with each other'.

– Afroz Taj

Often described as a 'melting pot' of cultures and languages, India, as a nation, is globally recognised for its diversity. It is the world's largest and most diverse democracy. Language, literature, culture, religion, and cuisine vary extensively as we traverse different parts of the country. These parameters of diversity are discussed below.

1.1 Multi-linguistic

Census 2011 recorded 19,569 mother-tongue names. However, all the 22 languages specified in the Eighth Schedule of our Constitution make up an overwhelming 96.72% of the Indian population, and the rest of the languages constitute 3.28% of the Indian population.

The Eighth Schedule of the Indian Constitution recognises 22 major languages in India. They are considered to be major literary languages in India, namely, Sanskrit, Assamese, Bangla, Bodo, Dogri, Gujarati, Hindi, Kashmiri, Kannada, Konkani, Maithili, Malayalam, Manipuri, Marathi, Nepali, Oriya, Punjabi, Tamil, Telugu, Santali, Sindhi and Urdu (Table 1.1).

All the States of India have different linguistic compositions, and all languages are minority languages in some States or others, depending on the number of speakers in a particular State. For example, Tamil is a major language in Tamil Nadu and Puducherry but a minority language in Odisha, West Bengal or any other State/UT beyond Tamil Nadu and Puducherry.

1.2 Multi-religious

The total population of the country in 2011 was 121.09 crores. Religion-wise population distribution is shown in Table 1.2.

All these religions and their practitioners have the freedom to flourish under a secular Constitution. It is important to note that these religions are not homogenous in nature. There is differentiation within these religious groups as well. For example, see Table 1.3.

S. No.	Language	Persons who returned the language as their mother tongue	Percentage to total population
1	Hindi	52,83,47,193	43.63
2	Bengali	9,72,37,669	8.03
3	Marathi	8,30,26,680	6.86
4	Telugu	8,11,27,740	6.70
5	Tamil	6,90,26,881	5.70
6	Gujarati	5,54,92,554	4.58
7	Urdu	5,07,72,631	4.19
8	Kannada	4,37,06,512	3.61
9	Odia	3,75,21,324	3.10

S. No.	Language	Persons who returned the language as their mother tongue	Percentage to total population
10	Malayalam	3,48,38,819	2.88
11	Punjabi	3,31,24,726	2.74
12	Assamese	1,53,11,351	1.26
13	Maithili	1,35,83,464	1.12
14	Santali	73,68,192	0.61
15	Kashmiri	67,97,587	0.56
16	Nepali	29,26, 168	0.24
17	Sindhi	27,72,264	0.23
18	Dogri	25,96,767	0.21
19	Konkani	22,56,502	0.19
20	Manipuri	17,61,079	0.15
21	Bodo	14,82,929	0.12
22	Sanskrit	24,821	N

Table 1.1 Scheduled Languages in Descending Order of Speakers' Strength - Census 2011 (N = Negligible)

Religions	Population in 2011 (cr)	Proportion of Population in %	Decadal change in proportion in % pts
Hindu	96.63	79.8	-0.7
Muslim	17.22	14.2	+0.8
Christian	2.78	2.3	No change
Sikh	2.08	1.7	-0.2
Buddhist	0.84	0.7	-0.1
Jain	0.45	0.4	No change
Others	0.79	0.7	-
Religion not Stated	0.29	0.2	-

Table 1.2 Religious Profile in India as per Census 2011

Religious Groups	Sects
Hindu	Vaishnavism, Shaivism, Bhakti and Shaktism
Muslim	Shia, Sunni, Alawites and Ahmadiyyas
Christian	Protestant and Catholic
Sikh	Khalsa, Namdhari and Nirankari

Table 1.3 Main Sects of Religious groups

1.3 Multi-racial

Race is a biological concept and refers to a group of people with similar inherited physical characteristics such as skin colour, facial features, type of hair, size of head, physique and blood groups.

In general, we use race and ethnicity in an interchanging way. In conceptual terms, race is different from ethnicity. The basic difference is that while race is biologically determined, ethnicity is culturally determined. Ethnicity refers to a group of people who identify each other on the basis of similarities such as common language, ancestry, religion, traditions, culture or nation.

Indian Anthropologist *B.S. Guha* classified the Indian population into six major racial groups. They are as follows (Fig. 1.1):

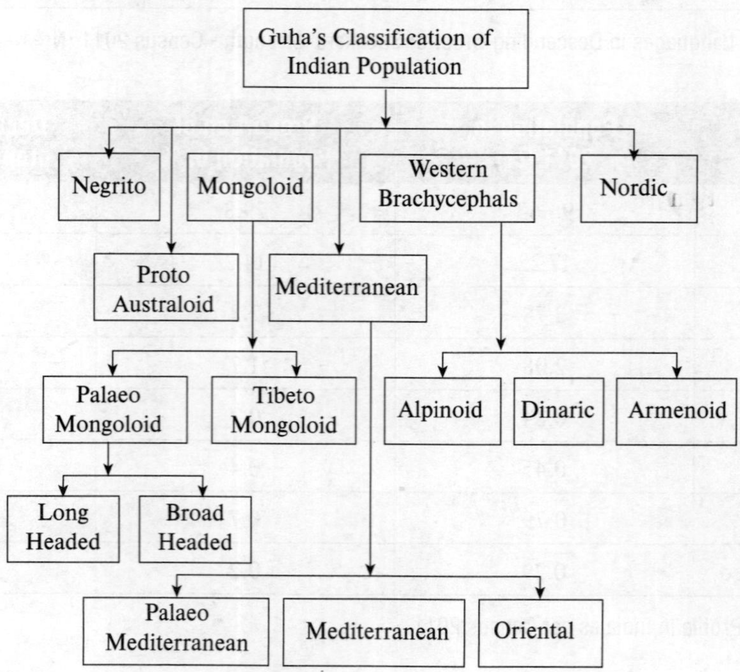

1. *The Negrito*: Perhaps they were the first group to arrive in the Indian sub-continent and are **considered** as true 'autochthones' of India. They settled in the hilly areas of Kerala and Andaman Islands. They have dark skin colour, spirally curved hair, small to broad head, flat or broad nose, and thick and everted lips.
2. *The Proto-Australoid*: Considered to be the second oldest oldest racial group to have settled in India, after the Negritos. The features of this racial group are found mainly among the tribal populations of Deccan, Central, Southern and Western India, e.g. Santhal, Bhil, Gond, Munda and Oraon tribes. They have short stature, dark brown to nearly black skin colour, broad and flat nose depressed at the root and wavy or curly hair.
3. *The Mongoloid*: They were originally from Mongolia (China). They came to India through passes in the northern and eastern mountain ranges. They are concentrated in the Himalayan region of Ladakh, Sikkim, Arunachal Pradesh and areas of Northeastern India. Their characteristic features include short height, scanty hair on the face and body, oblique eyes, flat face with prominent cheekbones, and straight hair. Its two sub-groups include:
   a. Paleo-Mongoloid Group: They are found mostly in Assam and the adjacent States.
   b. Tibeto-Mongoloid Group: They came from Tibet and are settled mainly in Bhutan, Sikkim and areas of the Northwestern Himalayas.
4. *The Mediterranean*: They arrived in India from Southwest Asia. This type has three sub-groups:
   a. Paleo-Mediterranean: They were the first racial group of this type to come to India. Perhaps they were one to have begun cultivation for the first time in north-west India.
   b. Mediterranean: They were linked to the Indus Valley civilisation and were believed to have initiated the bronze culture for the first time during 2500–1500 BC.
   c. Orientals: They are concentrated mainly in the region of Punjab and the north-west border of Pakistan. They are also found in Rajasthan and western Uttar Pradesh. They are represented by the Punjabis, the Chattris, the Bania of Rajasthan and the Pathans.

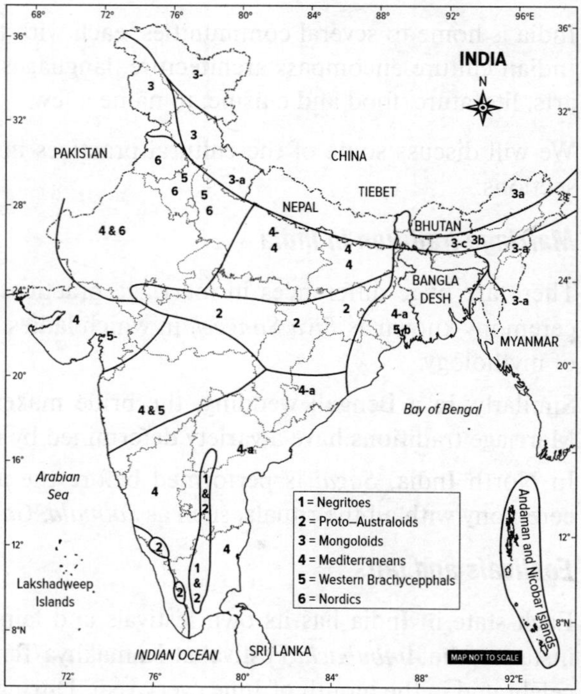

Fig. 1.1 Geographical Distribution of Racial Types among the People of India

(Source: B.S. Guha, *Census of India, 1931; Vol. 1- India; Part III-Ethnographical (A. Racial Affinities of the People of India)* (1935))

5. *The Western Brachycephals*: They were the ones with broad heads. They were divided into three groups:
   a. Alpinoid: The Bania of Gujarat and Kathi of Kathiawar represent this group.
   b. Dinaric: The people of Kathiawar, Coorg, represent this type.
   c. Armenoid: They are represented by the Parsis of Bombay, Vaidyas and Kayasthas (Bengal).
6. *The Nordics*: They were the last of the racial groups to have come to India. They had tall stature, long head and robust body built with fair complexion. They came to India probably from south-east Russia and south-west Siberia and entered India through Central Asia. They are mainly concentrated in the North-Western part of the country.

Debate Corner

"Is B.S. Guha's racial classification of India, developed in the early 20th century, still relevant for understanding the country's social and cultural diversity today, or does it reflect outdated perspectives in modern society?"

1.4 Multi-cultural

India is home to several communities, each with their own cultures and traditions. The elements of Indian culture encompass architecture, languages, films, music, handicrafts, visual and performing arts, literature, food and cuisine, to name a few.

We will discuss some of the cultural practices in India to appreciate the diversity in the following sections.

Marriage tradition in India

There are huge differences in marriage practices across India. For example, in Assam, there is a ceremony known as *Biya Sangeet,* in which ladies sing songs with ethical and moral values and tales of mythology.

Similarly, in a Bengali wedding, the bride makes entry by sitting on a *piri* lifted by two people. Marriage traditions have a variety determined by religion, caste, community and region.

In North India, *Sagai* is performed before the actual wedding. This is followed by the marriage ceremony with all the rituals, such as *Jaimala, Gathbandhan* and *Kanyadaan*.

Festivals and fairs

Each state in India has its own festivals and fairs. Importantly, each has its own significance. For instance, the *Ambubachi* Festival at Kamakhya Temple in Assam is the most important festival and is celebrated in the month of June every year. During this, the doors of the Kamakhya shrine are closed as it is believed that Goddess Kamakhya goes through her annual cycle of menstruation.

In the state of Bihar and Jharkhand, *Chhath* is the most important and revered festival. During this, devotees worship the Sun God (Surya) to show gratitude for sustaining life on earth.

While the Hornbill Festival is celebrated across Nagaland to encourage inter-tribal interactions and to protect, revive and promote the richness of the Naga heritage and traditions.

Apart from these, Onam in Kerala, Ganesh Chaturthi in Maharashtra, Baisakhi in Punjab and Pongal in Tamil Nadu are some of the most important festivals celebrated in India.

As far as fairs are concerned, the most notable ones include Kumbh Mela of Allahabad (now Prayagraj), UP, Pushkar Mela of Rajasthan, Sonepur Cattle Fair of Bihar, Surajkund Handicrafts Mela of Haryana, Medaram Jatara of Telangana, etc.

Food and cuisine

India's richness is in its culinary diversity. Each region is known for its specific dish with unique tastes, e.g. Vada Pav of Maharashtra, Litti Chokha of Bihar, Dal Baati Churma of Rajasthan, Dhokla of Gujarat, Masala Dosa of Tamil Nadu, etc.

Performing arts

Each State is known for its unique art form. Some States have classical dance as their treasure, while many regions are known for their folk art forms. For example, Bhangra of Punjab, Bihu of Assam, Ghoomar of Rajasthan and Lavani of Maharashtra are well-known folk dances.

Along with this, classical forms include Kathakali of Kerala, Kuchipudi of Andhra Pradesh, among others.

Despite the fact that this list is not exhaustive, it holds a mirror up to the cultural diversity of India. Such diversities can be seen in the fields of architecture, films, music, and visual arts as well, which we read about in the subject of Indian Culture.

2. Social Stratification in India: Caste, Tribe, Gender and Class

2.1 Caste

One of the most frequently used terms in India is 'caste'. Almost every Indian might be familiar with this term in one way or another, especially if one is from rural India. In rural areas, though, *Jati* is generally used in local connotation. The word 'caste' is derived from the Portuguese word *casta,* meaning pure breed.

Definition

Sociologists have defined 'caste' (locally referred to as '*Jati*') as 'hereditary, endogamous group', which is usually localised. It has a traditional association with an occupation and a particular position in the local hierarchy of castes.

From a historical perspective, the caste system as an institution is considered to be a characteristic of Hindu society. However, with time, the features of the caste system have extended even to non-Hindu communities such as Muslims, Sikhs and Christians.

One of the significant consequences of the presence of the caste system is that it creates social divisions. These social divisions have resulted in creating a 'stratified' society. Thus, people/groups have been ranked based on their caste status.

Social stratification, in simple words, means creating a hierarchy of people/group based on certain factors such as income and wealth, power, caste and gender.

Insight Box

Difference between *Varna* and *Jati*

Varna in Sanskrit means 'colour'. The first mention of *Varna* is found in the *Purusha Suktam* verse of the ancient Sanskrit *Rig Veda*. The term '*Jati*' is derived from the Sanskrit word '*jan,*' which literally translates 'to be born'. According to the classical Indian literature, the term '*Varna*' was used to define the caste structure. The Dharmashastras considered *Varnas* and *Jatis* to be the same. However, with time, it has been understood that the two terms are distinct from each other.

Varna came to be associated with 'social classes', while *Jati* came to be defined as a form of existence determined by birth. *Varna* is understood as an all-India phenomenon, while *Jati* is a localised endogamous group of families.

In numerical terms, there are only four *Varnas*, namely, *Brahmana, Kshatriya, Vaishya,* and *Shudra*, while on the other hand, there is no restriction on the number of Jatis. There are around 4000 Jatis in India.

There is no clear agreement on since when the caste system has been in existence. Various sociologists have different opinions on this. The four varna classification is considered to be around three thousand years old. However, it is to be understood that the meaning of 'caste system' has changed over different time periods.

For instance, in the late Vedic period, i.e. between 900 and 500 BC, the caste system consisted of only four major divisions. Theoretically speaking, caste system overlapped with the varna system. That is, it was a system of division based on occupation and had reasonable mobility. The social divisions in this period were not very elaborate or rigid. It was mainly based on division of labour and not determined by birth. Apart from this, people could move from one category to another, i.e. caste system behaved like an 'open system' in which social mobility was not only possible but also quite common. However, it was only in the post-Vedic period that caste became a rigid institution with strict rules for mobility.

Insight Box

Note: The term 'Scheduled Castes' is a legal designation. It was adopted as per the Government of India Act of 1935, which gave legal recognition to the lists or 'schedules' of castes and tribes. The British listed the lowest-ranking Hindu castes in a Schedule appended to the Government of India Act in order to provide statutory safeguards and other benefits. This is how the terms 'Scheduled Tribes' and 'Scheduled Castes' came into being.

Features of the caste system

The features of caste system are discussed below (Fig. 1.2):

1. *Caste is determined by birth*: A person inherits the caste of his father. It is not up to an individual to choose one's caste, change it, leave it or choose not to join it.
2. *Endogamy*: There are strict rules about marriage for the members of the caste. Generally, marriage is conducted between members of the same caste or sub-caste.
3. *Restrictions on inter-dining*: There are rules about the kind of food that could be eaten together or exchanged among castes.
4. *Hierarchy*: Caste involves a system in which people are arranged in a social and ritual hierarchy. A sense of superiority and inferiority is associated with this system. It is to be noted that hierarchical positions may vary from region to region. But hierarchy is the most socially salient aspect of the caste system.
5. *Segmental organisation of society*: It means that there can be sub-divisions within a particular caste. Thus, a caste may have sub-castes and sub-castes may also have sub-sub-castes.
6. *Occupational association*: Traditionally, each caste was linked to a particular occupation. They were even ranked on the basis of the purity of their occupations. The members of a caste could only enter an occupation associated with their caste. Members of other castes could not enter the occupation.

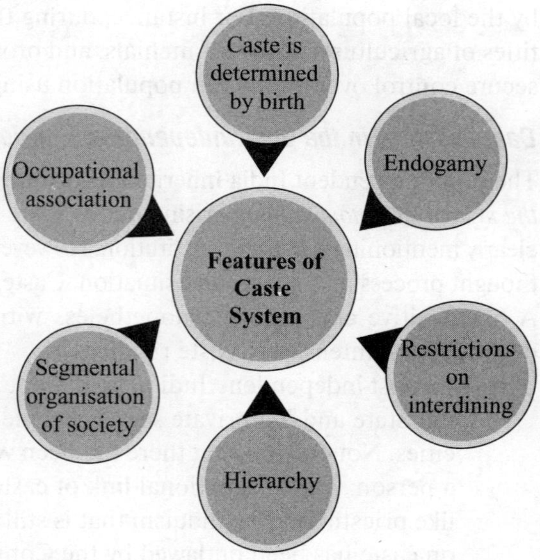

Fig. 1.2 Features of Caste System

One of the important features of the caste system that we can observe in the present day is the **formation of new castes**. This is mainly due to the adoption of new occupations by members of a caste. It results in new sub-divisions that ultimately become distinct castes. The Sadgops of Bengal were traditionally associated with cattle herding. In recent times, however, they separated themselves from a pastoral caste. They are now an independent agricultural caste.

Caste system during the colonial period

The colonial system significantly impacted the social institutions of India, particularly the institution of caste. For the first time, Britishers spent significant resources to categorise castes into a ranked system. Thus, the system of stratification became relatively more formalised. As a result of this, the rigidity of the caste system was further drilled deep into Indian society. The infusion of politics vis-à-vis the caste system further resulted in creating enormous and never-ending conflicts in Indian society. Historians believe that before the British invasion, caste system prevailed but it was flexible and mobility was relatively simple.

The British administration also conducted a census of the population. They categorised people as per their professions and even ranked them according to priority, whose weightage was determined by the local population. For instance, during the census of 1881, people were categorised under the titles of agricultural, artisans, menials, and professionals, among others. Such divisions were used to secure control over the Indian population using the policy of divide and rule.

Caste system in the post-independence period

The post-independent India inherited a system in which caste was a reality. The State wanted to *abolish the system of untouchability* arising out of caste discrimination and usher in social equity. It did so by clearly mentioning it in the Constitution. However, there were huge differences between the constitutional thought process and the ground situation. Caste, as a system, was resilient enough to survive.

A few positive changes were nonetheless witnessed in modern India. Such changes resulted in a decline in the intensity of caste rigidity.

- In post-independent India, significant development activities have been taken up by both the State and the private sector. People across castes worked together in industrial set-ups in cities. Not only this but there has been very little association between caste and occupation for a person. The occupational link of caste has significantly declined, but there are professions like priesthood in Hinduism that is still associated with specific castes. Discrimination based on caste has been outlawed by the Constitution.
- The positive discrimination policy, i.e. reservation policy in jobs and education, has ensured that members of the Dalit community are no longer considered polluted/impure in an organisation. Restrictions on food and drink no longer exist.
- The caste-based hamlets that we see in rural pockets are rare phenomena in urban set-up. In cities, people do not usually consider the caste of neighbours as economics becomes a more important factor as compared to other factors.
- Modern India opened up opportunities for higher education. The modern educated Indians were inspired by the liberal ideas of individualism and meritocracy and moved away from the traditional caste-based thought process. People are identified mainly on the basis of achievement, not caste identity.

However, as discussed above, the caste system was resilient enough. There were various avenues where the caste system was still prevalent.

- In the private sector, the employees were recruited on the basis of caste or kinship, whether it was the textile mills of Mumbai or the jute mills of Kolkata.
- Even though caste prejudice against the untouchables was not as strong as it was in rural India, it was still not absent in the city.
- One area where caste was still deeply instilled in the minds of people was in the cultural and domestic spheres. Marriage ceremonies took place mainly among the same caste, and this practice was largely unaffected by modernisation. Over the years, though, we have seen an *increase in inter-caste marriages*.
- Another sphere where caste has played a crucial role is democratic politics. In the Indian context, it is said that 'People don't cast their *votes*, but vote their *caste*'.

Debate Corner

Has modern India truly weakened the hold of caste, or has caste simply changed its form–shifting from occupation and purity to politics and identity?

Caste and politics

The Indian system of parliamentary democracy, adult franchise and democratic decentralisation through Panchayati Raj has taken politics down to the grassroots level. One of the key determining factors during an election is *caste.* Very often, candidates are fielded by political parties on the basis of their caste identity. It is assumed and believed to a great extent that voters prefer to vote for candidates from their own caste.

Just after independence, *land reforms* were initiated. In this process, the land was transferred from the upper caste elites to the intermediate castes. With land reforms, they acquired considerable economic power, while their large population also added to their advantage. Thus, economic power along with a large population gave them political power too in the era of electoral democracy based on universal adult franchise. They became dominant castes, and they significantly influenced Indian politics. Examples of such dominant castes include the Yadavs of Bihar and Uttar Pradesh, the Vokkaligas of Karnataka, the Reddys and Khammas of Andhra Pradesh, the Jats of Punjab, Haryana and Western Uttar Pradesh and the Patidars of Gujarat.

Apart from this, in India, democratic politics requires organised political parties, which in turn field their candidates. The organised political party requires support from its cadre. Here, caste provides a ready-made system of mobilisation and support for them. There are even organised political platforms based on caste, for example, the Kshatriya Sabha of Gujarat.

In this regard, the 1990s saw a significant shift in caste politics, especially the nature of vote bank politics. There was the rise of various caste-based regional political parties in North India.

Insight Box

Why is it difficult to eradicate the caste system in India?

1. **Political patronage:** As discussed above, caste and politics have a symbiotic relationship in the context of democratic politics in India. In India, caste identities influence politics, and electoral politics affect the caste system.
2. **Social practices:** Caste-based practices are deeply ingrained in psyches of individuals. Specifically in rural set-up, various practices are still based on caste identity. For example, during a marriage ceremony in a village, one can see people from different castes performing their respective roles.
3. **Economic benefits:** In India, there has been continuous demand for reservation in jobs and education by the socially influential castes. Such demands have only strengthened the caste-based mobilisation.

Apart from the caste-based mobilisation for political gain, it is also believed that there is a demand for reservation in order to ensure job security and overcome agrarian distress.

Since the caste system serves socio-political group alliances, it appears that it will be difficult to end the system in the near future. If we analyse the caste system, it seems that this system is resilient enough and has been able to survive through the ages.

Measures to prohibit caste discrimination

The Government of India has brought many reforms to improve the quality of life of the weaker sections of society. Some of them are as follows:

i. Constitutionally guaranteed fundamental rights;
ii. Abolition of untouchability (Article 17);
iii. Scheduled Caste and Scheduled Tribe (Prevention of Atrocities) Act, 1989;
iv. Provision of positive discrimination, i.e. reservation in educational institutions, employment and other opportunities;
v. Establishment of the Department of Social Welfare and National Commissions for the Welfare of Scheduled Castes and Tribes; and
vi. Protection of Civil Rights Act, 1976.

Dalit mobilisation and annihilation of caste

The word 'Dalit' is derived from the Sanskrit word *Dal*, meaning 'ground', 'suppressed', 'crushed', or 'broken to pieces'. It was first used by Jyotiba Phule, the founder of the Satya Shodak Samaj. Jyotiba Phule was referring to 'untouchables' and outcastes who had been victims of caste discrimination for centuries.

The Dalit movement can be understood as a social revolution against caste-based hierarchy, cultural exclusion, economic deprivation and political exploitation. Based on democratic ideals of liberty and social justice, this movement pushed for equality in social and political order.

Even before independence, the Dalit voices emerged strongly in E.V. Ramaswamy Periyar's Self-Respect Movement in Tamil Nadu, the Namashudra movement in Bengal and B.R. Ambedkar's movement in Maharashtra. Ambedkar emphasised how political independence would mean little for the untouchables without social reform and cultural liberation.

Post-independence, caste hierarchy and social oppression remained an unfortunate reality, despite the constitutional guarantee of equality and the abolition of untouchability. Meanwhile, increased access to education and employment opportunities brought some social and economic mobility to a section of Dalits. It led to the rise of movements that demanded equality of treatment and identity assertion among Dalits. A few such movements have been discussed below:

1. *Dr. B.R. Ambedkar and the Buddhist Dalit Movement:* Even seventy-five years after independence, Ambedkar remains the tallest leader of Dalit empowerment. He led movements such as the Mahad Satyagraha (1927) to demand dignity and access to resources for Dalits. He advocated for inter-caste marriages as a way to reduce the influence of caste in Indian society. Ambedkar, in his *Annihilation of Caste,* described caste as intrinsically related to religion and hence eventually saw conversion as the only hope for Dalit emancipation.
2. *Dalit Panther Movement*: The Dalit Panthers movement emerged in the early 1970s against persisting caste-based discrimination. Its leadership came from the first generation of Dalit graduates. The movement pointed out the inconsistency between the constitutional ideal of equality and the prevalence of social and economic inequality in society. It demanded

redistributive justice for Dalits as well as more effective implementation of government policies like reservation.

3. *Political Movement:* Dr. B.R. Ambedkar is the icon of 'politics of recognition', which is a major feature of the Dalit movement today. His ideas inspired the Kashi Ram-led Bahujan Samaj Party (BSP) in Uttar Pradesh. The political journey of the BSP was important because the scheduled castes in Uttar Pradesh had remained politically marginalised despite constituting around 20 per cent of the State's population.

The primary focus of the BSP was the upliftment of downtrodden people, with the principal goal of social transformation in the Bahujan Samaj. However, critics have noted how this 'politics of recognition' without emphasis on redistributive justice was insufficient in empowering Dalits.

The Dalit movement has no doubt brought about a major social change in the traditional hierarchy of Indian society. It raised issues related to identity and reservations in government jobs and political positions.

It has brought the Dalits into mainstream politics and allowed them to hold important political and administrative posts. A glorious example would be Smt. Droupadi Murmu, the first person belonging to a tribal community to hold Presidential office. She won the Presidential campaign as a BJP candidate in 2022.

Social scientists have commented on the paradox of identity-based caste politics, wherein movements have digressed from their goal of caste annihilation due to the nature of caste based politics. Caste is perhaps the most easily identifiable vote bank in a diverse country like India. Caste-based movements, on the one hand, have culturally and politically empowered hitherto marginalised sections like the Dalits but have also sharpened caste consciousness. Formation of caste-based groups for the demand of reservation and frequent demands of caste census in some States is an example of this increased consciousness. Needless to say, caste has transformed instead of disintegrating in the face of modernity.

Insight Box

Horizontal Reservation versus Vertical Reservation

In the recent times, there has been a demand for horizontal reservations for transgender people. In this context, let's understand the meaning of horizontal and vertical reservations.

Vertical Reservation means the reservation provided to Scheduled Castes, Scheduled Tribes, and Other Backward Classes separately as per the law.

Horizontal Reservation means the reservation provided to various categories of beneficiaries such as women, transgender, differently abled, cutting through the vertical categories. For eg, if women have 33% horizontal reservation, then in each vertical quota category, there should be 33% women i.e 33% of all selected open category candidates will be women, 33% of all selected SC candidates will have to be women, and so on.

Society Today

Caste Census

Caste Census simply means recording caste identity of all citizens during the National Census. In the Indian scenario, caste plays a very crucial role in the socio-economic and political life of individuals. Hence, caste data can help policy makers in understanding the socio-economic profile of various caste groups. This will ultimately help in better policy making in order to promote social justice in the society.

Historical context

During the British period, caste census used to be conducted regularly from 1881 to 1931. During these censuses, data on all castes, including Other Backward Classes (OBCs) used to be collected in a comprehensive way. After independence, though, the Government of India, headed by Prime Minister Jawaharlal Nehru, decided to discontinue this practice of collecting caste data during national census, except data on Scheduled Castes (SCs) and Scheduled Tribes (STs). This was done in order to prevent further social division in the Indian society.

In 1961, though, the Government of India allowed the States to do their own-survey and collect data on OBCs, if they desire. But, there was no green signal to conduct caste census at national level.

Demand for national caste census

Over time, the demand for a national caste census grew, particularly after the Mandal Commission Report in 1980. Mandal Commission, in its report, recommended 27% reservation for OBCs in central government jobs and educational institutions. The basis for recommendation was the fact that there was 52% population of OBCs in the country. It is important to note that the population percentage was based on the *1931 census data*.

Prior to the Mandal commission, few other commissions were also set-up to discuss the issue of welfare measures and reservation policy for the backward classes viz. Kaka Kalelkar Commission, Mungeri Lal Commission. However, none of the committees had updated data, after 1931 census data, based on which effective recommendations could be made regarding welfare measures for the OBCs. Consequently, the discussion also gave rise to the demand for fresh and more relevant data, driven by the need for improved policy-making.

In 2011, the then Government of India made effort to collect caste data through ***Socio-Economic and Caste Census (SECC)***. However, the data on caste population was never released, except the number of SCs and STs. This was because of the lack of quality, credible and usable data as people identified their castes in a very different manner.

Some suggested their sub-caste, while many others identified their caste based on the communities to which they belong. Even people belonging to similar castes registered their castes in a different way, causing significant administrative challenge to classify such a huge population in similar caste categories. In fact, the 2011 SECC registered 46.7 lakh castes/sub-castes, with around 8.2 crore errors. This was mainly because the government did not provide a caste-registry for the people to mark their castes specifically while carrying out the census.

Recent caste surveys by State Governments

In recent years, in the absence of national caste census, few States have carried out their own surveys.

1. **Bihar Caste Survey (2022):** The caste survey findings got released in 2023. The image below shows the data of various caste categories. Bihar Government, based on the fact that OBCs and Extremely Backward Classes (EBCs) together constitute more than 63% of the population of Bihar, raised reservations for SCs, STs, OBCs, and EBCs from 50% to 65%, apart from the 10% reservation for Economically Weaker Section (EWS). As a result, the total quota increased to 75% in Bihar.

   This move breached the reservation limit of 50% set by the Supreme Court in the Indra Sawhney Judgment (1992). The Patna High Court, therefore, struck down the increased quota calling it unconstitutional. The case is now pending in the Supreme Court.

Bihar population	130,725,310
Category	Share in population (%)
OBC	27.13
EBC	36.01
SC	19.65
ST	1.68
Unreserved/ General	15.52

2. **Karnataka Socio-Economic and Educational Survey, 2024:** Even though the survey was conducted in 2015, its report was accepted in 2024, nearly after a decade. The survey was conducted by the Karnataka State Commission for Backward Classes..

   The Survey found OBCs to be constituting 69.6% of the total population, while the SCs and STs accounted for 18.2% and 7.1% respectively. The general category population constitute around 4.9% of the population.

   Based on this, the Commission recommended increasing reservation for backward class from 32% to 51%. Adding 24% reservation for SC/STs and 10% for EWS, the total reservation in the State will move up to 85%. It may invite legal scrutiny, in case Karnataka moves ahead with this. The report has also generated criticisms from various quarters, including some political groups. They pointed various issues with the survey viz. all households were not covered during the survey, issues relating to categorising sub-castes, data being too old, among others.

3. **Telangana Caste Census 2024:** Officially, it was called the 'Socio- Economic, Educational, Employment, Political and Caste Survey' (SEEEPC). In this survey, it was found that OBCs

constitute around 56% of the population, while SCs and STs account for around 17% and 10% respectively.

Telangana Caste Count Findings

96.9% Households surveyed	**35,477,554** Individuals covered

Population Distribution

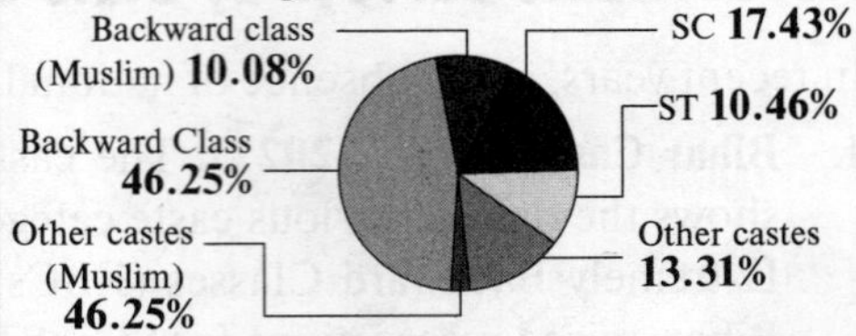

The Telangana government, based on the survey data, increased reservations for Backward Classes (BCs) to 42% in education, employment, and local body elections. A bill in this regard was subsequently passed in both the State Legislative Assembly and the Legislative Council. The Bill also proposes 18% quota for SCs and 10% for STs, taking the total quota to 70%. The state government has requested the Central government to place this bill in the Ninth Schedule of the Indian Constitution to make it immune from the judicial scrutiny.

Benefits of Caste Census	Challenges/Issues
1. Updation of caste records; since 1931 no census collected caste-based data, except SCs and STs	1. It may reinforce caste identities and create factions in the society on caste lines. The ultimate goal to create a casteless society will take a backseat
2. Can help bring the extremely marginalised in the mainstream by formulating specific policies for them based on caste data and their socio-economic and political status	2. Identity and vote-bank based politics may rise in the country
3. Re-defining policy on reservation; caste census will further help in sub-categorisation of caste groups for the purpose of reservation	3. Administrative and logistical challenges; People have different way of identifying their own caste/sub-caste, creating administrative challenge of categorising them in similar caste categories. This can also affect data quality
4. Will help the policy makers in knowing whether the schemes and social programmes have helped in reducing socio-economic inequality	4. If caste census results in increase in reservation quota beyond 50%, it may invite legal scrutiny

A caste census holds the potential to empower marginalised and underrepresented sections of society by enabling the formulation of more inclusive policies that improve their access to education and employment. However, it is equally important to ensure that such an exercise does not become a tool for social division or political appeasement that could threaten national unity.

2.2 Tribal Communities

For a long time, tribal communities were seen as undifferentiated and egalitarian in nature with communal ownership of land. However, contemporary empirical studies by scholars such as Ghanshyam Shah, A. R. Desai, amongst others, have shown that tribal communities are also differentiated and stratified based on age, sex, family and kinship.

In tribal societies, the positions of the clan, families and individuals are taken into consideration for the purpose of ranking in the same tribal groups. These studies also point out that it is only a myth that tribal societies were egalitarian.

Features of tribal communities

The term *tribe* can be broadly defined as a group of people tied together by blood and marriage. In the Indian context, the constitutional term Scheduled Tribes (STs) is used to refer to the many tribal communities across the country. Scheduled Tribes constitute approximately 8.6% of the population of India, numbering around 10.4 crore (2011 census).

Apart from kinship, the **Lokur Committee (1965)** suggested five characteristics that define tribal communities, namely,

1. primitive traits
2. distinct culture
3. geographical isolation
4. shyness of contact
5. backwardness

Article 342 of the Indian Constitution empowers the President to notify Scheduled Tribes in consultation with the government. **Article 366** of the Constitution States that tribes notified under Article 342 are to be treated as Scheduled Tribes. There are over 730 Scheduled Tribes notified under Article 342 of the Constitution of India.

It is undeniable that tribal communities have great cultural and customary diversity. But equally significant are some key characteristics that are common among the indigenous people. Broadly, these are as follows:

1. *Community orientation:* Kinship ties are the broad foundation of tribal communities. Most tribes claim their origin from a common ancestor. They can be further subdivided into clans. Usually, marriages outside the tribe and within the clan are socially forbidden. There is much emphasis on community in the tribal culture. Tribal folklores see the clan as one big family. Conflicts are resolved by discussion among elders and consensus.

2. *Worshipping of natural phenomena:* Some form of worship of natural elements is found in most tribal communities. In the Northern Sahyadri tribal belt of Maharashtra, the Warli tribes worship Hirva dev, literally the God of nature and greenery. The Bhumia tribe of Koraput district in Odisha is known to worship the sun god. The Niyamgiri Hill spread across Kalahandi and Rayagada districts of Odisha is sacred for the Dongria Kondh, who reveres the hills as the abode of the Niyam Raja, the deity of this area.

There is great reverence for nature and its elements in tribal culture. Sacred groves in dense tribal-inhabited forests are another example of this reverence. These sacred groves are known as Devrai in the western part of Maharashtra and Devgudi in the eastern belt of Maharashtra. This regard for nature also manifests in the preservation of forests and their beings by tribals. There is emphasis on living in harmony with nature instead of a resource-extraction mindset.

3. *Geographical isolation:* Though tribal communities are spread all over the country, they can be particularly located in remote hilly and densely forested regions. The Great Andamanese, Jarawa and Sentinelese of Andaman and Nicobar Islands are some of the most isolated tribal communities. North-east India has a great number of tribes that reside in the Eastern Himalayas. This geographical isolation partly explains the continuation of unique tribal cultures and customs.
4. *Unique culture and philosophy:* A tribe is defined not just by kinship but also by its unique culture, dialect, customs, beliefs and folklore. The Warli tribes of Maharashtra are famous for their Warli paintings, which were traditionally painted on mud huts. The Korku community from Amravati region in Maharashtra speak Korku, which is completely different from Marathi. Even marriage traditions in tribal communities are different compared to those of other communities.
5. *Jatras and festivals:* Jatras are a uniting feature of tribal communities across India. The *Kachargad Yatra in Gondia district* of Maharashtra attracts Gonds from 18 States of India. The Kachargad caves are considered the origin point of the Gond tribe. The Medaram Jatra is one of the largest fairs celebrated by the Koya tribes of Telangana for four days. This once-in-two-year festival is believed to attract the largest number of devotees after the Kumbh Mela.
6. *Indigenous knowledge system:* It is important to preserve traditional knowledge of tribal communities as it is inter-generational wisdom. Whether it be food, medicine or agriculture, all tribal communities have their unique indigenous knowledge system, which has been relied upon for thousands of years. Knowledge about medicinal plants and their usage is preserved through traditional healers in tribal communities.

   Some tribes possess various artistic and handcrafted skills. For example, the Bhotiya tribes of the Garhwal region make natural dyes from native plant species, and this technique is a very sustainable alternative that has been used for centuries. Similarly, Konyak Nagas from northeast India are considered to be expert gunsmiths. Most tribal knowledge is transmitted orally and hence is at risk of extinction. State governments have established Tribal Research Institutions (TRIs) to document such traditional knowledge and cultural practices.
7. *Socio-economic backwardness:* There is a general consensus that the socio-economic development of tribal communities is less than desirable. Most States with a high proportion of tribal affairs have dedicated departments to monitor and improve the socio-economic progress of tribal communities. The socio-economic challenges faced by tribal communities are discussed in detail in the next section.

Geographical distribution of tribal communities

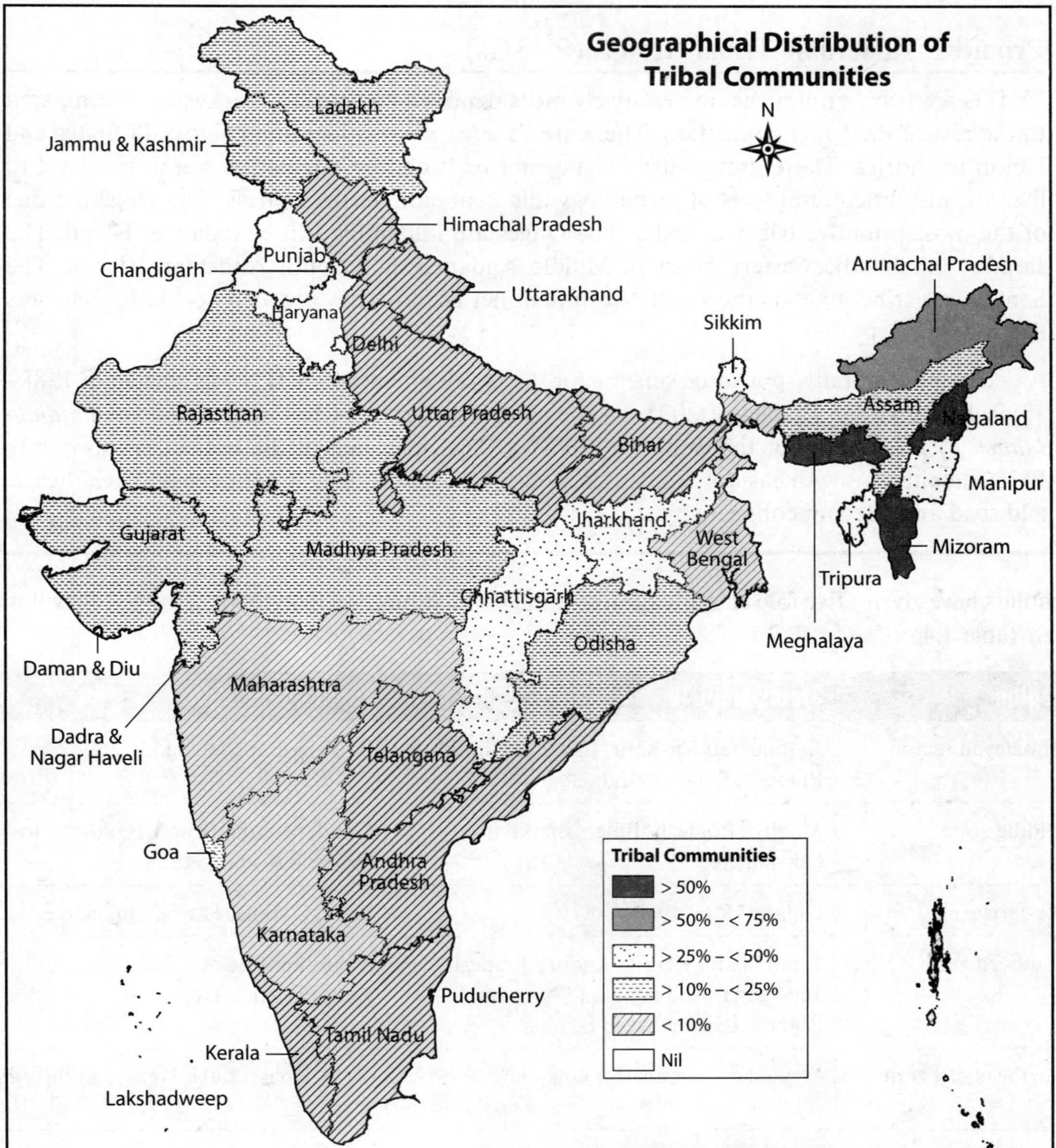

Insight Box

Primitive Vulnerable Tribal Groups (PVTGs)

PVTGs are tribal groups that are relatively more deprived and socially backward as compared to the rest of the tribal population. There are 75 such PVTGs identified across 18 States and Union territories. These groups have a stagnant or declining population trend, low level of literacy, pre-agricultural level of technology and economic backwardness. The Onge are one of the most primitive tribes in India. The Onges are inhabiting Little Andaman Island. The Jarawas inhabit the western coast of Middle Andaman and South Andaman Islands. The Sentinelese tribe inhabits the small North Sentinel Island. They are also hostile to outsiders like the Jarawas.

A dedicated, centrally sponsored scheme for the development of PVTGs was started in 1988–1999. In the Union Budget of 2023–24 the central government has announced the *Pradhan Mantri PVTG mission* for the welfare of PVTGs. The main aim of the project is to saturate PVTG habitations with basic amenities like housing, clean drinking water, access to healthcare, and road and telecom connectivity.

Scholars have given a five-fold classification of tribal populations based on their territorial distribution (See Table 1.4).

Region	States and UTs	Tribal Communities
Himalayan region	Jammu and Kashmir, Ladakh, Himachal Pradesh, Uttarakhand, etc.	Bhotiya, Lepcha, Gaddi, etc.
Middle zone	Madhya Pradesh, Bihar, Jharkhand, Odisha, etc.	Gond, Munda, Oraon, Santhal, Ho, Dongria Kondh, etc.
Western zone	Gujarat, Rajasthan	Bhils, Dhodia, Pawra, Dubla, etc.
Southern zone	Tamil Nadu, Kerala, Andhra Pradesh, Telangana, Andaman and Nicobar Islands, Lakshadweep Islands	Irulas, Sentinelese, Toda, Jarawas, Kattunayakan, etc.
Northeastern zone	Meghalaya, Assam, Sikkim, Nagaland, Manipur, etc.	Garo, Khasi, Kuki, Naga, Jaintia, etc.

Table 1.4 Main Tribal Communities across various regions of India

Challenges

1. *Educational backwardness:* As per Census 2011, the literacy rate of Scheduled Tribes (STs) was 59%, whereas the overall literacy rate was 73% at all levels in India. The low economic development and nomadic nature of some tribal and remote tribal habitations are partly responsible for this educational backwardness. Some State governments like Maharashtra and Odisha run residential schools called Ashram schools to improve the educational status of tribal communities. Similarly, the Government of India runs Ekalvya Model Residential Schools (EMRS) to support the Scheduled Tribes.
2. *Health and malnutrition challenges:* The life expectancy at birth for the ST population in India is 63.9 years, as against the average life expectancy of 67 years in India (Census 2011). Even more recent data suggests that tribal populations have poorer health indicators and high burden of morbidity. Early marriage, premature child birth, low BMI and higher incidence of anaemia lead to high maternal mortality among tribal women. Child mortality is also higher due to the higher prevalence of malnutrition and sickle cell anemia.

According to the **Report of the Expert Committee on Health,** the tribal population suffers from a triple burden of communicable diseases like malaria, an increasing prevalence of non-communicable diseases like heart diseases and poor mental health due to alcoholism and addiction.

3. *Development induced displacement:* In the post-independence period, there was much emphasis on industrialisation and infrastructure projects. Huge dams, thermal power plants, ports and highway projects were initiated all across the country. Unfortunately, large sections of tribal communities have been dislocated by such projects. Data suggests that by 1990, tribals constituted 40% of the total project-affected families which were displaced by 3300 dams built all across the country.

The Narmada Bachao Andolan and the anti-mining protests in Niyamgiri hills of Odisha have highlighted this question of displacement, which leads to the loss of livelihood, culture and autonomy of tribal communities.

The **Land Acquisition and Rehabilitation Act 2013** recognises the need for fair distribution of gains from development. For the first time ever, this Act gives equal emphasis to resettlement and also has a social impact assessment clause to assess and redress damage to communities from large projects.

- As per Section 41(1) of this Act, as far as possible, no acquisition of land shall be made in the Scheduled Areas.
- As per Section 41(2), where such acquisition does take place, it shall be done only as a demonstrable last resort.

4. *Erosion of culture:* Tribal culture is the backbone of tribal identity, and its erosion negatively impacts a sense of self-respect and autonomy among tribals. Urbanisation and the increasing inroads of modernisation have eroded tribal culture. One example is the extinction of tribal dialects.

Similarly, the traditional institutions of tribal communities have been eroded by the new political administrative system. The constitutional provisions of classifying scheduled areas into the Fifth and Sixth schedules have been brought in as measures to prevent such erosion.

5. *Landlessness and reliance on primitive agricultural techniques:* A large section of the tribal population are marginal land holders or landless. Some are hunter-gatherers, pastoralists, nomadic herders and artisans. Generally, tribal communities are resource poor and low on the economic development ladder.
6. *Addiction and alcohol use disorder:* Both globally and in India, studies have found higher consumption of alcohol among tribal communities. Traditionally, communities manufacture their own alcohol from rice and forest produce like *mahua* flowers. Higher alcohol and tobacco consumption among tribal communities leads to higher disease burden, lower productivity and even law and order issues at times.

Landmark Judgements

Landmark judgements regarding tribal rights

1. *Samatha versus State of Andhra Pradesh (1997):* The question before the court was regarding the grant of mining leases to private entities in scheduled areas. The court cancelled all leases and underscored that development activities must be sustainable and require the compulsory participation of local tribals.
2. *Union of India versus Rakesh Kumar (2010):* In this case, the court held that reserving the seat of chairperson for Scheduled Tribe (ST) individuals in ST areas does not violate the constitutional right to equality guaranteed under Article 14. The court highlighted that equality under Article 14 must be seen in a substantive sense, and the principle of distributive justice behind such reservations must be appreciated.
3. *Orissa Mineral Corporation Limited versus Ministry of Environment and Forests (2013):* In this judgement, the court highlighted that tribal communities enjoy distinct spiritual relationships with nature, which must be respected while pursuing development activities. This judgement empowered the Gram Sabha to decide about the social and economic viability of projects. Informed consent from Gram Sabha has since become necessary for approval of all large infrastructure projects.

Protective measures

1. *Constitutional provisions:* ***"Constitutional provisions for safeguards of tribals"*** follows right after this section.

2. *The Scheduled Tribes and Other Traditional Forest Dwellers (Recognition of Forest Rights) Act, 2006:* The Forest Rights Act is a landmark Act that has recognised the symbiotic relationship between forests and tribals. Broadly, the Act provides for the grant of Individual Forest Rights (IFR) patta and Community Forest Rights (CFR) patta to tribal and other traditional forest dwellers. It brought relief to tribals all across India who were facing livelihood loss and eviction, apart from constant conflicts with the forest department. The Act is a land reform measure in the sense that it granted cultivation rights to many hitherto landless tribals.
3. *Tribal Sub-Plan:* The Tribal Sub-Plan guarantees that States allocate dedicated budgets for tribal communities in proportion to their populations. In some States, there are dedicated agencies called the Integrated Tribal Development Project (ITDP)/agency to monitor the implementation of the tribal sub-plan expenditure. The TSP strategy ensures that State governments spend on tribal welfare in a planned, dedicated and consistent manner.
4. *Grants under Article 275 (1) of the Indian Constitution:* Under Article 275 (1), grants are distributed to 26 tribal dominant States and Union Territories (UTs) by the central government for the welfare of tribal communities. It is 100% supported by the central government, and needs-based projects on infrastructure, livelihood and agriculture are supported under this scheme.
5. *Panchayat (extension to scheduled areas):* PESA is an Act to provide for the extension of the provisions of Part IX of the Constitution relating to the Panchayats to the Scheduled Areas. The Act strives to implement tribal self-governance in Schedule V areas. It empowers Gram Sabha to take decisions regarding the control and monitoring of local resources like minerals, forest produce, water bodies and the like. Though the Act has a long way to go in terms of actual implementation, it is a powerful tool for local democracy and participatory governance in tribal areas.
6. *Anti-land alienation measures:* Land being a State subject, most States with tribal populations have a law to prevent land alienation among tribals, e.g. Maharashtra Restoration of Lands to Scheduled Tribes Act, 1974.
7. *The Scheduled Castes and Scheduled Tribes (Prevention of Atrocities) Act, 1989:* It has been enacted to deter the commission of atrocities against members of the SCs and STs. It provides for a special court for the trial of such offences and for the relief and rehabilitation of the victims.

Constitutional provisions for safeguards of tribals

Educational, economic and public employment

Article 15: Prohibition of discrimination on grounds of religion, race, caste, sex or place of birth

Article 16: Equality of opportunity in matters of public employment

Article 19: Protection of certain rights regarding freedom of speech and expression, to practise any profession, etc.

Article 46: Promotion of educational and economic interests of Scheduled Castes, Scheduled Tribes and other weaker sections

Article 335: Claims of Scheduled Castes and Scheduled Tribes to services and posts

Political safeguards

Article 330: Reservation of seats for Scheduled Castes and Scheduled Tribes in the House of the People

Article 332: Reservation of seats for Scheduled Castes and Scheduled Tribes in the Legislative Assemblies of the States

Article 334: Reservation of seats and special representation to cease after sixty years

Article 243D: Reservation of seats (in Panchayats)

Article 243T: Reservation of seats

Fifth and Sixth Schedules of the Constitution

The primary purpose of both of these schedules is to ensure the preservation of tribal culture and extend political autonomy to the tribal community.

The Fifth Schedule provides for decentralisation of various powers as well as the constitution of a Tribal Advisory Council (TAC).

The Sixth schedule provides for the constitution of autonomous district councils. Most of the Northeastern States have such district councils. For example, Mizoram has Lai autonomous district council. Meghalaya has a Jaintia Hill autonomous district council.

Agency for monitoring safeguards

Article 338A: National Commission for Scheduled Tribe

Society Today

Sub-Categorisation of Scheduled Castes and Scheduled Tribes

The Preamble of the Indian Constitution commits to securing justice - social, economic and political - for all its citizens. Reservations to socially and educationally backward sections of society are an important component of social justice architecture envisaged by the Indian constitution. In recent years, the question of which castes and communities qualify as 'socially and educationally backward' has become increasingly contested.

On one hand, several dominant communities have increasingly demanded reservation, citing rising agrarian distress and shrinking economic opportunities. On the other hand, concerns have been raised about identifying the truly `genuine and deserving beneficiaries', as well as addressing the issue of relative deprivation within the Scheduled Castes and Scheduled Tribes themselves.

Against this backdrop, a seven-judge bench of the Supreme Court was called to adjudicate upon the Constitutionality of sub-categorisation of Scheduled Castes (SC) and Scheduled Tribes (STs) in the ***State of Punjab and Others Vs Davinder Singh and others (2024)***.

Article 341 of the Constitution empowers the President to designate certain castes and tribes as SCs and STs. The question of sub-categorisation among SCs and STs was earlier considered in ***EV Chinnaiah vs State of Andhra Pradesh (2004)***. In this judgement, the Court opined that sub-categorisation among SCs and STs would be unconstitutional as it would amount to tinkering with the Presidential order under Article 341. The court further held that SCs and groups constitute a homogenous group, and any sub-categorisation would be unconstitutional and impermissible under Article 14.

However, in the State of Punjab and Other Vs Davinder Singh and others, with a 6:1 majority, the Supreme Court held that sub-categorisation of SCs and STs does not amount to violation of Article 14 and Article 341 of the Constitution. The Court held that the relative backwardness of sub-castes and tribes can be a basis for sub-categorisation. Thus, this judgement over-ruled the five-judge bench decision in E.V. Chinaiah v State of Andhra Pradesh (2004).

Opinion of the Supreme Court

- The Court pointed out that owing to different historical and social struggles, SCs and STs do not constitute a homogenous group. Such sub-categorisation of SCs and STs has to be based on empirical data and reservations cannot be exclusively allocated to any specific scheduled caste or tribe.
- The Court pointed out that the most disadvantaged and marginalised have not benefitted much from the reservation policy. Instead, it is the most affluent or urbanised castes who are able to access higher education and get benefitted from reservation, causing persistent inequality. One of the justices even suggested that reservation should be restricted to first generation beneficiaries in the family.
- The Court also noted that State must "evolve a policy for identifying the *creamy layer* even from the Scheduled Castes and Scheduled Tribes so as to exclude them from the benefit of affirmative action." The 'creamy layer' principle is an exclusionary principle which excludes socially and educationally advanced castes from the purview of other backward class reservation. The court held that the basis for assessing *'creamy layer'* for SCs/STs should be different from that of OBCs.
- One of the judges had a *dissenting* opinion. She held that any sub-categorisation of scheduled castes and scheduled tribes would amount to tinkering with Presidential Order under Article 341 and this is beyond power of the States.

The judgement has evoked mixed responses from various sections of society and subject experts.

- Some scheduled castes and tribes' organisation deem the judgement divisive and one leading to dilution of the reservation policy.
- The reference to *creamy layer* by the majority opinion has also been criticised as adjudication upon same was never sought in the original plea.
- Critics of the judgement have also pointed out that the so-called better off individuals or castes are only marginally better off than others and their relative exclusion is not justified. Others fear that such relative exclusion may reverse social and educational gains which have been made due to seventy plus years of affirmative action.

- It has also been pointed out that the judgement may be appropriated for appeasement of specific castes and the good intentions of the judgement may be undermined by vote bank politics.
- On the positive side, though, sub-categorisation can help in addressing the issue of *elite capture of reservation*. It can provide better opportunities for the most backward sub-castes to uplift themselves.

Perhaps, one of the most critical questions which states face is settling the basis of sub-categorisation of scheduled castes. Because reservation as a policy of social justice is based on broader principles of socio-economic and political justice and cannot be assessed simply based on the narrow domain of economic backwardness. It is important to note here that States, such as Haryana and Telangana, have already implemented the court judgement in this regard. Even Karnataka has started a survey for the purpose of sub-classification of SCs.

Another question is how the sub-categorisation principle will be applied to Scheduled Tribes whose socio-economic deprivation has different structure and history compared to scheduled castes.

Overall, the Davinder Singh judgement has provided scope to the state governments to focus on the *extremely marginalised* within the disadvantaged groups. The judgement opens discussion on *targeted social justice*. However, it is clear that the judgement has a long and arduous journey before it can be implemented in practice. Sub-categorisation will have to be based on well researched empirical and scientific data. Yet, exclusion will always remain contentious and difficult in times when clamour for reservation is only rising.

Insight Box

Categorisation of Scheduled Castes (SCs) by Telangana State

Following the verdict by Supreme Court, Telangana government has notified the Telangana Scheduled Castes (Rationalisation of Reservations) Act 2025. As per this Act, the SCs have been divided into 3 groups- Group I, Group II and Group III- for the purpose of providing reservation to each such group.

The Government took into consideration socio-economic, political, educational and employment status of the SC communities before deciding the groups.

- Out of the total 59 sub-castes in SC category, 15 most backward sub-castes forms part of Group I. 1% reservation has been provided to this group.
- 18 sub-castes, who have received marginal benefits, has been provided with 9% reservation in Group II.
- Rest 26 sub-castes, who are relatively well-off and have better opportunities, have been placed in Group III with 5% reservation.

Insight Box

Categorisation of Scheduled Castes (SCs) by Haryana

Haryana, apart from Telangana, also implemented the Supreme Court Judgement on sub-classification. Based on the Haryana Scheduled Castes (SC) Commission report, the government decided to divide SCs into two categories: Deprived Scheduled Castes (DSCs) and Other Scheduled Castes (OSCs).

- Deprived Scheduled Castes (DSCs): There are 36 sub-castes in DSCs such as Dhanaks, Balmikis, Bazigar, Mazhabi Sikhs, and Sapera. Out of the total 20% quota for SCs in the state, half of it i.e 10% to be reserved for DSCs. DSCs are relatively more backward among the SCs.
- Rest 10% to be reserved for Other Scheduled Castes (OSCs), which includes sub-cases like Jatavs, Ravidas, Ramdasi, Chamar, among others. This group, historically, have had better socio-economic representation.

2.3 Class-based Stratification

A social class is a group of individuals who possess more or less similar wealth. In class-based stratification, *wealth* is the determining factor. In modern societies, with economic development, class-based stratification has become an important phenomenon apart from caste-based stratification. Indian society can be divided into Upper Class, Middle Class (Upper middle class, Middle middle class, Lower middle class) and Lower Class.

One of the important characteristics of class-based hierarchy is that by acquiring more wealth, one can change their position and can move from lower class to upper class. This is not possible in the caste-based system, as the caste of an individual is determined at birth.

2.4 Gender-based Stratification

In India, gender-based stratification is a reality in the sense that women and men have differential and adverse access to resources, opportunities and rights. Also, there is a difference in the status of women and men in society. This is mainly due to the patriarchal nature of society, wherein the nature of work is also decided on the basis of gender to some extent.

For instance, men are considered breadwinners and women are supposed to do household work. In terms of access to resources, there is a huge difference between men and women. As per the fifth National Family Health Survey (NFHS), in India, in 2020–21, there were 22.7% of women on whose name a house or land was registered.

3. Family System in India

Family, marriage and kinship are universal institutions. However, there are variations in these institutions based on region, religion, language, caste, class and occupation. That is why it is difficult to make generalisations about these institutions. Here, we will discuss some of the aspects of these institutions.

3.1 Institution of Family in India

The term family is derived from the Latin word '*familia*'. It refers to a 'group of individuals living together during important phases of their lifetime and bound to each other by biological and/or social and psychological relationship'.

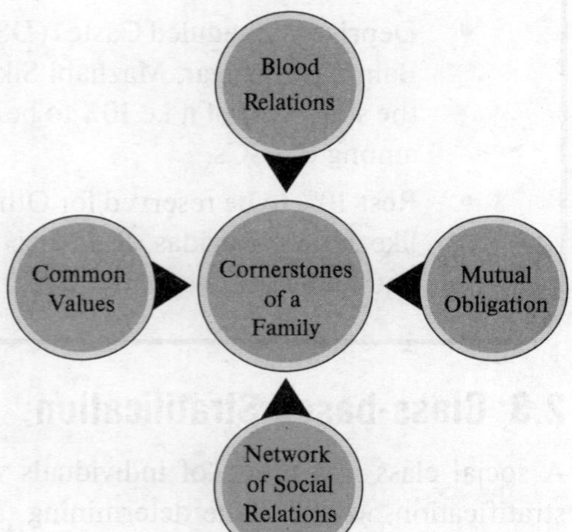

The family is an essential institution in Indian society. In India, the identity of an individual is generally associated with the family to which she belongs. Also, an individual is dependent on family for emotional support, financial, educational and safety needs.

The family system can be discussed in terms of structure and function.

3.2 Structure of Family in India

Conventionally, the family system in India was understood in terms of a joint family system. An extended family (commonly known as the 'joint family') can take different forms but has more than one couple, and often more than two generations, living together. This could be a set of brothers with their individual families or an elderly couple with their sons and grandsons and their respective families. Such traditional families form the oldest social institution that has survived through the ages. Yet this is by no means the dominant form, now or earlier. Some studies have shown that the conventional joint family is found only in land-owning and trading castes.

With time, there has been a rise in *nuclear families* due to the practical demands of modern life. A nuclear family consists of only one set of parents and their children. Many factors are responsible for the shift towards the *nuclear family system*. These include:

1. *Increase in levels of education*: Increased education and employment opportunities, especially among women, explain the increasing prevalence of nuclear families. The joint family system tends to have a traditional, household-oriented role for women, which may not be compatible with the aspirations of modern women.

2. *Urbanisation and related economic pressures*: Growing urbanisation and rising expenditures force families to shift to dual incomes. Families also seek to limit responsibilities and expenditures in the face of economic pressure.
3. *Migration patterns*: As opposed to the rural agrarian economy of the last century, nearly one-third of India's population is now in urban areas, and cities are seen as economic growth engines. As per sociologists, urbanisation, migration and nuclearisation go hand in hand, as nuclear families are more geographically mobile than the joint families.
4. *Rising spirit of individualism:* The joint family system places much emphasis on family rules, consent of elders and obedience. It is not aligned with the growing trend of individualism and self-assertion. Hence, individuals shift to the nuclear family system for freedom and personal space.

The division of the joint family into smaller units is not a symbol of people rejecting the traditional structure. It is to be kept in mind that even though families have become nuclear in nature, the 'jointness' still remains. Even in this nuclear family structure, it is common to find elderly parents or younger siblings staying with the family for prolonged periods. Families who migrate for work keep close ties with their ancestral village and participate in ritual ceremonies.

Family continues to hold strong psychological and ideological significance in Indian society, with a deep sense of obligation often reinforced by religious values. Even in urban areas, nuclear families frequently seek guidance from elders on major decisions such as marriage, functioning more as an extension of the joint family than as an entirely separate unit. Therefore, a rigid distinction between nuclear and joint families may not accurately reflect the social reality in India.

Forms of Family	Description
Patriarchal	Men exercise authority and dominance
Matriarchal	Women exercise authority and play dominant role
Patrilineal	Son inherits property from father
Matrilineal	Daughter inherits property from mother
Patrilocal	Newly married couple lives with the man's parents
Matrilocal	Newly married couple stays with the woman's parents

3.3 Functions of Family

1. *Ritual and ceremonial:* Members participate in religious functions and ceremonies together. A Hindu marriage ceremony requires necessary participation of the bride's parents at the time of '*kanyadan*'.
2. *Transmission of values and behaviours across generations*: Elders and grandparents are keystones in transferring the norms, moral values and traditions of society. This helps in the proper socialisation of children. From food choices to marriage, the institution of family influences an individual from cradle to grave.

3. *Fulfils sexual needs*: Marriage is traditionally viewed as a legitimate institution fulfilling the essential need for the continuation of the human race through procreation.
4. *Rearing of children*: Family, through its members, contributes to the proper growth and development of children.
5. *Protection and security*: Apart from financial support, family members act as a cushion against any unwanted incident in the life of a member. They provide an emotional and physical safety net.

Apart from these, family performs other functions too: providing a home to its members, providing educational support and performing psychological functions.

3.4 Contemporary Trends and Issues

Dual-income households

It is increasingly common to find both sets of parents to be working individuals. While it has increased the disposable incomes of households, having an employed wife and an employed mother requires adjustments to the traditional role of the woman as the main care-giver. In families where such adjustment is absent, women find themselves with the double burden of office and household work. The problem of balancing career and ambition with parenting responsibilities persists even for women in the upper echelons of the corporate world. Former CEO of Pepsico, Smt. Indra Nooyi, has openly commented about the impossibility of balancing both work and family as a woman and how 'mom guilt' constantly afflicted her as she rose to the topmost position.

Work from home

Post-COVID, the traditional norm of working from office space has been revisited. The rising trend of freelancing and gig economy is also encouraging corporations to explore the possibility of 'remote working', which implies employees don't need to be in office space and may not need to follow any structured office timings.

The flexibility, saving of commute time and expenditure and the implied trust in the employee working from home are its advantages. However, studies have warned that the work-from-home culture can reduce quality time with family and even cause health problems due to the long hours of working in the name of flexible hours.

Live-in relations and family

Live-in relations can be defined as adult, hetero/homo sexual, non-marital, or cohabitational arrangements. With growing personal and sexual autonomy in urban areas, couples are choosing to enter into non-marital but exclusive relations as a form of experimentation. The legal status of live-in relationships remains in the grey zone.

Landmark Judgements

In *Payal Sharma versus Nari Niketan (2001)*, the Allahabad High Court highlighted that society may consider adult men and women living together without marriage as immoral, but it is by no means illegal. The same was reiterated by the Supreme Court in *Lata Singh versus State of Uttar Pradesh (2006)*. The Protection of Women from Domestic Violence Act, 2005, is the first act to recognise relations that are 'in the nature of marriage'.

The Supreme Court in *Kattukandi Edathil Krishnan versus Kattukandi Edathil Valsan (2022)* held that children born out of such relations can be considered legitimate, provided the couple has been living together for a prolonged period. Such children are entitled to inherit property from their parents.

Despite such indirect references, there is no clarity on the rights and obligations of partners in a live-in arrangement. Given the social and ceremonial importance attached to the institution of marriage in India, whether or not live-in relations should get legal protection is also contested.

Insight Box

Live-in Relationships - Social Issues

Social Censure: Live-in relationships often face stigma in conservative sections of Indian society, where cohabitation without marriage is viewed as morally unacceptable or against cultural norms.

Question about the Social and Legal Legitimacy of Children: While courts have clarified that children born from long-term live-in relationships can be considered legitimate, societal acceptance and clarity in matters like naming rights, school admissions, and inheritance still pose challenges.

Risk of Abuse from a Partner, Especially for Women: Women in live-in relationships may be more vulnerable to emotional, physical, or financial abuse due to the lack of formal legal protections traditionally associated with marriage. However, legislations such as the Protection of Women from Domestic Violence Act (PWDVA), 2005 have begun to bridge this gap.

Inheritance and Financial Rights of the Partner: Unlike legally married spouses, partners in live-in relationships often struggle to claim property, maintenance, or other financial rights unless they can prove the relationship was "in the nature of marriage," as recognized by the courts.

Patriarchy and family

It results in gender stratification. In this set-up, men have higher status than women counterparts. Men take all major decisions in a family, including financial decisions. Women are either given responsibility for household chores or are made to participate in minor decisions such as buying household items.

Decline in fertility

It has directly impacted a reduction in family size. Moreover, with the increasing cost of bearing children, families prefer to have less children as well. It will have a significant impact on the demography of India.

4. Institution of Marriage in India

Marriage is a universal social institution in India. Marriage in India is considered as unification of not only two individuals but of two families as well. Children born out of such unification are considered legitimate, and this legitimacy is important for inheritance and succession. Marriage is also considered as a legitimate institution for the sexual gratification of members. There is great diversity in the rituals and cultural customs of marriage all over India.

Forms of Marriage	Description
Monogamy	Marrying only one partner at a time
Polygamy	Man or woman having more than one spouse (either polygyny or polyandry)
Polygyny	A man marrying more than one woman at a time
Polyandry	A woman marrying more than one man at a time

4.1 Issues Related to Marriage in India

Early marriage of a girl child in India

There are a few reasons for the same:

1. One of the main reasons for early marriage is the desire to preserve the chastity or purity of women.
2. Safety concerns with respect to women also push parents to marry their daughters at an early age.
3. Poverty is another important factor. Since daughters in India are considered as *paraya dhan,* parents prefer marrying a daughter at an early age so that they do not have to spend much resources on her.
4. Cultural traditions of marrying a girl child just after the onset of puberty as she becomes capable of attaining motherhood.

Increasing divorce rate in India

Divorce is an emotional issue in the Indian context. It affects marriage partners, their respective families and their children, if any. It is a difficult decision to make for the marriage partners. It also affects family structure as it may result in a single-parent family. It can also result in divorced individuals living with their family members for the rest of their lives without marrying again.

In the modern scenario, the divorce rate in India, even though it is low, is increasing mainly because of the following reasons:

1. *Financial empowerment of women*: There is no dependency on a male partner financially, as used to be the case a few decades ago. Thus, women take decisions for themselves. If the marriage turns sour for some reason, women exit the relationship, considering their mental well-being.
2. *Lack of attention from partners*: In the modern financial set-up, both partners work in their respective professions. As a result, they are unable to provide sufficient attention to each other. This creates friction in the long term.
3. *Trust and compatibility factor*: One of the key factors is the trust deficit and compatibility issues between two individuals. Trust deficits can occur due to suspicion of infidelity and other personal reasons. Compatibility issues can result from differences in personalities.

Dowry in marriage

Dowry can be defined as any property or valuables given or agreed to be given by one party to another as part of marriage arrangement. Deep-rooted patriarchal norms and widespread social acceptance of dowry have meant that this practice has survived despite a clear prohibition as per law. *As per NCRB Data (2022), as many as 6450 dowry deaths were reported with the highest number of cases from Uttar Pradesh and Bihar.*

Insight Box

Why does dowry as a cultural practise still persist?

1. There is a gender bias in society, which makes an unmarried daughter a liability for the family. Most families wish to marry their daughter as early as possible, and dowry is seen as a way to secure quick and decent match.
2. Legal lacunae such as that exception in the 1961 Act, which allows for 'gifts' to be given to the bride.
3. Unfortunately, dowry-related issues are still seen as a 'family matter', and public outcry against the practise is sporadic and not universal. Its existence is so pervasive that demanding and accepting dowry is still not perceived as a crime.
4. Under-reporting of cases and the difficulty of conviction in dowry-related cases are another reason why deterrence is not strong.
5. Dowry and extravagant marriages are now seen as status symbols and ways to assert one's position in the hierarchy.
6. There is an increasing trend towards a consumerist and materialist mindset in India, which has made dowry an essential component of arranged marriages.

The practise of dowry cannot be abolished by law alone. Gender-sensitive education and awareness activities, along with full educational and employment opportunities for women, can aid in weeding out this cultural evil.

Insight Box

Legal Provisions against Dowry

1. Dowry Prohibition Act, 1961: Direct or indirect demand of dowry to be punished with fine and imprisonment of up to two years.
2. Criminal Law Act 1983: It added Section 498A to the Indian Penal Code, which recognises cruelty by a husband or relatives as an offence. It is a non-bailable and cognizable offence.
3. The Dowry Prohibition (Amendment) Act, 1984: This Act addressed lacunae of the 1961 Act and recognised the concept of dowry death, which had become a menace in the 1970s and 1980s. It also shifted the burden of proof to the accused, and hence the legal protection against dowry became much stronger.
4. Protection of Women from Domestic Violence Act, 2005 This is a comprehensive law that protects women from all kinds of violence.
5. All India Service Rules: Rule 11 of the AIS rules prohibits any member of the service from demanding and receiving dowry directly or indirectly.

Marital rape in India

Debate Corner

Should India criminalize marital rape, or does doing so risk undermining the sanctity of marriage as traditionally understood in Indian society?

It can be defined as non-consensual sexual acts between a man and his spouse. As per Section 375 of the Indian Penal Code (IPC), sexual intercourse between a man and his wife, who is above 15 years of age, does not constitute rape. This is an exception to the rape law in India. Some argue that criminalising marital rape will weaken the family structure, and the act of marriage itself implies consent. They also point out the difficulty of proving innocence on the part of the husband as the act takes place in a private space.

However, the **J.S. Verma Committee of 2013** recommended that the exception to marital rape be removed. The committee argues that marriage should not be considered as a valid defence against sexual crimes like rape.

Others argue that not criminalising marital rape undermines the concept of consent and women's right to bodily integrity and dignity.

4.2 Contemporary Trends

Intercaste marriages

Since intercaste marriages are recognised by law, couples are at liberty to make their own choice, and hence such marriages take place on a larger scale than before. It is important to note that caste endogamy is still a popular practice.

Marriage by choice or 'love marriages'

Though the majority of marriages are still decided by parents or elders, the pattern of selection of spouse has undergone a change. It is not uncommon to see couples deciding for themselves and selecting their own partners.

Online matrimonial matching

Traditionally, one saw that searching for a prospective groom/bride was done using family and social networks. In the last few years, though, many matrimonial websites have come up where prospective brides and grooms display their profiles. Matching is then done based on various factors, viz. income of the spouse, facial characteristics, caste, religion, among others.

Same-sex marriage

In the landmark case *Navtej Singh Johar versus Union of India (2018)*, the court decriminalised homosexuality by striking down Section 377 of the Indian Penal Code (IPC). However, same-sex marriages still do not have legal recognition in the country. Activists have argued that legal recognition is necessary for same-sex marriages to get equivalent rights, privileges and obligations as those enjoyed by heterosexual marriages. Besides, it is argued that the right to choose a partner is part of the personal autonomy and privacy guaranteed under Articles 14, 15, 19 and 21 of the Indian Constitution.

Others have cautioned that while individual autonomy is important, the State has a legitimate right to regulate marriages of all kinds. It is to be noted that changes in as many as 160 laws may be required to give constitutional protection to same-sex marriage, and hence it is held that such major social reform is best driven by the legislature.

In October 2023, the Supreme Court held that there is no fundamental right to marry, and in 3:2 verdict, the court ruled against same-sex marriages. The top court was of the view that the legislature or Parliament must take a call on bringing in same-sex marriage.

Increasing age of marriage

There is an increasing tendency to postpone marriage. This is mainly due to individuals aspiring for higher education and achieving goals. It results in a declining fertility rate and, thus, reduction in family size as well.

5. Kinship System in India

5.1 Definition

The kinship system refers to a set of persons recognised as relatives either by virtue of a blood relationship called consanguinity or by virtue of a marriage relationship called affinity. For example, the relationships between mother and daughter, sister and brother are consanguinal relations, while relationships between father-in-law and son-in-law are affinal relations.

5.2 Functions of Kinship

- It helps in determining family tree and lineage, i.e. it provides identity to a person by assigning him as a member of a particular kin group.
- Kinship is an important tool in the socialisation of children and the emotional fulfilment of an individual.
- Kinship helps in assigning appropriate and acceptable behaviour among people, e.g. father-son, brother-sister.
- It provides guidelines to forge new marriage relationships between people and decides who is socially acceptable for marriage purposes. Briefly, families in South India prefer to marry within the kinship network, while in North India, marriage outside one's kinship network is preferred.
- It helps to determine the rights and obligations of the members in all religious practices, right from birth to the death of a person.
- As opposed to contractual relations, kinship ties are more stable and long-lasting in nature. A villager's status is determined not just by his *Jati* but also by his kin whom he can mobilise as his supporters.
- It helps in determining succession and the transfer of property to descendants.

6. Village/Rural Life

The Indian population primarily resides in villages/rural society even though urbanisation is growing. As per Census 2011, 68.8 per cent, i.e. more than two-thirds of the population live in rural areas in India. In India, all areas that are not characterised as urban area are considered as rural area. Most of the people in rural area make their living through agriculture or other allied activities.

Land is the primary asset that people possess. However, land is not just a form of property, nor is agriculture just a form of livelihood. Rather, people have emotional connection with their lands, and agriculture is a way of life for many. In fact, many of our cultural practices can also be traced to our agrarian backgrounds. For example, festivals such as Bihu in Assam and Baisakhi in Punjab celebrate the harvest season and the beginning of the new agricultural season.

6.1 Characteristics of Village Life

1. Caste plays a key role in the daily lives of people. The answer to the questions- who will till the land, who will conduct ritual ceremonies, who are major landowners- have caste linkages. Caste-based hamlets can still be seen in Indian villages.
2. Villagers maintain both physical unity as well as social solidarity. Families exhibit solidarity even though they belong to different castes and are not related. However, in a dispute between members of two different castes, one caste stands united against the other.
3. As far as the family system is concerned, joint families are more commonly found in villages. It is to be noted that joint families are found mainly among the economically well-off higher castes rather than the poor lower and untouchable castes. Thus, joint family phenomena are related to the economy of households.
4. In terms of marital relations, North India follows village exogamy, i.e. a woman cannot be married to a man of the same village. While in South India, marriages do take place within the village.
5. The commercialisation of agriculture is taking place even in rural areas. However, it is only medium and large farmers who are able to benefit from the revolution in agriculture as input costs are high and technology is affordable only for them. Thus, these farmers are able to produce for the market. While small landowners can produce only for their own consumption.
6. Seasonal migration is one of the characteristics of rural India. Small landowners and agricultural labourers have less income during the non-farming season. Rural households utilise the migration of their members as a mechanism to improve their income and well-being.

7. Unity across Diverse Groups: Tolerance and Love

Unity implies integration among diverse groups. It means socio-psychological ties that bind all the members together in a society.

Since ancient times, India has seen an influx of various religious, linguistic and ethnic groups. All the groups have assimilated so well that India is truly believed to be the 'cradle of human civilisations'. India maintains and truly follows the spirit of tolerance and love for all.

Even in present times, one can find that in spite of various internal and external threats from various agencies, such as ISIS, left-wing extremist groups and communal groups, India has been able to maintain both territorial and psychological unity across groups.

B. Continuity and Changes in the Indian Society

In India, traditional social values are, to a great extent, derivative of social institutions. Social values such as obedience to elders, importance to family and performance of religious rituals at the village level are transmitted and internalised through institutions such as family, religion and caste.

8. Continuity and Change of Traditional Values through Social Institutions

8.1 Caste System

Continuity

1. *Endogamy*: Still, members of society prefer to marry within their own caste. One can see that even on matrimonial websites, prospective groom/bride specify their preference with respect to the caste of the spouse.
2. *Hierarchy*: The value system of '*unch-nic*h' is still prevalent in our society, especially in rural India.
3. *Caste-based rituals and ceremonies*: For instance, the 'twice-born caste' conducts the ritual of 'sacred thread wearing ceremony' or *Janeu* ceremony for its members.

Changes

1. *Disintegration of occupational linkage to caste*: Due to the constitutional right to equality and growing urbanisation, nearly all fields of employment are open to all.
2. *Reduced observance of purity-pollution norms:* The attitudinal shift and exigencies of modern life make it inconvenient and unacceptable to observe such norms. Hence, inter-dining at public places is common now.

8.2 Family System

Continuity

1. Emotional and financial dependence on family still continues.
2. Practice of respecting and obeying elders in the family.
3. Marriage decisions are still largely determined by the family.

Changes

1. Increasing individualism and space to exercise personal autonomy, e.g. career choice decision, age of marriage.

2. Consumeristic value has increased significantly, e.g. shopping mall culture in India.
3. Shift towards having a lesser number of children, especially in urban India.

8.3 Religion

Continuity

1. *Belief in supernatural force*: In the modern time, when there is much complexity and uncertainty in public life, individuals tend to take part in religious activity because it provides solace.
2. *Following religion-based practices:* For instance, going to a temple or a mosque for praying, as well as the style of praying of various religions, have been continuing for centuries.
3. *Following social norms based on religion:* An individual is socialised by observing specific social practices at home. There is an intrinsic societal expectation for him to follow such norms, e.g. a devout Hindu avoids eating beef.

Changes

1. *Outlawing of inhumane religious-based practices*: This includes the practice of sati or human sacrifices.
2. Traditionally, because of a relatively simple life and the availability of time, one would go to temples or religious places to conduct pujas. However, now one can see that even online services are being adopted to conduct pujas because of hectic life schedules.

8.4 Village Life

Continuity

1. Caste and religious norms are strongly observed in villages even today. Interactions, habitation patterns, inter-dining are based on caste norms.
2. Marriages are generally not conducted within a village, i.e. village exogamy is still practiced to a great extent.

Changes

1. There is continuous interaction between villages and cities due to migration, connectivity facilities, information and communication technology revolution. As a result, urban values like individualism and materialism have penetrated in the rural areas too.

C. Diversity and Challenges

It is true that India has been able to maintain unity across its diverse groups to a great extent. It is due to the fact that India has emerged as a successful and vibrant democracy. However, India has also been facing a few challenges in this regard. Some of them are as follows:

1. *Threat to integrity*: India has seen instances when religious and linguistic groups have made efforts and demanded secession, thus posing a challenge to the territorial integrity of India.
2. *Divisive politics*: Sometimes, political groups, for the purpose of gaining votes, try to lure voters from specific groups by creating division among various religious, ethnic and linguistic groups.
3. *Psychological disunity*: Diversity makes it difficult for people to believe in the idea of 'one-ness of all'. In India, people still identify themselves on the basis of their caste, religion, etc. It, therefore, becomes difficult to build India as a nation in a 'psychological sense'.
4. *Ethnic conflict*: India has also witnessed cases of ethnic conflict. For example, the recent violence in Manipur is a case in point.
5. *Communal violence*: Because of religious diversity, India becomes vulnerable to communal violence. Since the time of the partition of India, there have been various communal incidents, e.g. *Babri Masjid* case, Anti-Sikh Riots.

Society Today

Manipur Ethnic issue

Since May 2023, the state of Manipur has witnessed severe ethnic clashes between the Meitei community and the Kuki tribal groups. The Meiteis constitute about 53% of the total population in the State and primarily reside in the Imphal Valley, whereas the tribal communities - mainly the Kuki and Naga - make up around 40% and inhabit the surrounding hill districts. Notably, the Meiteis are predominantly Hindu, while the tribal communities largely follow Christianity.

Causes for Friction

1. **Historical disputes:** Long-standing issues exist between the tribal communities and the majority Meitei community regarding political representation, land ownership and ethnic identity.
2. **Land ownership:** In Manipur, while tribals can buy land in the valley, the Meitei are prohibited from buying land in the hills. This has generated perception among the tribals that Meitei intend to take over the tribal lands in the hills, causing perennial distrust. Meitei, however, argue that they are restricted to only 10% of the area in the State while the tribals hold over 90% of the same.

3. **Development disparities:** Even though 90% of the areas fall in the tribal-dominated hill districts, tribals say that most of the developmental works and funds are devolved in the Meitei-dominated Imphal Valley.
4. **Law and security concerns:** The Kuki tribal group have been alleged to be involved in drug trafficking, forest encroachment and harbouring illegal migrants, causing further mistrust between the communities.
5. **Scheduled Tribe (ST) Status Demand:** The constant demand by the Meitei community since 2012 for ST status is another cause of tension between the Meitei and tribal communities.
6. **Immediate cause:** The most immediate cause was the stance taken by Manipur High Court in March 2023 regarding ST status of Meitei. The Court directed the State Government to consider the case of inclusion of the Meitei community in the ST list. This triggered intense protest and ultimately escalated into violent conflict.

It is important to highlight that the Manipur High Court, in Feb 2024, deleted the paragraph in its March 2023 order which recommended ST status for the Meiteis community. The High Court said that its ruling was passed in "misconception of law".

Impact and Government response: As per various published reports, the ethnic clash has resulted in the killing of more than 250 people and displacement of around 60,000 people. After two years of intense clash, the Central Government imposed President's Rule in the State in February 2025 to bring the situation under control. After application of President's Rule, the Government need to -

- disarm both the communities, including militant outfits, militias and village defence groups and establish law and order
- immediately rehabilitate and re-settle the victims of the violence
- bring all parties - Meitei, Kuki, Naga, and other stakeholders - together for negotiations and peace talks regarding rights of the tribals and other communities in the State

Additional Readings

1. *Language Atlas of India 2011.*
2. Census of India 2011: Language.
3. *NCERT Class XII Sociology.*
4. Indira Gandhi National Open University, Ethnic elements in Indian Population (Unit 5).
5. B.S. Guha, *Census of India, 1931; Vol. 1–India; Part III–Ethnographical (A. Racial Affinities of the People of India)* (1935).
6. Indira Gandhi National Open University, Caste System In India, Module IV, Chapter 27.
7. A.a. macdonell, the early history of caste. *the american historical review* 19: 230–244 (1914).
8. L. Dushkin, Scheduled caste policy in India: History, problems, prospects. *Asian Survey* 7: 626–623 (1967).

9. Ministry of Tribal Affairs, Annual Report 2021-2022.
10. Ministry of Health and Family Welfare and Ministry of Tribal Affairs, Report of the Expert Committee on Tribal Health (2018).
11. NFHS Report: Dip in women owning property, but better financial, social autonomy.
12. P.R. Bannerjee, Dowry in 21st Century India. *Trauma, Violence, & Abuse* 15: 34 (2014).
13. S.A. Freed and R.S. Freed, Changing family types in India. *Ethnology* 21:189 (1982).
14. P. Puschmann and A. Solli, Household and family during urbanization and industrialization: Efforts to shed new light on an old debate.
15. B. Gupta, Modernity and the Hindu joint family system: A problematic interaction. *International Journal on World Peace* 11: 37 (1994).
16. S. Kakar, Family matters. *India International Centre Quarterly* 33: 214 (2007).
17. N. Kumar, Dalit and Shudra politics and anti-Brahmin movement. *Economic and Political Weekly* 35: 3977 (2000).
18. N.K. Bose, *Tribal Life in India* (National Book Trust, 2017).

Previous Years' Questions

Diversity of India

1. Describe any four cultural elements of diversity in India and rate their relative significance in building a national identity. (2015)
2. In the context of the diversity of India, can it be said that the regions form cultural units rather than the States? Give reasons with examples for your viewpoint. (2017)
3. Do we have cultural pockets of small India all over the nation? Elaborate with examples. (2019)

Caste

1. Debate the issue of whether and how contemporary movements for assertion of Dalit identity work towards annihilation of caste. (2015)
2. "Caste system is assuming new identities and associational forms. Hence caste system cannot be eradicated in India." Comment. (2018)
3. Has caste lost its relevance in understanding the multi-cultural Indian Society? Elaborate your answer with illustrations. (2020)
4. Why is caste identity in India both fluid and static? (2023)

Tribals

1. How do you explain the statistics that show that the sex ratio in Tribes in India is more favourable to women than the sex ratio among Scheduled Castes? (2015)
2. Why are the tribals in India referred to as 'the Scheduled Tribes'? Indicate the major provisions enshrined in the Constitution of India for their upliftment. (2016)

3. What are the two major legal initiatives by the State since Independence addressing discrimination against Scheduled Tribes (STs)? (2017)
4. Examine the uniqueness of tribal knowledge systems when compared with mainstream knowledge and cultural systems. (2021)
5. Given the diversities among tribal communities in India, in which specific contexts should they be considered as a single category? (2022)
6. How did the colonial rule affect the tribals in India and what was the tribal response to the colonial oppression? (2023)

Multi-cultural

1. What makes the Indian society unique in sustaining its culture? Discuss. (2019)
2. Customs and traditions suppress reason leading to obscurantism. Do you agree? (2020)
3. The spirit of tolerance and love is not only an interesting feature of Indian society from very early times, but it is also playing an important part at the present. Elaborate. (2017)
4. Analyse the salience of 'sect' in Indian society vis-a-vis caste, region and religion. (2022)

Family, Marriage and Kinship

1. The life cycle of a joint family depends on economic factors rather than social values. Discuss. (2014)
2. Why do some of the most prosperous regions of India have an adverse sex ratio for women? Give your arguments. (2014)
3. How does patriarchy impact the position of a middle class working woman in India? (2014)
4. Explore and evaluate the impact of 'Work From Home' on family relationships. (2022)
5. Do you think marriage as a sacrament is losing its value in Modern India? (2023)
6. Explain why suicide among young women is increasing in Indian society. (2023)
7. Child cuddling is now being replaced by mobile phones. Discuss its impact on the socialization of children. (2023)

Continuity and Changes in Indian Society

1. How does Indian society maintain continuity in traditional social values? Enumerate the changes taking place in it. (2021)

Indian Society and New Technology

1. What is Cryptocurrency? How does it affect global society? Has it been affecting Indian society also? (2021)

UPSC CSE 2025

1. Does tribal development in India centre around two axes, those of displacement and of rehabilitation? Give your opinion. (250 Words | 15 Marks)

Model Answer

Tribal development in India has often revolved around the twin axes of displacement and rehabilitation, as noted by the **Xaxa Committee Report** of 2014. Although tribal communities constitute only 8.6 percent of India's population, they account for more than 40 percent of those displaced by large projects such as dams, mines, industries, and conservation efforts.

Axis One: Displacement

1. **Dams and Hydropower Projects:** Projects like the Narmada Valley Development Project and Polavaram Irrigation Project displaced lakhs of tribals.
2. **Mining and Industries:** Tribes such as the Santhals in Jharkhand and the Dongria Kondhs in Odisha lost ancestral lands to coal and bauxite mining.
3. **Conservation Projects:** Baigas and Gonds were uprooted from tiger reserves, often without village assembly consent, despite the Forest Rights Act of 2006.
4. **Urban Development:** Migrant tribals face eviction from slums in cities like Delhi and Mumbai.

Axis Two: Rehabilitation

1. **Tokenism:** Cash compensation overlooks cultural and community ties.
2. **Policy Gaps:** The National Rehabilitation and Resettlement Policy of 2007 and the Land Acquisition, Rehabilitation and Resettlement Act of 2013 mandate participatory rehabilitation, but implementation remains weak.
3. **Cultural Erosion:** Resettlement colonies disrupt kinship networks and traditions.

Beyond Displacement and Rehabilitation

1. **Resistance Movements:** The Narmada Bachao Andolan and Niyamgiri movement demand consent-based, inclusive development.
2. **Positive Measures:** The Panchayats (Extension to Scheduled Areas) Act of 1996, the Minimum Support Price scheme for Minor Forest Produce, the Vanbandhu Kalyan Yojana, and the Tribal Cooperative Marketing Development Federation of India strengthen livelihoods.

As affirmed in *Samatha versus State of Andhra Pradesh* (1997), land is central to tribal identity. True development must move beyond displacement and partial rehabilitation towards participatory governance, livelihood security, and cultural preservation, ensuring justice and empowerment.

2. The ethos of Civil Services in India stands for the combination of Professionalism with nationalistic consciousness. Elucidate. (150 Words | 10 Marks)

Model Answer

Civil services are regarded as the "steel frame" of Indian democracy. Their ethos rests on two pillars - **professionalism**, rooted in neutrality and efficiency, and **nationalistic consciousness**, anchored in constitutional values and democratic nation-building.

1. **Professionalism**
   - **Impartiality & Neutrality:** Following *Max Weber's bureaucratic* model, civil servants must act with legality, objectivity, and ethical conduct.
   - **Efficiency in Implementation:** Neutral execution of schemes such as MGNREGA and the COVID-19 vaccination drive.
   - **Accountability & Reforms:** Electoral reforms under T.N. Seshan, transparency through the RTI Act, and digital innovations like Aadhaar and the JAM Trinity.
   - Capacity Building: Institutions such as LBSNAA, SVPNPA inculcate professional competence.

2. **Nationalistic Consciousness**
   - **People-Centric Governance:** Inspired by *Gandhian trusteeship*, officers act as trustees of unity, equity, and justice.
   - **Developmental Role:** Contribution to affirmative action, Green Revolution, and rural transformation.
   - **Safeguarding Sovereignty:** Service in insurgency-prone and border areas strengthens national security.
   - **Nation-building in Crises:** Relief during floods, and pandemics reflects commitment to public welfare.

The ethos of civil services lies in combining professionalism with nationalistic consciousness - delivering neutral yet empathetic governance, upholding constitutional morality, and ensuring India's democratic aspirations remain strong.

UPSC CSE 2024

1. Inter-caste marriages between castes which have socio-economic parity have increased, to some extent, but this is less true of inter-religious marriages. Discuss. (150 words | 10 Marks)

Model Answer

Marriage patterns in India are traditionally governed by caste and religion. While caste barriers have softened slightly due to social mobility, religious boundaries remain more rigid.

1. **Reasons for increasing Inter-caste Marriages**
    - Younger generations are mostly driven by personal aspirations, modern values, economic stability, partner compatibility rather than caste principles, especially when it comes to selection of partner for marriages.
    - Urbanisation and higher education have ensured interaction among various caste groups in similar workplace with similar socio-economic status. For example: Marriage among IT professionals in Bengaluru.
    - Lesser resistance from families if the couple has a similar socio-economic background i.e, economic compatibility overtakes caste considerations.
    - States like Maharashtra, Rajasthan, Tamil Nadu offer incentives for inter-caste couples, boosting acceptance.
    - Yet, such marriages remain rare in rural areas due to fear of social ostracism and honour crimes.

> As per the India Human Development Survey (IHDS-2, 2011–12), about 5% of marriages are inter-caste.

> *Dr. Savita Ben Ambedkar Inter-caste Marriage Scheme of Rajasthan Government:* Rs 10 lakh is provided as an incentive to couples entering inter-caste marriages.

2. **Reasons for less Inter-religious Marriages**
    - Such marriages face deeper resistance due to concerns over religious identity, community honour and doctrinal rigidity.
    - Complicated legal procedures under the Special Marriage Act, including 30-day notice, often deter couples.
    - Socio-political narratives (e.g., "love jihad") further discourage acceptance, especially in North India.

> Only 2–2.5% of marriages are inter-faith (IHDS-2).

While class mobility enables some inter-caste unions, true social integration requires dismantling both caste and religious barriers.

Source:

1. The IT Caste: Love and Arranged Marriages in the IT Industry of Bangalore By Michiel Baas (2009, South Asia: Journal of South Asian Studies)
2. Rajasthan govt hikes inter-caste marriage incentive to Rs 10 lakhs (The Economic Times: March 2023)

2. Critically analyse the proposition that there is a high correlation between India's cultural diversities and socio-economic marginalities. (250 words | 15 Marks)

Model Answer

India's rich Mcultural diversity - spanning religion, language, ethnicity, caste and tribal identities - forms the bedrock of its pluralistic society. However, many of these culturally distinct groups also experience socio-economic marginalisation, raising the question of whether diversity structurally correlates with disadvantage.

This manifests in multiple dimensions:

1. **Tribal Communities marginalisation:**
   - As per Census 2011, the literacy rate of Scheduled Tribes (STs) was 59% against the national average of 73%.
   - They face poverty, displacement and limited access to services.
   - Many are landless or marginal landholders, engaged in traditional occupations like hunting, pastoralism, and artisanal work.
   - Regions like Bastar and the North-East illustrate this overlap between cultural isolation and development exclusion.
2. **Religious Minorities and socio-economic backwardness:**
   - The *Sachar Committee Report (2006)* highlighted that Muslims face poor access to education, employment, and credit.
   - Discrimination and ghettoisation worsen their economic vulnerability.
3. **Caste diversities and marginalisation:**
   - The literacy rate of SCs was 66.1% (Census 2011).
   - SCs and STs remain overrepresented among the rural poor and urban slum populations.
   - Despite legal prohibition, most manual scavengers still belong to the SC community.
   - Dalit women face compounded marginalisation due to caste and gender.
4. **Marginalisation of De-notified and Nomadic Tribes:**
   - Communities like the *Sapera and Madari*, with mobile and unique livelihoods, face exclusion from welfare schemes and lack access to land, education, and services.
5. **Ethnic and Linguistic Minorities:**
   - Groups like the Bodos, Nagas, and Gorkhas maintain distinct identities but feel economically neglected, fuelling demands for autonomy.

However, there are notable exceptions and emerging trends that challenge this correlation -

1. **Socio-economically empowered minorities**
   - Groups like Parsis, Jains, and Jews retain cultural uniqueness yet are economically advanced.
2. **Affirmative action and caste groups upliftment**
   - As per AISHE 2021-22, SC and ST student enrolment rose by 44% and 65.2% respectively since 2014-15.

In sum, while cultural diversity often overlaps with marginality, it is not deterministic. Inclusive, identity-sensitive development is vital to addressing structural inequities.

Source:

1. Ministry of Education releases All India Survey on Higher Education (AISHE) 2020-2021 (PIB: Jan 2023)

2 Role of Women and Women's Organisation

1. Status of Women in India

Overcoming gender disparity is a major developmental goal for any emerging economy like India. Even though there has been progress and significant empowerment of women in the seventy-five years of independence, there is still a lot to achieve. Women face various forms of discrimination across their life cycle, and violence against women is still rampant.

As per the World Economic Forum's Global Gender Gap Report (2024), India ranked 129 among 146 countries in terms of gender parity. This ranking is a wake-up call as India cannot achieve its economic potential if the women of the country can't realise their full potential as equal citizens. To understand the various burdens imposed by gender discrimination, we must assess women's status in the fields of education, health, economic and political empowerment and enjoyment of safe, violence-free space. The following section is an appraisal of the women's position in various fields and major challenges therein.

1.1 Sex Ratio in India

One of the major parameters responsible for India's low rank in the Gender Gap Report is the skewed sex ratio of the country. The National Family Health Survey (NFHS-5) shows that the sex ratio at birth in India has improved from 919 females per 1,000 males in 2015–2016 to 929 females per 1,000 males in 2019–2020. The natural standard is the birth of 952 females per 1,000 male births.

Urban areas showed a poorer ratio compared to rural areas, indicating that access to sex-determination technology is distorting the sex ratio in urban areas. The reasons for this skewed sex ratio are discussed in detail as follows:

1. Systemic son preference as sons are seen as essential for carrying forward family names and inheriting family property.
2. Prevalence of daughter aversion because daughters are seen as liabilities. Ensuring their safety and well-being is perceived as a burden.
3. The institution of marriage is influenced by patriarchal norms. The hefty dowry requirement is another reason families do not want a girl child.
4. With modernisation and urbanisation, family sizes are becoming smaller. Families are using sex-determination technology to abort a girl child and ensure a male heir.
5. Even after birth, a girl child may have to suffer deprivation and neglection, which may at times lead to death.

Insight Box

The Pre-Conception and Pre-Natal Diagnostic Techniques Act (PC-PNDT) of 1994 was enacted with the primary aim of prohibiting prenatal diagnostic methods specifically used for determining the sex of the foetus, ultimately combatting female foeticide. Its fundamental objective was to curb the practice of female foeticide.

The Act has been designed and implemented to serve as a deterrent, targeting individuals engaged in the practice of sex determination. Violation of provisions can lead to the suspension of registration, filing of criminal cases and the sealing of machines. Besides, criminal prosecution will also result in the suspension and cancellation of registration granted by the State Medical Council.

1.2 Women and Education

Education has long been recognised as a key enabler of women's empowerment. Quality education paves the way not just for skills and competency but also for good self-esteem. In the context of an emerging economy like India, education is critical for the achievement of many social goals, such as good maternal health and sanitation.

Even though the importance of female education is well recognised, progress is less than desirable. As per the NFHS-5 data, the overall literacy rate for men stands at 84% while the rate for women lags behind at 72%. The average figures hide much diversity. An educationally advanced state like Kerala has an almost universal literacy rate, while in Bihar, the male literacy rate stands at 76% and the female literacy rate is dismal at 55% (NFHS-5). It is important to note that literacy is only the starting point of education.

With increased awareness and penetration of government and private schools, more and more girls are getting enrolled in schools, but some major barriers to education can be enumerated as follows:

1. Financial constraints in families.
2. A patriarchal mindset creates a preference for educating boys over girls, and fewer efforts and resources are available for girl-child education.
3. Care burden, whereby the girl child is burdened with household chores and the caretaking of younger siblings.
4. The lack of access to functional toilets has been identified as a major reason for the dropout of girl children.
5. At times, the lack of a safe environment at school and transport-related challenges become reasons for dropping out.

Both supply-side interventions, such as scholarships, access to functional toilets, safe transport and improved infrastructure in schools, and demand-side interventions, such as engaging parents and transforming patriarchal attitudes, are required to address these issues. Apart from enrolment, ensuring the attendance of girl children and good learning outcomes are continuing challenges in this field.

Insight Box

Schemes and Initiatives

- Samagra Shiksha Abhiyan
- Beti Bachao Beti Padhao
- Kasturba Gandhi Balika Vidyala (a residential school with female staff)
- Ladli Behan Scheme (MP)
- Mazhi Kanya Bhagyashree

Gender inequality in primary education has significantly declined in the past decade due to initiatives like Sarva Shiksha Abhiyan, the introduction of the right to compulsory and free primary education (Article 21A), and the Mid-day Meal Scheme. However, ensuring the transition of girls to secondary education and preventing dropouts remains a challenge.

Following are some barriers that cause a drop at the secondary level:

1. While primary schools are available in or near the village, secondary schools are at some distance. A lack of safe and reliable transportation is a challenge.
2. There is increased insecurity among parents regarding the safety of adolescent girls.
3. Research has shown that a lack of female teachers can be a major reason for dropouts at the secondary level.

4. Infrastructural inadequacy, such as a lack of functional toilets, drinking water and waiting hall.
5. High cost of private senior secondary education.
6. Lack of government hostels is also a factor as it may be impractical for children from remote or densely forested areas to undertake an unsafe commute daily.

There is a notable difference between urban and rural secondary school participation among girl children, indicating that there is a need for greater attention to reducing dropouts in rural areas. The rural location is strongly correlated with other disadvantages, like lower parental literacy rate and economic vulnerability. Hence, there is a clear need to push the universalisation of secondary and higher secondary education for girl children, particularly those in rural areas.

As per the *All India Survey on Higher Education (AISHE)* 2021-22, *female enrolment has increased to 2.07 crore in 2021-22 from 1.57 crore in 2014-15 (an increase of 50 lakh students, 32% increase).* While this shows an overall increasing demand for higher education among women, there is scope for improvement. Women's enrolment in post-graduate and technical education courses is lagging behind.

Needless to say, women's participation in education must be seen beyond enrolment. It must translate into quality education and competency in the labour market. Education has a positive correlation with women's health and is a key enabler for women to make informed maternal health choices.

Insight Box

Cycling to School: Increasing High School Enrolment for Girls in Bihar

The Bihar government introduced the *Mukhyamantri Balika Cycle Yojana* in 2006. This initiative aimed to provide a cash grant to every girl entering the ninth grade, enabling them to purchase a cycle for commuting to school. The rationale behind this scheme was to address the issue of low school density and reduce the dropout rate among girls by minimising travel time to distant schools. By providing cycles, the intention was to effectively bring schools closer without requiring substantial investments. The initial assessments of the program were highly positive, showing promising outcomes. It operated efficiently with minimal misuse: the first year witnessed a remarkable increase of over 30% in enrolment, and the scheme experienced leakages of less than 5%.

It was found that the cycle program was substantially more cost-effective at increasing girls' enrolment. This program may have resulted in additional positive outcomes beyond the cash value of the programme, including improved safety for girls cycling to school in groups and changes in patriarchal social norms that proscribed female mobility outside the village.

1.3 Women in the Workforce

Participation of women in the labour force has both economic and social value for India. Women constitute about half of the population and one third of the labour force in the country as of now. Female Labour Force Participation Rate (LFPR) has gone up from 30% in 2019-20 to 41.7% in 2023-24. There is a notable rise in Rural Female Labour Force Participation Rate from 33 % in 2019-20 to 47.6% in 2023-24, showing *increasing contribution of women in rural production.* LFPR is the share of the working-age population (aged 15 years and above) that is employed or unemployed, willing and looking for employment.

As seen in Table 2.1, *rural female labour force participation* has been consistently higher than urban female labour force participation. So the discussion of Indian women at work must start in rural India, where women are predominantly engaged in agriculture and allied activities.

Indicator	Rural	Urban	Rural + Urban
LFPR (PLFS 2023-2024)	Female: 47.6 Male: 80.2	Female: 28.0 Male: 75.6	Female: 41.7 Male: 78.8
LFPR (PLFS 2022-2023)	Female: 41.5 Male: 80.2	Female: 25.4 Male: 74.5	Female: 37.0 Male: 78.5
LFPR (PLFS 2021-2022)	Female: 36.6 Male: 78.2	Female: 23.8 Male: 74.7	Female: 32.8 Male: 77.2
LFPR (PLFS 2020-2021)	Female: 36.5 Male: 78.1	Female: 23.2 Male: 74.6	Female: 32.5 Male: 77.0
LFPR (PLFS 2019-2020)	Female: 33.0 Male: 77.9	Female: 23.3 Male: 74.6	Female: 30.0 Male: 76.8

Table 2.1: Rural and Urban Female Labour Force Participation
Note: PLFS *is the Periodic Labour Force Survey*

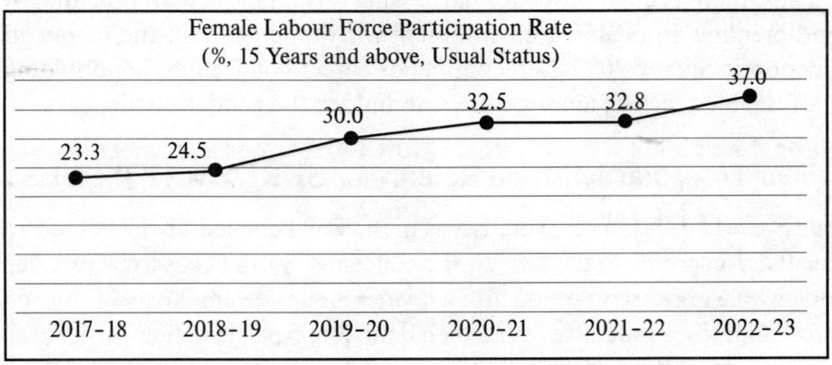

Source: PIB

The ICAR-Central Institute for Women in Agriculture (CIWA) acknowledges that women are the invisible face of agriculture in India. Although women farmers contribute significantly to agricultural work, they operate only 11.72% of the total operated area in the country, as per the Agriculture Census 2015-16. This reflects a stark disparity in land ownership and creates significant barriers for women in accessing agriculture-related benefits such as crop loans, insurance, and subsidies. Since land is the primary asset in rural areas, limited ownership makes women farmers more vulnerable to eviction and poverty. Moreover, most women landowners fall within the small and marginal category, where subsistence farming is prevalent, further limiting their economic security and agricultural productivity.

After the liberalisation reforms of the 1990s, a significant share of the male work force transitioned to the secondary and tertiary sectors of the economy due to better education and employment opportunities. But a similar transition has not happened for the female work force, which remains largely concentrated in the primary sector- agriculture and allied activities. This sector is particularly vulnerable to climate change and major price fluctuations. Therefore, it is essential to consider the needs of all women farmers when formulating policies. Schemes and agricultural mechanisation tools tailored to women can provide much-needed recognition and support. Additionally, a policy push to enable more women to own or share the land they cultivate would be a crucial step toward empowering them economically and socially.

Going ahead, if we shift our focus to urban *female labour force participation*, it becomes evident from the above table that although it has shown an upward trend in recent years, it still lags behind rural female labour force participation. According to the PLFS 2023-24, the urban female labour force participation rate stands at 28.0%. Several factors contribute to this disparity, including deeply rooted societal norms that disproportionately assign household responsibilities to women, persistent labour market discrimination, mismatch between women's skills and the demands of the urban job market, focus on higher education delaying workforce entry, among others.

Overall, if we look at the female labour force participation in India, it is encouraging to note an increasing trend over the last few years. As per the PFLS 2023-24, it is around 41.7%, a significant rise from earlier years. However, it still remains below the global average female labour force participation of around 52.4% and significantly below when compared to some East Asian economies, where it is as high as 66%. Thus, there is great scope for harnessing this latent human potential by empowering more women and creating an enabling environment for women to join the labour market. In this direction, the Economic Survey 2022-23 recommends career counselling/handholding, lodging and transportation, affordable creches, among others, to unlock the gender dividend.

Female Labour Force Participation Rate: MEASUREMENT ISSUES

The **Economic Survey 2022-23** points out issues in the way Female Labour Force Participation Rate is calculated. According to the Survey, the concept of work needs to be broadened. Work should include whole universe of productive activities alongside employment. As per the latest ILO standards, limiting productive work to labour force participation is narrow and only measures work as a market product. It does not include the value of women's unpaid domestic work, which can be seen as expenditure-saving work such as collecting firewood, cooking, tutoring children, etc, and contributes significantly to the household's standard of living.

Debate Corner

To what extent is the underrepresentation of women in India's workforce driven by societal and systemic constraints, as opposed to individual choices and economic factors?

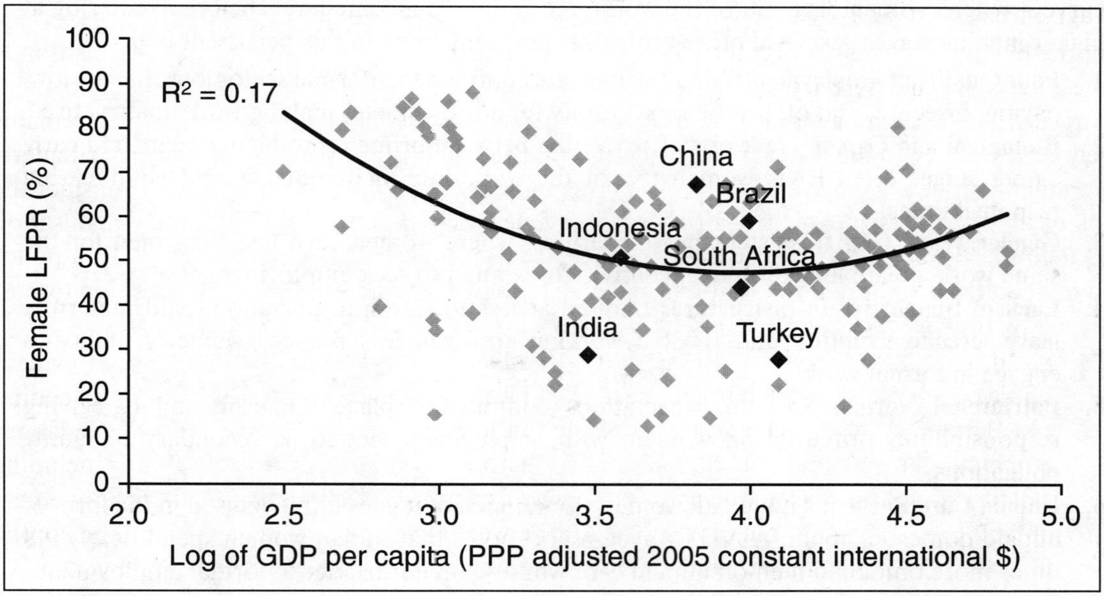

Fig. 2.1 The U-Shaped Curve for Female LFPR
(Source: ILO Model Estimates, ILOSTAT)

Sometimes the U-shaped curve is used to analyse the decline/slow improvement in female labour force participation in India (see Fig. 2.1).

The curve shows that female labour force participation is higher in underdeveloped economies. Such participation is borne out of necessity as women work to financially support their families.

As an economy transitions to a developing and intermediate stage, women withdraw from the workforce as a single income becomes adequate to support the family. Attitudes towards employment and labour demand patterns change, so women choose to focus on domestic responsibilities.

However, with further rise in female education and increasing value of labour, women move back into the labour force, and this rising part of the curve is known as the *substitution effect.*

Insight Box

Understanding the low Female Labour Force Participation in Urban India

Despite economic growth and rising educational attainment, female labour force participation in urban India remains stagnant. While some experts explain this trend using the U-shaped curve – where women drop out of the workforce at middle-income levels before re-entering at higher income stages – several other critical factors contribute to this persistent issue:

1. **Poor Quality of Employment:** Many women are confined to informal sector jobs that are low-paying, insecure, and offer little opportunity for advancement, making work unattractive.
2. **Biological and Career Trade-offs:** The overlap between prime reproductive years and early career stages often leads women to exit the workforce for pregnancy and child-rearing responsibilities.
3. **Gender Wage Gap:** Persistent pay disparities, where women earn less than men for the same work, create long-term disincentives for women to seek employment.
4. **Lack of Supportive Infrastructure:** Limited access to safe transportation, paid maternity leave, crèche facilities, and flexible working arrangements reduces women's ability to engage in formal work.
5. **Patriarchal Norms:** Societal expectations continue to place domestic and caregiving responsibilities primarily on women, with employment viewed as secondary to family obligations.
6. **Unpaid Care Burden:** Though all women work, much of it goes unrecognised in the form of unpaid domestic labour. A NITI Aayog report notes that Indian women spend nearly 9.8 times more time than men on unpaid care work – a major barrier to formal employment.
7. **Safety and Lack of Agency:** Concerns over safety in public spaces often lead families to restrict women's mobility, limiting their freedom to pursue work outside the home.

These overlapping structural, social, and economic barriers collectively hinder women's economic participation and call for urgent policy intervention to create a more inclusive and enabling environment.

Insight Box

Role of Women in Pink Collar Jobs

Over the years, the issue of women being over-represented in certain job profiles has been raised. Most of these jobs involve some form of care work and for various socio-economic factors, such jobs are considered more suitable for women. Teaching, nursing, social work and the beauty industry are classic examples of such jobs, and together, they are popularly known as pink collar jobs. While women's labour force participation in any form is welcome, it is also important that they are represented in traditionally male-dominated jobs like scientists, technology industry and the like.

Landmark Judgements

1. *Air India v. Nargesh Mirza (1981)*

Justices Syed Murtaza Fazali, A Varadarajan, AP Sen

Air India once enforced policies requiring female flight attendants to resign upon marriage, retire at age 35, or leave after becoming pregnant. These practices were challenged by an employee who argued they unfairly targeted women.

The nation's highest court ruled that these employment conditions were unreasonable and violated constitutional rights to equality. This decision established an important precedent for combating workplace discrimination and protecting women's rights in professional settings.

The ruling emphasized that employers cannot impose arbitrary restrictions based on gender and reinforced the principle of equal treatment in the workplace. It marked a significant step forward in addressing unfair labour practices and promoting gender equality in employment.

2. *Neera Mathur v. Life Insurance Corporation of India and Another (1991)*

Justices K Jagannath Shetty and Yogeshwar Dayal

An employee of Life Insurance Corporation of India (LIC) named Neera Mathur was dismissed from her job for not disclosing her pregnancy on the employment declaration form. She challenged this decision in the Supreme Court, arguing that the termination was discriminatory and humiliating.

The Supreme Court ruled in Mathur's favor, stating that such intrusive and irrelevant questions about a woman's personal health were unconstitutional and violated Article 14 of the Indian Constitution. The court recommended removing such declarations from employment forms to ensure dignity and privacy for women in the workplace.

This ruling set an important precedent for workplace equality and women's rights in India. It emphasized that employers, including major corporations like LIC, cannot discriminate based on pregnancy or require disclosure of personal health information unrelated to job performance.

1.4 Women and Health

Good health and access to health institutions are crucial for longevity and obtaining social and economic opportunities. Women's health is also important because it directly influences the health of the next generation. Many studies have shown that gender-related barriers hamper women's health-seeking behaviour. These are discussed in detail in the next section.

The prevalence of anaemia among adolescent girls and pregnant and menstruating women has been a major concern for at least two decades. Unfortunately, recent data suggest that the number of women and children impacted by anaemia has only increased. NFHS-5 (2019–2020) shows that 57% of women, 59.1% of adolescent girls and 52.2% of pregnant women suffer from anaemia.

Increasing anaemia among all sections of women is a challenge and reflects issues of poor dietary choices even among educated and financially well-off families. It is even more worrisome that nearly half of all pregnant women suffer from anaemia, and it has lifelong implications for the baby. Research has shown that children with anaemic mothers are at risk of inter-generational deprivation and poor physical and cognitive development.

NITI Aayog has highlighted how this vicious circle of poor nutrition can lead to inter-generational poverty and an increased burden of malnutrition in the country.

Initiatives for Anaemia Mukt Bharat

1. Iron and folic acid supplementation for all target groups
2. Testing with a special focus on pregnant women and adolescent girls
3. Behaviour change like promoting consumption of local iron-rich foods through *Poshan Maah*
4. Addressing non-nutritional causes of anaemia like endemic malaria and fluorosis
5. Incentives to ASHA workers for follow-up in high-priority districts

The *National Sickle Cell Anaemia Elimination* programme launched by the Union Budget 2023 to target sickle cell anaemia, especially among tribal populations.

Apart from the prevalence of anaemia, **maternal health-related challenges** are faced by most women. Some reasons for this are discussed below:

1. Lack of financial resources to avail health facilities.
2. Women, especially in rural areas, do not have decision-making power regarding their own health. They are dependent on elders or a male figure in such matters. The use of contraceptives and family planning is a classic example in this regard.
3. There is a lack of awareness and knowledge among women. For example, many myths are still prevalent regarding pregnancy and breast feeding.
4. Customs or traditional practices may negatively impact women's health. For example, menstruation is still a taboo topic in many regions. The taboo and superstitions deprived women and girls of period hygiene products.
5. Women's and girl's well-being is not a priority for most families. The practice of women eating last in most households symbolically reflects this issue. Research has shown that one eating last gets less or lower quality food.
6. Health infrastructure and manpower-related challenges are also an issue. In rural and remote areas, a lack of female doctors may discourage women from seeking medical help.

In the discussion regarding women's health, their **mental health** is a neglected area. Research has shown that women are more likely to be exposed to risk factors for poor mental health, such as violence, childhood neglect, financial insecurity and loss of a loved one.

Social scientists also discuss women's paradoxical situation, where women are getting empowerment through education and employment but still getting treated like second-grade citizens in private and public spaces. This paradoxical situation also makes women more vulnerable to mental health challenges.

The Indian Women's Health Report 2021 surveyed working women and found that women feel unsupported in managing health issues at work. Educational institutions and workplaces need to destigmatise women's health issues and ensure that health challenges do not become the reason for women dropping out.

Landmark Judgements

1. *Suchita Srivastava and Another v. Chandigarh Administration (2009)*

Chief Justice KG Balakrishnan and Justices BS Chauhan and P Satharivam

This case involved a woman's right to terminate her pregnancy under India's Medical Termination of Pregnancy Act, 1971. The Supreme Court ruled that the decision to end a pregnancy falls within a woman's right to privacy and personal autonomy, as protected by Article 21 of the Indian Constitution.

The judgment reinforced the principle that reproductive choices are a fundamental right for women in India. It emphasized that women have the autonomy to make decisions about their own bodies and reproductive health without undue interference.

This ruling has significant implications for women's rights and healthcare in India. It strengthens legal protections for women seeking abortions and upholds their right to make personal medical decisions.

2. *The Principal Secretary Health and Family Welfare Department, Delhi NCT Government and Another (2022)*

Justices: DY Chandrachud, AS Bopanna, and JB Pardiwala

This case expanded abortion rights in India by ruling that unmarried women are also entitled to seek medical termination of pregnancy up to 24 weeks, just like married women. The Supreme Court held that denying this right to unmarried women in consensual relationships while allowing it for married women violates the constitutional right to equality under Article 14.

The Court emphasized that the Medical Termination of Pregnancy (MTP) Act should be interpreted liberally to uphold reproductive rights. This ruling reinforces the principle that reproductive choices are fundamental rights for all women, regardless of marital status.

This decision has significant implications for women's healthcare and reproductive rights in India. It removes a discriminatory barrier and ensures more equitable access to abortion services for unmarried women.

1.5 Pandemic and Women

The report **Women and Girls Left Behind (2021)** by UN Women has shown the disproportionate impact of the pandemic on women. Women were at greater risk of permanent job loss due to the lockdowns imposed in the wake of the pandemic. Many surveys have shown how the pandemic worsened the gender poverty gap and that women were forced to hold insecure, low-paying informal jobs during the pandemic. In general, women faced an increased burden of unpaid care work during the pandemic.

An alarming rise in complaints of domestic and sexual violence was reported during the lockdown. The term **'shadow pandemic'** was coined to describe this silent emergency wherein violence against women, especially in private spaces, increased manifold. The strict lockdown and social isolation norms made it difficult for women struggling with violence to seek support. Poor mental health and increased violence against women have been widely recognised as unintended consequences of the pandemic-induced lockdowns.

1.6 Women and Leadership Role

Women's political participation is a key measure of gender equality in any society. India is an exception, where the right to vote was extended to women without much political debate. In that sense, women's right to self-determination was easily recognised. But how far has this right enabled women to access higher echelons of power? This is a question to which there are no easy answers.

A quantitative analysis of women's political participation reveals significant progress over the decades. The 2019 Lok Sabha elections marked a historic moment, as women's voter turnout (67.18%) marginally surpassed that of men (67.01%) for the first time since Independence. This is particularly noteworthy when compared to the 1962 general elections, where women's turnout lagged behind men by over 16%.

This growing electoral participation has sparked interest in the concept of a distinct female vote bank. Earlier, it was widely assumed that women's political choices were influenced or determined by male family members. However, in recent years, political parties have increasingly tailored their outreach towards women. Initiatives such as 'pink manifestos', dedicated women's wings in parties, and gender-based welfare promises reflect this shift. Even policies like liquor prohibition have been framed as measures that resonate with women voters, especially considering the impact of alcohol abuse on domestic violence and household finances.

Additionally, offering reservations for women in state services has been interpreted as another strategy to attract female support. Nonetheless, experts caution that due to the intersecting influences of caste, class, and regional identities, women in India cannot be viewed as a uniform electoral bloc. Their diverse lived experiences make political alignment more nuanced than the idea of a monolithic vote bank suggests.

While women as voters have claimed increasing political space, the same cannot be said for women's share in the country's highest political institutions. The 2019 Lok Sabha had the highest share of women in history, but even this was less than 15%. As of June 2025, share of women legislators in the Rajya Sabha stands at a mere 16.3%. Tables 2.2 and 2.3 demonstrate the share of women in Parliament over the years.

Year of General Election	Total Contestants	Women Contestants (Number)	Women Contestants (%)	Total Seats	Women Elected (Number)	Women Elected (%)
1999	4648	284	6.1	543	49	9.0
2004	5435	355	6.5	543	45	8.3
2009	8070	536	6.9	543	59	10.9
2014	8251	668	8.0	543	62	11.4
2019	8054	726	9.0	543	78	14.4
2024	8360	800	9.6	543	74	13.6

Table 2.2 Number and Percentage of Women Contestants and Women Elected over Total Seats in Last 5 General Elections to Lok Sabha

(Source: ECI Releases Granular Data of Lok Sabha Elections 2024 (PIB: Dec 2024))

Year	Women Member (Number)	Women Member (%)
2012	24	9.8
2014	31	12.8
2016	27	11.0
2018	28	11.4
2019	26	10.83
2021	29	12.24
2025	40	16.33

Table 2.3 Representation of Women Elected/Nominated in Rajya Sabha during 2012 to 2025 (June)

> **Debate Corner**
> Does the low representation of women in leadership positions in India reflect a lack of opportunity—or a deeper, systemic reluctance to accept women as leaders?

The situation regarding women's participation in legislative assembly varies across states. But with the exception of a handful of states like Uttar Pradesh, Rajasthan, Chattisgarh, Jharkhand and West Bengal, the percentage of female legislators is at or below 10%, indicating that women's political representation is lagging behind at the state level. Political experts have pointed out that the poor representation of women is partly explained by the continued hesitation in fielding female candidates. In the 2024 Lok Sabha elections, out of the 8360 contestants, less than 10% were women. Although progress has been made, electoral politics is still largely dominated by men.

Another issue that has been raised regarding women's political representation is the issue of dynasties. It has been argued that most women in Parliament and legislative assemblies have been enabled by their political background, specifically by political stalwart fathers, husband, brothers and so on. This is a undeniable trend in entire South Asia because a political family brings the advantage of legitimacy and institutional support to any candidate. But still, there are examples of women who entered politics as party workers and made their own way in the corridors of power.

The above analysis suggests that education, growing political awareness, efforts of the women's movement and inclusion initiatives of the Election Commission have translated into increased political participation by women. However, there are institutional and attitudinal barriers that inhibit women from contesting and winning elections, especially at the state and national levels. Even when elected in large numbers as seen in local governance bodies, women may struggle to reach full potential as leaders due to such barriers. Some of these barriers are discussed below:

1. *Lack of Information and awareness*: This challenge is felt most in the case of women leaders at the local level, like gram panchayats, panchayat samiti and the like. While the 73rd Constitution Amendment Act bestowed political leadership on women, all are not adequately educated and prepared for the responsibilities. For many, this is the first time they are venturing into public space, and hence, public communication may be a challenge. All such barriers inhibit effective women's leadership at the ground level and encourage proxies like *Sarpanch Pati* to take over decision-making.
2. *Domestic responsibilities and care burden:* Women continue to be responsible for household chores and child-rearing. Political careers and related work suffer as women struggle to balance both.
3. *Attitudinal barriers*: In some families, it may be considered inappropriate for women to participate in politics. It may be considered undesirable for a woman to interact with the outside world without the supervision of male members. Similar women leaders themselves may lack political consciousness and not consider their political future very seriously.
4. *Patriarchal norms in political parties*: As already discussed, the average Indian political party is dominated by male decision-makers. It is hard to get support as a female candidate. The financial resources required to contest elections make it difficult for women to contest as independent candidates.
5. *Criminalisation of politics*: The increasing prevalence of violence and criminalisation of politics is another factor driving away women from active political participation.

6. *Stereotyping of female leaders*: Women leaders may have to suffer unsavoury controversies and even character assassination, which acts as deterrence for other women.

Need for reforms

Needless to say, efforts to improve both the quantity and quality of women's participation are required to ensure women get an effective role in decision-making. It's an essential condition to realise both development goals and substantive democracy in the country.

One landmark reform in the field of gender-inclusive politics is the recently passed Constitution (One Hundred and Twenty-Eighth Amendment) Bill, 2023. This historic legislation reserves 1/3rd of the total seats for women in the Lok Sabha, state legislative assemblies and the Delhi Assembly. The bill has a sub-quota for women belonging to Scheduled Castes and Scheduled Tribes. The reserved seats shall be allotted in rotation, and as per the Act, reservation of seats shall cease to exist 15 years after commencement.

To appreciate the significance of this legislation, one must know that only 15 out of some 389 members of the Constituent Assembly were women. The Assembly did not guarantee any political reservation to women because it was assumed that the civil rights guaranteed by the Constitution would be enough to enable women's participation. As discussed above, women's marginal representation in Lok Sabha and state assemblies has falsified this assumption.

Women were given political representation in rural and urban local bodies, but the 81st Constitution Amendment Bill for the reservation of seats in Parliament was not passed. After this, the Bill was sent to the Joint Parliamentary Committee headed by Geeta Mukherjee for observations and building consensus. Between 1998 and 2003, the bill lapsed atleast four times.

Finally, in a specially convened parliamentary session in September 2023, the Bill was passed in both the Rajya Sabha and Lok Sabha with almost unanimity. The Act is undoubtedly a significant landmark for women's political empowerment. With its passage, India has achieved parity with most of its south Asian counterparts, like Nepal (33%) and Bangladesh (50%), who already have reservations for women.

But it must be noted that passage of the Bill is only one of the many steps that are needed to bring the Act to its logical conclusion.

- First, the issue of delimitation must be sorted out, and the exercise must be done in a transparent and consensual manner.
- Second, political parties must adopt a voluntary quota and focus sincerely on nurturing female political participation throughout the ranks and file.

Political parties being the main source of politics and representation, it has been suggested that reforms are needed to ensure parties give a fair chance to women.

The experience of Rwanda, the country with the highest number of female lawmakers at nearly 62%, is pertinent for India. Political reservation for women helped the country dramatically improve women's representation in national politics. But social acceptance of women leaders and adequate capacity building are works in progress. Another concern is that the benefits of this reservation must be accessible to all women and not be limited to women from political dynasties.

Any discussion of women as leaders must touch upon the presence of women in public service and corporation. A UNDP report titled 'Gender Equality in Public Administration' has pointed out that women's share in top leadership is an abysmal 12%. Between 1950 and 2020, women made up just 13% of the Indian Administrative Service. India has yet to appoint a woman as Cabinet Secretary–the highest-ranking bureaucratic position in the country. Only a few states have had women serve as Chief Secretary or Director General of Police, reflecting the continuing gender gap in top administrative roles.

The report, **Diversity in the Boardroom** (Ernst & Young) has shown that gender diversity on the boards of companies has improved over the years. Almost 95% of NIFTY500 companies have at least one female board member. This same figure was a shocking 6% in 2013, so the representation of women in the top echelons has increased rapidly. Less than 5% of these 500 companies have female heads, showing that there is a long way to go. In this context, the example of Indra Nooyi, the first ever female CEO of PepsiCo, is both inspiring and relevant. She has talked about the clash between career and the biological clock of a woman, and the need for supportive strategies to make corporations more inclusive.

1.7 Women and Media

Media influences public perceptions of issues. Hence, it is important to question whether the media portrayal of women is aligned with norms of gender sensitivity. Bollywood is one of the world's most successful media industries. It is not uncommon to hear female leads complain about male-centric scripts and the lack of quality roles for females in Bollywood movies.

Another problem that can easily be observed is the stereotypical portrayal of women in the media. Women are often portrayed as submissive, docile and vulnerable. TV serials showcasing women in traditional roles can be held most guilty in this regard. Such serials also tend to show relationships determined by patriarchal norms, where men are shown as powerful and authoritative.

Indecent representation of women especially in digital media is also an issue that demands serious attention. Such content can lead to dehumanisation of women in the minds of consumers and can potentially lead to increased violence against women. The issue of unrealistic body standards, which create unnecessary pressure on a woman to look a certain way, has also been highlighted recently.

It is high time that the media and associated industries resolve to portray women in a gender-inclusive manner.

1.8 Violence Against Women

Violence against women, such as physical, sexual and mental, has been a major manifestation of patriarchy. Such violence is a major human rights violation and a barrier to women obtaining their full rights as equal citizens. As per NFHS-5 data, 30% of women in the 18-49 age group had experienced some form of violence.

Major forms of violence against women are discussed below:

1. Domestic violence against women: Physical and mental abuse of women is a common form of violence against women. It is hard to tackle because perpetrators are known and loved ones. Second, it happens in the private sphere making it difficult to identify and support the victims leading to them remaining invisible.
2. Sexual violence against women by both intimate partners and non partners is a grave problem. Such violence, like rape and sexual assault, are underpinned by patriarchal mindsets which objectifies women's bodies. As per NCRB data, India registered 31,677 cases of rape in 2021. Not all forms of sexual violence against women is reported as there is considerable stigma around the issue. Victims of sexual violence also struggle to get adequate rehabilitation support.
3. Commercial sexual exploitation of women and girl children is another serious security threat. India is both a source as well as destination for trafficking of young women and children. Women are trafficked from source countries like Bangladesh, Nepal and Myanmar in the name of job opportunities and better lifestyle. Notably, women are trafficked not just for sexual exploitation but also cheap labour, especially as domestic help. There have been incidents of international trafficking in the name of marriage as well. Government of India is providing assistance to all States for setting up Anti Human Trafficking Units (AHTUs) and special assistance to border States for combatting this menace.
4. Violence against women in conflict zones: Women and children tend to be worst impacted in situations of conflict. The United Nations has acknowledged that women may face violence, sexual violence, torture and forced marriage during conflict situations.
5. Sexual Harassment at workplace has been recognised as major barrier in women's work force participation. Women are vulnerable to unwanted sexual advances at workplace and it is difficult to resist these due to power asymmetry of the workplace.

   The 'Me Too' movement has highlighted this issue in India and across the world. The Prevention of Sexual Harassment at Workplace (POSH), 2013 Act has been brought to address sexual harassment at workplace.

> **Debate Corner**
>
> Is the current legal and institutional framework in India sufficient to protect women from systemic violence, or is a radical restructuring needed to dismantle deeply rooted patriarchal norms?

Landmark Judgements

Vishaka and Others v. State of Rajasthan and Other (1997)

Chief Justice JS Verma, Justices Sujata V. Manohar, and BN Kirpal

This landmark case arose from the gang-rape of a social worker in Rajasthan, prompting women's rights groups to petition the Supreme Court for legal protections against workplace sexual harassment.

In response, the Supreme Court established comprehensive guidelines, known as the Vishaka Guidelines, to prevent and address sexual harassment in workplaces. The Court ruled that such harassment violated women's fundamental rights to equality, dignity, and a safe working environment under Articles 14, 15, and 21 of the Indian Constitution.

This judgment was pivotal in recognizing sexual harassment as a serious workplace issue and led to the eventual enactment of the Sexual Harassment of Women at Workplace (Prevention, Prohibition and Redressal) Act, 2013, **commonly known as the POSH Act.**

2. Main Initiative of the MWCD

The Ministry of Women and Child Development (MWCD) has launched Mission Shakti, an integrated scheme for safety, security and empowerment of women for the 15th Finance Commission period (2021–2022 to 2025–2026). The scheme caters to women's needs on a life-cycle basis and has two sub-schemes:

1. Sambal sub-scheme is for the safety and security of women.
2. Samarthya sub-scheme is for the empowerment of women.

2.1 Sambal Sub-scheme

1. One-stop centre to provide legal help and psychosocial counselling to women in need under one roof.
2. Women helpline (181-WHL) is an emergency toll-free number helpful for women.
3. *Beti Bachao Beti Padhao* is a scheme for behavioural and mindset change in favour of girls.
4. *Nari Adalat* is to provide women with an alternate dispute redressal platform for petty disputes.

2.2 Samarthya Sub-scheme

1. *Shakti Sadans* are integrated relief and rehabilitation centres for victims of trafficking, etc.
2. *Sakhi Niwas* is aimed at providing secure hostels to working women in cities.
3. *Palna Ghar* is to provide creche facilities to women and enable increase female labour force participation.
4. *Pradhan Mantri Matru Vandana Yojana* is a scheme that compensates women for lost wages due to pregnancy and seeks to promote better health-seeking behaviour among women. Now the benefit of the scheme also extends to the second child, even if the child is a girl.

The Ministry has also conceptualised national, state and district hubs for the empowerment of women.

2.3 Gender Budgeting

Gender budgeting has been globally recognised as a powerful tool to ensure gender-responsive planning and budgeting processes. The Government of India has also adopted gender budgeting under Mission Shakti. The Ministry of Women and Child Development (MWCD) is the Nodal Ministry for Gender Budgeting (Fig. 2.2).

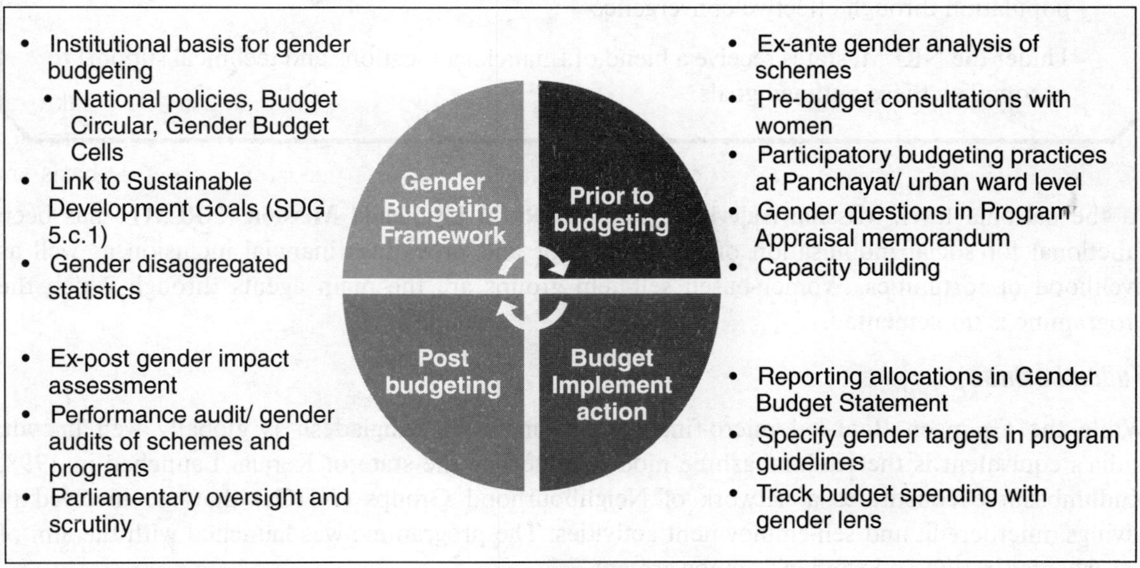

Fig. 2.2 Gender Budgeting Framework

3. Role of Women and Women's Organisation

3.1 Self-Help Groups (SHGs) and Women-led Development

Insight Box

The Deendayal Antyodaya Yojana-National Rural Livelihoods Mission (DAY-NRLM) was launched in June 2011 by the Government of India. The new programme design was based on the experiences gained from the large-scale community-based projects in the states of Andhra Pradesh, Telangana, Bihar, Kerala and Tamil Nadu.

The DAY-NRLM initiative aims to implement a holistic livelihood strategy that involves four interconnected objectives:

1. Mobilising rural, impoverished households to form functional self-help groups (SHGs) and SHG federations.
2. Facilitating access to credit, along with other financial, technical, and marketing services.
3. Developing capabilities and expertise for sustainable and profitable livelihoods.
4. Enhancing the delivery of social and economic support services to the impoverished population through effective convergence.

   Under the NRLM, states receive a blend of financial allocations and technical support to accomplish these outlined goals..

At the national level, **Mission Aajevika - National Rural Livelihood Mission (NRLM)** - has been functional for social mobilisation of the rural poor and providing financial inclusion as well as livelihood opportunities. Women-based self-help groups are the main agents through which the programme is implemented.

Kudumbashree

While the Grameen Bank-led micro-finance movement in Bangladesh is globally well known, India's equivalent is the Kudumbashree model piloted by the state of Kerala. Launched in 1998, Kudumbashree constitutes a network of Neighbourhood Groups (NHGs) that are involved in savings, microcredit and self-employment activities. The programme was launched with the aim of poverty eradication and women's empowerment.

The Kudumbashree movement and other such SHG-based movements in various states have been hailed as harbingers of not just economic but also social and political empowerment for women. Following are some of the important ways in which SHGs have enabled women' empowerment:

1. It has given women access to institutional finance (microcredit) and thus enabled economic participation. Kudumbashree women have established many micro-enterprises of their own ranging from canteens to farm produce shops. Kudumbashree women organised 1000+ Onam market fairs across the state to cater to the festive season.
2. Being part of the SHG movement gave women more control over monetary decision making in the household. Research has documented how income from microfinance is utilised for productive expenditures like health and education for children.
3. Most SHG members were previously confined to the household. Participation in group activities has given them a better voice, even in domestic decision-making as their confidence and self-esteem grew with group activities.
4. Studies have noted how SHGs are a platform for the political mobilisation of women. The study conducted in Tamil Nadu shows how SHG members mobilised and lobbied for local demands like the construction of roads.
5. The SHG network gives women access to information and awareness. A study conducted in Andhra Pradesh found that SHG members had shown improvement in nutritional status, although the nature of improvement varied across the group.
6. SHG space is also one where women seek and give emotional support to one another. A study conducted in Tamil Nadu found that being part of the network lessened feelings of exclusion among the widows.

The SHG movement has not seen the same success in all states and contexts. Group cohesion is fragile in the initial years and can be disturbed by caste and other conflicts. Further, poor communication and a lack of trust in leadership can hamper progress.

Overall, it is important that SHGs are carefully nurtured and adequately empowered so that they can truly act as vehicles of social and economic change for women.

3.2 Women's Movement

The women's movement in India can be visualised as a diverse group of organisations and collectives advocating for a broad range of women's rights. It includes both large, structured organisations and small, at times localised groups, with no clear hierarchy.

At the outset, it must be clarified that there is hardly any single, homogenous movement, rather various currents and ideologies that have flourished under the broad umbrella of the women's movement. It is also important to appreciate the trajectory of the movement since pre-independence days to understand the evolution of organisations and agendas.

The women's question first became an issue of public debate and action during the 19th century. The colonial rulers used women's socially and economically marginalised position as a justification for colonial rule. The critique by colonial rulers led to self-reflection and attempts to bring about social reforms so as to alleviate the position of women.

These social reform movements of the early 19th century were led by educated males who were inspired by Western ideals of equality and liberty. Raja Ram Mohan Roy famously advocated for the abolition of Sati and successfully persuaded colonial rulers to enact a law for outlawing the practise of Sati in 1829. Similarly, Ishwar Chandra Vidya Sagar used Sanskrit texts to justify widow remarriage, which was granted legal sanction through an Act in 1856.

The likes of D.K. Karve, M.G. Ranade and Shaikh Muhammad Abdullah advocated for women's education. The justification for women's rights was located at times in liberal principles and in the 'lost' glorious tradition of ancient India in other times. Mahatma Jyotiba Phule and his wife, Savitribai Phule, advocated a more radical stand and pioneered women's education in India by establishing the first ever schools for girls in Pune in 1848.

Broadly, the women's movements of the early 19th century were led by educated male social reformers and were based on the assumption that the '*bhadralok*' best understood women's interests. Ironically, women's faces were missing from the movement at this juncture. This began to change in the second half of the 19th century, when, supported by education, women started building own forums.

The Indian National Social Conference was founded by M.G. Ranade and Raghunath Rao to work on social evils like child marriage. Ramabai Ranade founded the Bharat Mahila Parishad under the aegis of the National Social Conference. The organisation worked to combat dowry, child marriage and other such social evils. The Arya Mahila Samaj was founded by Rambai Saraswati. The Ladies Society was established in 1882 by Swarnakumari Debi to economically empower widows by imparting livelihood skills.

Notably, such women-led reformist groups came up across religions. The *Stri Zarthosti Mandal* (Parsi Women's Circle) was formed to advocate for Parsi women's rights. Begum Rokeya founded the *Anjuman-e-Khwateen-e-Isam* in the 20th century to support women's education. The Bharat Stree Maha Mandal was founded in 1910 by Sarala Devi Chaudharani to support female education.

A broad assessment of the movement during this period shows that agendas like female education, opposition to the purdah system, child marriage prevention and support for widow remarriage were influenced by liberal principles of equality, liberty and humanism. The movement did not advocate for any radical ideas and lacked grassroots support.

The 20th century saw rise of mass-based women's organisations led by educated women. The Women's India Association (WIA), founded in 1917, was one of the first to have membership across caste, class and religion. Apart from philanthropic activities, it promoted female education. The likes of Annie

Besant and Margaret cousins worked with the WIA, and it brought out its own journal called the Stri Dharma. It is remembered as being among the first to demand the right to vote for women.

The two organisations, National Council for Women in India (NCWI) and the All India Women's Conference (AIWC), also played key roles in the women's movement of the 20th century. The NCWI was comprised of women from wealthy families who submitted petitions and memoranda on various women's issues. The AIWC had its first session in 1927 and had female education as its topmost priority, but it also advocated for women's equality in property matters.

In the 1930s and 1940s, the independence movement was at its peak and the women's movement advocated for rights for women in independent India. The principle of Universal Adult Franchise, which allows all women to vote irrespective of caste, class and education is a major contribution of the women's movement.

Another major accomplishment of the movement was the establishment of the Women Subcommittee under the National Planning Committee (1938). The visionary committee had demanded various political, economic and social rights for women. It sought to change the patriarchal image of 'man striding forward to conquer new worlds, woman following wearily behind with a baby in her arms' in favour of one where man and woman walk together as comrades.

For almost two decades after independence, the women's movement was lulled into inertia by the false belief that a liberal, democratic state guided by a modern ethos was sufficient to protect women's interests. Apart from the passage of the Hindu Code Bill in 1956, very few significant achievements from this period can be recounted. This too can be credited more to Dr. B.R. Ambedkar's push for a civil code than anything else. While the women's movement lay dormant, women continued to face the conflict between rights guaranteed by the Constitution and deeply entrenched patriarchal norms.

The first eye-opener regarding this conflict came when the Committee on the Status of Women published its report, 'Towards Equality', 1974. The report is widely recognised as a pioneer of the post-independence women's movement. Analysing women's socio-economic deprivation, the report highlighted the gap between laws and reality. It noted the widespread prevalence of dowry, polygamy, child marriage and rapid decline in the sex ratio. Noting the invisibility of women's work, it advocated for the economic empowerment of women. Most importantly, the report made it obvious that the modernisation model doesn't necessarily protect women's interests and that women need to mobilise for their cause.

Against the backdrop of the Towards Equality report, growing violence against women became a key agenda of the women's movement in the 1970s and 1980s. While practise of dowry had continued unabated despite the Dowry Prohibition Act (1961), the new menace of 'dowry deaths' and 'bride burning' raised its ugly head during this period. Brides were tortured for extorting maximum dowry, and in cases where the demands were not satisfied, dowry-related deaths of the bride were shown as suicides or accidents. The ineffectiveness of the Dowry Prohibition Act could be gauged from the fact that nearly 21 years after its passage, the Act had led to only one conviction.

Women's organisations like the *Dahej Virodhi Chetna Manch* advocated for stronger legal deterrence and the proactive role of the State in preventing dowry deaths. These protests and women's mobilisation were landmark developments because dowry and treatment of a newlywed were hitherto seen as a private matter wherein the state had no business. The movement led to the passing of the Criminal Law (Second Amendment) Act, which inserted section 498A in the Indian Penal Code (IPC). The section protects woman against cruelty by husband and relatives and explicitly prohibits dowry-related harassment.

The issue of sexual violence against women, especially against women from vulnerable communities, was highlighted by the *Mathura Rape* case. Apart from the issue of endemic violence against women, the incident highlighted deep-seated prejudice and a patriarchal mindset even among educated sections of society.

Many women's group like the Forum Against Oppression of Women (FAOW) mobilised in light of the Supreme Court judgement acquitting the accused, and the question of consent for sexual relations was fiercely debated. The civil society movement ultimately led to reforms in rape laws and the introduction of custodial rape as a punishable offence.

In the 1970s and early 1980s, the women's movement successfully brought about positive legal and policy changes. But in the late 1980s and 1990s, issues of caste and religion threatened the cohesiveness of the movement. The first example in this regard is the *Shah Bano case*. In this case, the Supreme Court held that a Muslim woman is entitled to alimony for lifetime if she is unable to provide for herself. In contrast, the Muslim personal laws had provision for alimony only during the period of *iddat*. The Supreme Court in this case held that personal laws do not override constitutional safeguards.

While this instance of judicial activism was endorsed by most women's organisation, the gains were quickly reversed by the Muslim Women (Protection of Rights on Divorce) Act 1986, which again made alimony rights subject to personal laws. The Act, which was widely seen as an act of political expediency, led to fresh debates regarding women's rights and their ethnocultural identity, as well as the legitimacy of state interference to correct discriminatory practices.

Another inflection point was the shocking *Roop Kanwar sati* case, in which Kanwar was burned alive on her husband's funeral pyre. While the practice of Sati had long been abolished, the incident was disturbing as it led to the glorification of a crime and inhuman practises. Roop Kanwar was held up as an example of ideal womanhood by some. It legitimised the patriarchal notion that a woman had no identity or purpose after her husband and hence must leave this life alongside her husband. In the 1980s and thereafter, women remained primary targets in ethno-religious clashes due to the patriarchal concept that family and community honour are tied to women's bodies.

Any discussion of the women's movement in the 1970s and 1980s shall remain incomplete without reference to the Chipko Movement and the rise of what was called 'Eco-feminism'. The Chipko

Movement in the hills of Uttarakhand is a perfect example of grassroots activism by women to protect nature. The movement resisted a masculinist, extractive mentality and favoured living in harmony with nature and all its beings. Advocates of ecofeminism like Vandana Shiva have held that women are custodians of divine feminine creative energy, and they must protect nature from careless commercialisation and exploitation. The Anti-Arrack movement in the state of Andhra Pradesh is also another remarkable example of a grassroots women's movement against the social evils of alcoholism and addiction.

Women and their economic welfare found a separate place in national planning only as late as in the 1980s, when the Sixth Five-Year Plan had a chapter on women and development. In this period, women led various movements against price rises. In the 1990s, apart from questions of identity, the movement was forced to reckon with liberalisation and the growing impact of globalisation.

The question of the invisibility of women's unpaid domestic work and the crowding of women in the informal sector began to draw attention even in the 1980s. The report of the National Commission on Self-Employed Women and Women in the Informal Sector, popularly known as the Shram Shakti Report, highlighted the plight of women. It pointed out that women had to labour hard at construction sites, in tea gardens and as weavers, but without equal pay and without any social insurance. The report highlighted that developmental processes need to be inclusive and that both the quantity and quality of women's employment need to improve.

In the first decade of the 21st century, the enactment of the Protection of Women from Domestic Violence Act 2005 (PWDVA) was seen as a significant achievement of the Women's Movement. The PWDVA is a milestone as it covers relations in the 'nature of marriage'.

The Act recognises women's right to a shared household and protects against the range of violence, including economic deprivation. Importantly, the law provides for the rehabilitation of domestic violence victims through protection officers, shelter homes and medico-legal counselling. The National Commission for Women (NCW) engaged with the Lawyers' Collective and a women's group to bring forth comprehensive legislation.

The Internet and the rise of social media have given as a new life to all social mobilisations, including the women's movement. The internet has emerged as a new force to give voice to the voiceless and galvanise individuals with similar opinions on any issue. The most significant event that highlighted this was the *Nirbhaya gang rape* (December 2012) case and the spontaneous protests that broke out in the aftermath of the gruesome incident. The iconic protest at Jantar Mantar had diffused leadership and comprised of young men and women, most of whom were students. The incident led to the setting up of the Justice Verma Committee and some landmark changes in rape-related criminal laws in the country.

Insight Box

State Feminism: This concept has been used to explain policies and legal measures that are aimed at gender justice and the empowerment of women. The late 1990s saw the launch of many *pro-women measures* like the Mahila Samakhya programme which was brought for the education and empowerment of women in rural areas, particularly women from socially and economically marginalised groups. Similarly, state-backed Self-Help Group Movements like the Kudumbashree Movement and Mission Aajeevika have been cited as examples of state feminism. Through such measures, democratic states seek to improve women's status and well-being and give them full citizenship rights.

More recently, the *#MeToo Movement* captured national attention as many women confessed years of sexual abuse by men of influence and how such abuse was perpetuated with unabated impunity. The movement was largely social media-based and was also critiqued as elitist by a few. Nonetheless, it reignited the question of toxic authority and how many women still do not have access to a safe working environment.

As can be gathered from the above discussion, the women's movement in India has traversed many domains and it is hard to conceive of a single movement. Rather, there are many movements, interest groups, women's collectives and women's organisations. While some question and critique state policy, others actively collaborate with the state to bring about gender-just policies and laws.

Additional Readings

1. Report on Status of Women in India by Economic Advisory Council to the Prime Minister (2022).
2. Report on Tackling Violence Against Women : A Study of State Intervention Measures by Bhartiya Stree Shakti (March 2017).
3. M. Mukherjee, Women and work in the shadow of globalisation. *Indian Journal of Gender Studies*, 11(3), 275–290 (2004).
4. Women's Reservation Bill 2023 [The Constitution (One Hundred Twenty-Eighth Amendment) Bill, 2023].
5. Women's Representation on Indian Boards has Tripled in 10 Years: EY Report.
6. Recalling the Origins of Kudumbashree on Its Silver Jubilee.
7. Women Reservation in Parliament and State Assemblies.
8. *Women in Indian Society,* Neera Desai and Usha Thakkar, National Book Trust
9. Electoral Participation of Women in india: Key Determinants and Barriers by Praveen Rai
10. Women's Studies and the Women's Movement in India: An overview by Vina Mazumdar
11. Women's Issues in India: Role and importance of Media by Purnima Ojha

12. Women's Movement Groups in State Policy Formulation: Addressing Violence Against Women in India by Mangala Subramaniam, Preethi Krishnan, Christopher Bunka (2014).
13. Indian Paradox : Rising education, declining women's employment by Esha Chatterjee, Sonalde Desai, Reeve Vanneman (2018).

Previous Years' Questions

1. "Male membership needs to be encouraged in order to make women's organisation free from gender bias." Comment. (2013)
2. Discuss the various economic and socio-cultural forces that are driving increasing feminisation of agriculture in India. (2014)
3. "Women's movement in India has not addressed the issues of women of lower social strata." Substantiate your view. (2018)
4. What are the continued challenges for women in India against time and space? (2019)

UPSC CSE 2024

1. Distinguish between gender equality, gender equity and women's empowerment. Why is it important to take gender concerns into account in programme design and implementation?
(150 words | 10 Marks)

Model Answer

Gender-related concepts are crucial to ensuring inclusive and just development. While often used interchangeably, they have distinct meanings.

Key Differences between gender equality, gender equity and women's empowerment:

Gender Equality	Gender Equity	Women's Empowerment
Refers to equal rights, responsibilities, and opportunities for all genders	Involves fairness of treatment by considering different needs	Enhancing women's agency to make decisions and access resources
Example: Equal pay for equal work, regardless of gender	*Example*: Providing separate toilets for girls in schools to ensure attendance	*Example:* SHGs in India promoting financial independence among rural women

Importance of Gender Concerns in Programmes design and implementation:

1. **Improves effectiveness and sustainability of welfare schemes -** Programmes that account for ground realities, such as childcare for women, yield better outcomes. For eg. crèche facilities in *MGNREGA* enable rural women to work, boosting participation and income.
2. **Ensures social equity -** Gender-sensitive policies ensure equitable access to opportunities and resources. For eg. *PM Awas Yojana* prioritizes property in women's names to enhance security and decision-making power.
3. **Corrects historical disadvantages-** Women have faced marginalisation in health, education, and employment. Gender-sensitive design improves outcomes in these areas. *For instance, Ujjwala Yojana* reduced indoor air pollution and enhanced women's dignity and safety.
4. **Promotes inclusive development-** Such policies address the diverse needs of all genders, leaving no one behind. E.g., Gender Budgeting ensures fair resource distribution across genders.

Mainstreaming gender ensures inclusive, effective, and equitable development–key to achieving Sustainable Developmental Goals (SDG 5 - Achieve gender equality and empower all women and girls) and constitutional ideals.

3 Population and Associated Issues

1. Demographic Structure of Indian Society

Demography is the scientific and systematic study of the human population in terms of its size, structure and movement. The term 'demography' is of Greek origin and is composed of two words, *demos* (people) and *graphein* (describe), meaning the description of people.

1.1 Population Trends in India

Size and growth of India's population

As per the 2011 Census, India was the second most populous country with a population of 121 crores.

As per a recent report (*UNFPA's State of World Population Report 2023*), India has surpassed China to become the world's most populous country. As per this report, India's population is estimated at 142.8 crore, slightly higher than China's 142.5 crore. It is estimated that India's population will continue to grow for nearly three decades before it peaks at 165 crore and then will start declining.

Growth rate: As far as the decadal growth of the population in India is concerned, it has varied inconsistently over the decades. It is important to note that in the last four decades, i.e. since 1971, the growth rate of the population in India has been declining consistently (Fig. 3.1).

Similarly, there is no consistent pattern with respect to the annual growth rate of the population in India. However, if we look at the Table 3.1, we can easily identify that there has been a consistent decline in the annual growth rate since 1981.

Census Year	Population (in crores)	Average annual growth rate
1901	23.84	-
1911	25.21	0.56
1921	25.13	-0.03
1931	27.90	1.04
1941	31.87	1.33
1951	36.11	1.25
1961	43.92	1.96
1971	54.81	2.20
1981	68.33	2.22
1991	84.33	2.16
2001	102.70	1.97
2011	121.02	1.66

Table 3.1 Average annual growth rate of population in India

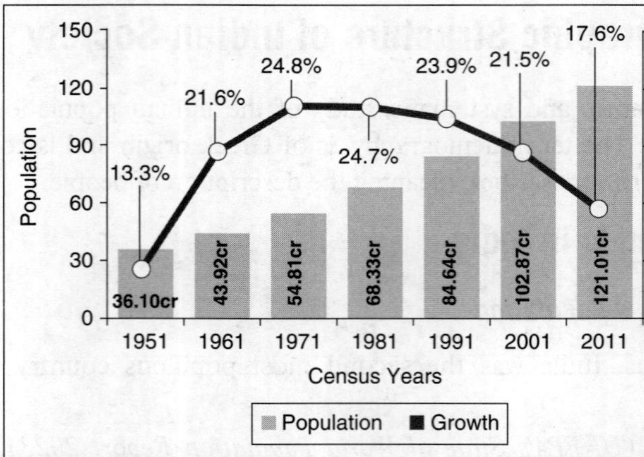

Fig. 3.1 Decadal Growth Rate of Population in India

Changing age structure of India's populations

Age structure: It refers to the proportion of population in various age groups with respect to total population. The age structure of a society varies in response to the level of development and average life expectancy. In India, 'Report of the Technical Group on Population Projections' by the Ministry of Health and Family Welfare compared the age structure of the Indian population in 2011 and after 25 years, i.e. in 2036 (Figs. 3.2 and 3.3).

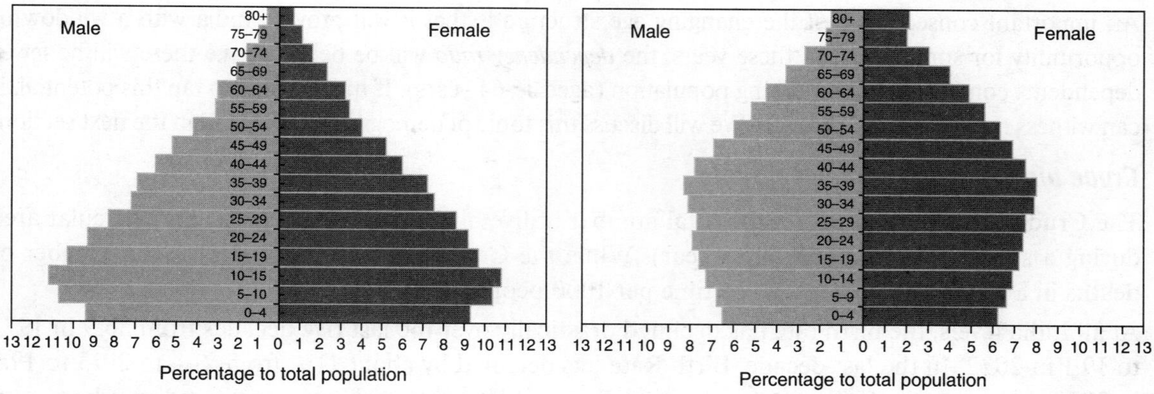

Fig. 3.2 Proportion of Population in Various Age Groups: 2011 and 2036

Source: Report of the Technical Group on Population Projections, July 2020 by National Commission of Population, Ministry of Health and Family Welfare.

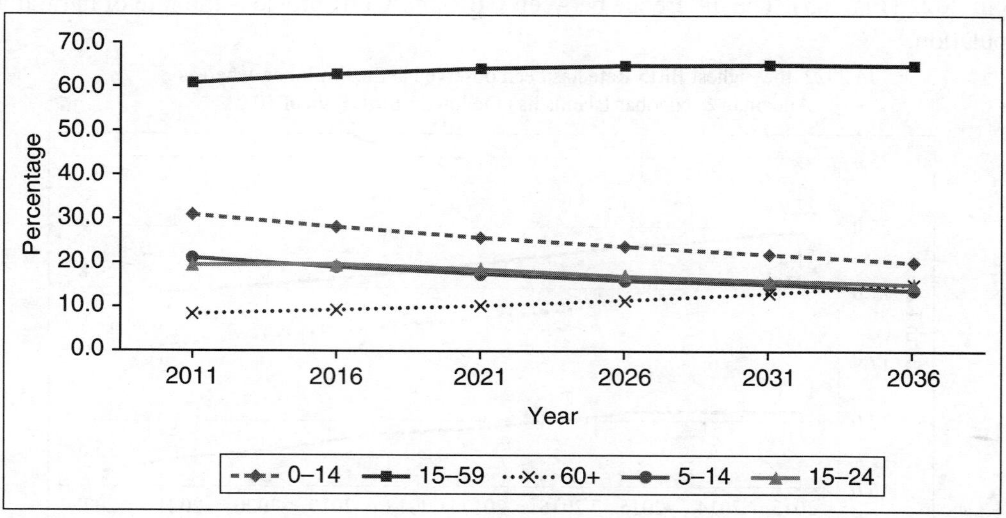

Fig. 3.3 Percentage of Population by Broad Age Groups, India: 2011–2036

Source: Report of the Technical Group on Population Projections, July 2020 by National Commission of Population, Ministry of Health and Family Welfare.

1. *Brief analysis:* As society develops in terms of better technology and medical facilities, life expectancy improves. Hence, over time, a larger population will be in the older age group as compared to the younger age group. Thus, there will be *ageing population*. This is also very evident from the above graphs.

It is also important to note that in India, age structure is different in different states as the level of development varies. For example, Kerala has an age structure similar to a developed country with a greater population in the middle and older-age groups. While states like Uttar Pradesh is having higher population in the younger age group and a relatively lesser population among the aged.

An important consequence of the changing age structure is that it will provide India with a window of opportunity for some years. In these years, the *dependency ratio* will be below 50, i.e there will be fewer dependents compared to the working population (aged 15-64 years). If India is able to tap this potential, it can witness rapid economic growth. We will discuss this topic of demographic dividend in the next section.

Crude birth rate and crude death rate

The Crude Birth Rate (CBR) is the total number of live births per 1000 people in a particular area during a specified period (usually a year). While the Crude Death Rate (CDR) is the number of deaths in a given area during a given time per 1000 people.

At all India levels, the birth rate has declined drastically over the last five decades from 36.9 in 1971 to 19.1 in 2022. In the last decade, Birth Rate has declined by about 11%, from 21.4 in 2013 to 19.1 in 2022. However, the birth rate has continued to be higher in rural areas compared to urban areas in the last five decades (Fig. 3.4).

In the last five decades, the death rate in India has also witnessed a significant decline from 14.9 in 1971 to 6.8 in 2022 (Fig. 3.5). The difference between CBR and CDR provides the rate of natural increase of population.

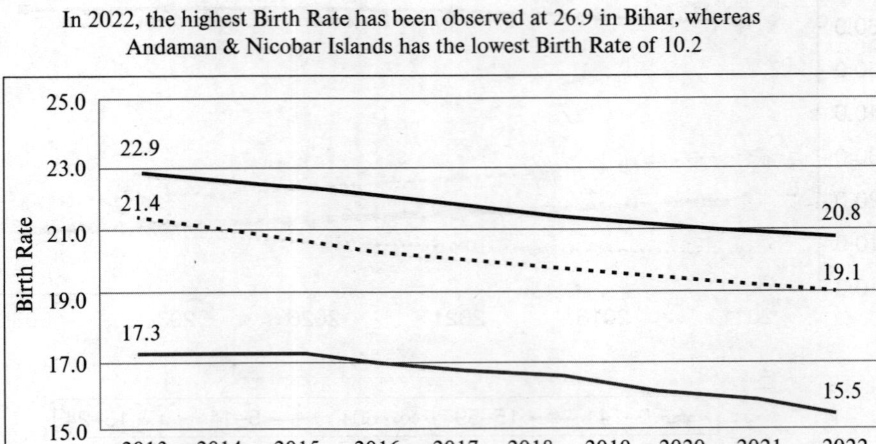

Fig. 3.4 Crude Birth Rate (2013-2022)

Source: SRS Bulletin 2022, Volume 57 No. 1; June 2025, Office of the Registrar General & Census Commissioner, India (ORGI).

In 2022, Chhattisgarh recorded the highest Death Rate of 9.0, whereas the lowest Death Rate has been recorded in Chandigarh at 4.2.

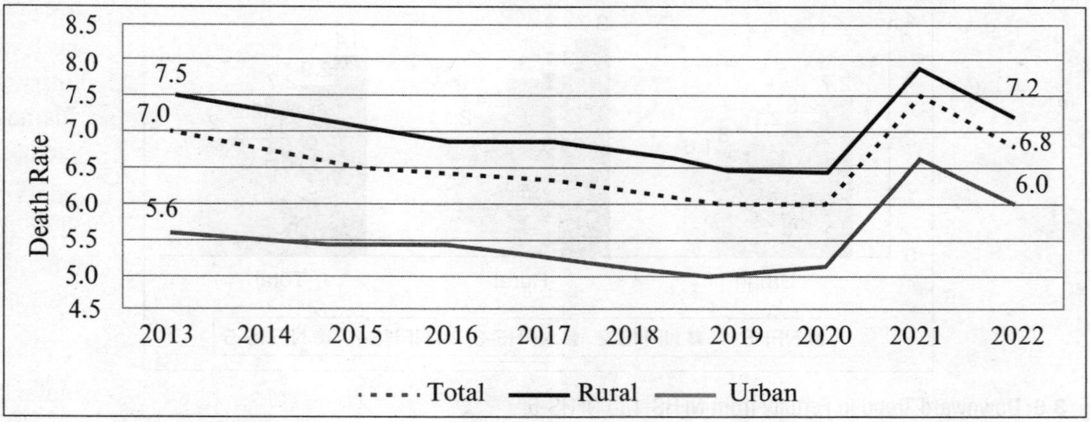

Fig. 3.5 Crude Death Rate (2013-2022)

Source: SRS Bulletin 2022, Volume 57 No. 1; June 2025, Office of the Registrar General & Census Commissioner, India (ORGI).

Total fertility rate (TFR) in India

It refers to the number of live births per 1000 women in the child-bearing age group, usually taken to be 15 to 49 years. The fertility rate determines the growth of the population. India, over the years, has been successful in reducing the fertility rate. Falling TFR signals that our population will not grow in the long term and will get stabilised.

As per the fifth round of the *National Family Health Survey (NFHS),* conducted by the Ministry of Health and Family Welfare (MoHFW), the fertility rate in India is 2.0 at the national level, which is below the replacement level of 2.1 (Fig. 3.6). It is to be noted that, on average, women in rural areas have higher fertility compared to women in urban areas (TFR of 2.1 and 1.6, respectively). Replacement level is the fertility rate at which a population exactly replaces itself from one generation to the next, without migration.

The survey says that there are only five states in India that have yet to achieve replacement levels of fertility. They are Bihar, Meghalaya, Uttar Pradesh, Jharkhand and Manipur.

Sl. No.	Indicator	NFHS 5 (2019–2021)	NFHS 4 (2015–2016)
1	Total Fertility Rate (TFR)	2.0	2.2

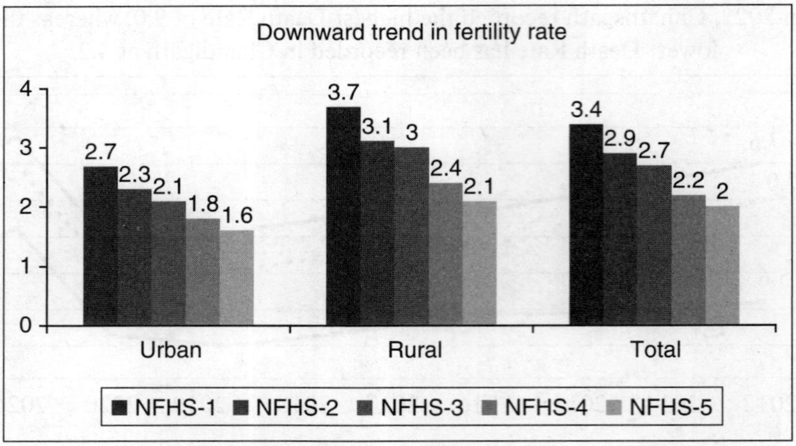

Fig. 3.6 Downward Trend in Fertility from NFHS-1 to NFHS-5
Source: National Family Health Survey (NFHS-5)

Insight Box

Declining fertility rate in Southern India: cause of concern?

Recently, a few States such as Andhra Pradesh and Tamil Nadu have raised concerns about the declining birth rates and its potential consequences. As per the Sample Registration System Statistical Report 2021, the TFR in Southern States of India is: Tamil Nadu (1.5), Kerala (1.5), Andhra Pradesh (1.5), Karnataka (1.6) and Telangana (1.6). Some challenges with this trend include:

1. **Ageing population:** A falling birth rate will result in a smaller working-age population to contribute to the economy and increase the proportion of the elderly population. This ageing population will require pensions and healthcare support, thereby putting financial stress on the State exchequer. Worldwide, countries such as Japan, China and some parts of Europe are already facing the issue of ageing.
2. **Issue regarding representation in Lok Sabha:** India is scheduled to carry out delimitation of parliamentary constituencies based on population data from the first census after 2026. The Southern States are concerned that declining population growth may have a negative impact on their representation in the Lok Sabha.

Infant mortality rate (IMR) in India

It is defined as the number of infant deaths (below one year) per 1000 live births in a given time period for a given region. IMR data signifies the overall health situation of the country. In the last five decades, the IMR in India has witnessed more than three-fourth decline from 129 in 1971 to 26 in 2022.

As per the Sample Registration System (SRS) survey, the IMR at the national level has declined from 40 to 26 in the last decade, i.e. decline of 35%. From Fig. 3.7, it is to be noted that there is a huge disparity in IMR data between urban and rural India.

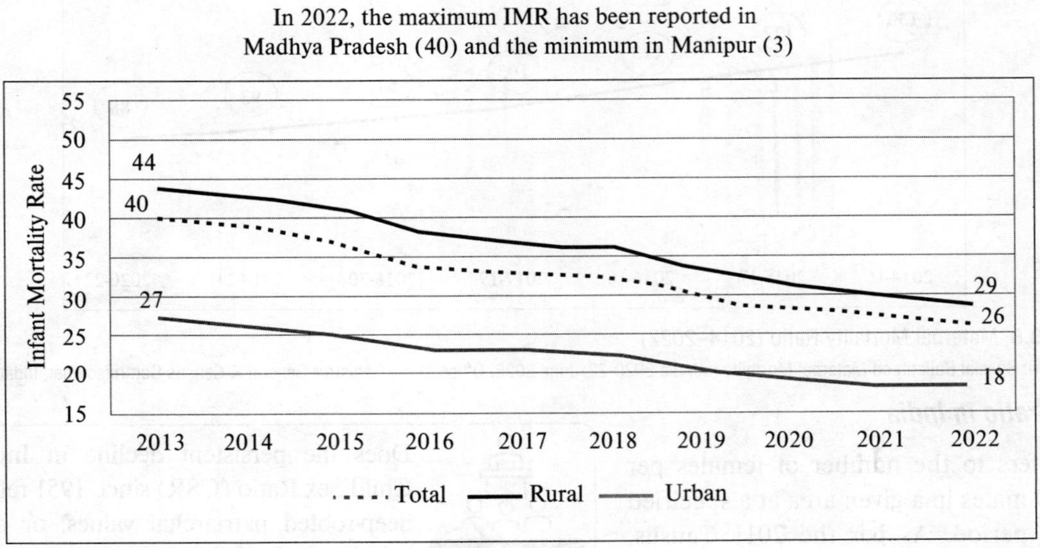

Fig. 3.7 Infant Mortality Rate (2013-2022)

Source: SRS Bulletin 2022, Volume 57 No. 1; June 2025, Office of the Registrar General & Census Commissioner, India (ORGI).

It is important to note the significant inter-state variations in Infant Mortality Rate (IMR). Progressive states like Kerala (IMR-7), Goa (IMR-5), and Sikkim (IMR-5) have achieved remarkable reductions in infant deaths. In contrast, relatively less developed states such as Assam (IMR-32), Madhya Pradesh (IMR-40), and Uttar Pradesh (IMR-38) continue to face serious challenges in bringing down their IMR.

Maternal mortality ratio (MMR) in India

It is the number of maternal deaths during a given time period per 100,000 live births during the same time period. It is encouraging to note that as per the Sample Registration System (SRS) survey, MMR in India has declined from 130 in 2014-16 to 88 in 2020-22, as indicated in Fig. 3.8.

> As per World Health Organization, "**Maternal death** is the death of a woman while pregnant or within 42 days of termination of pregnancy, irrespective of the duration and site of the pregnancy, from any cause related to or aggravated by the pregnancy or its management but not from accidental or incidental causes".

Notably, with this progress, India has achieved the National Health Policy (NHP) target of reducing the Maternal Mortality Ratio (MMR) to below 100 per 100,000 live births. The country is also well-positioned to meet

Sustainable Development Goal (SDG) Target 3.1, which aims to bring the global MMR below 70 per 100,000 live births.

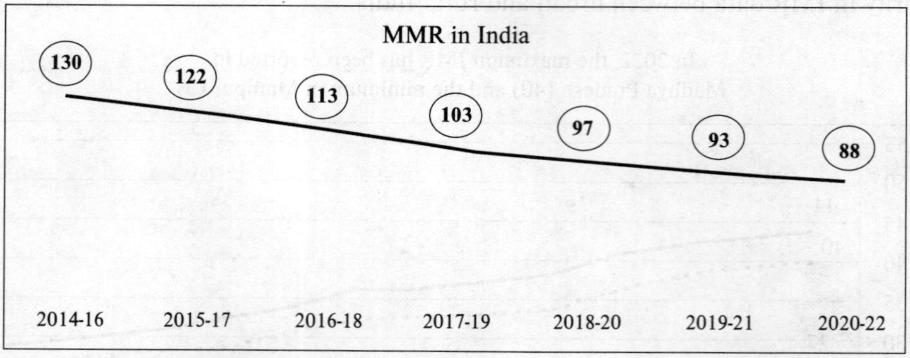

Fig. 3.8 Maternal Mortality Ratio (2014–2022)
Source: Special Bulletin on Maternal Mortality in India 2020-22; June 2025, Office of the Registrar General & Census Commissioner, India (ORGI)

Sex ratio in India

It refers to the number of females per 1000 males in a given area at a specified time period. As per the 2011 Census, the overall sex ratio was 943. The recent National Family Health Survey (NFHS-5) 2019–2021, though, reported that the overall sex ratio in India was 1020.

> **Debate Corner**
> Does the persistent decline in India's Child Sex Ratio (CSR) since 1951 reflect deep-rooted patriarchal values, or does it indicate the failure of legal and policy interventions to effectively curb gender-biased practices?

It is better to clarify here that there is variation between census data and NFHS data. Things would be clearer when the next census data will be released. Nonetheless, it is certain that the overall sex ratio has improved over the last three decades, i.e. since 1991.

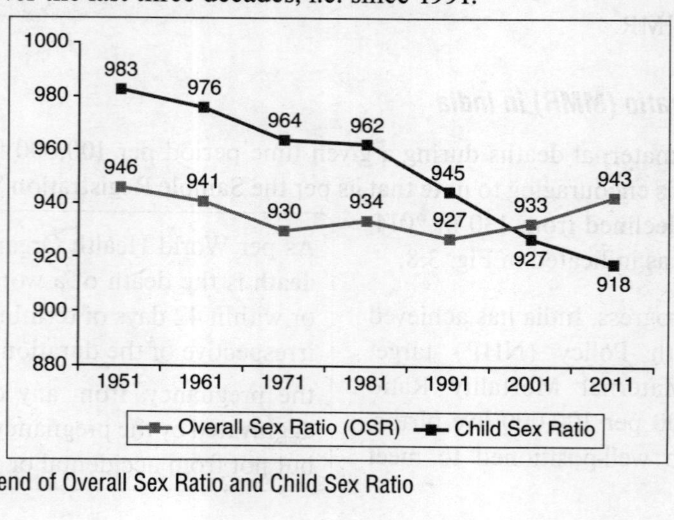

Fig. 3.9 Comparative Trend of Overall Sex Ratio and Child Sex Ratio

However, there is concern when it comes to Child Sex Ratio (CSR). CSR is the number of females per 1000 males in the age group of 0–6 years in a given population. From Fig. 3.9, it is very clear that CSR has been continuously declining since 1951.

Insight Box

Factors Behind Adverse Sex Ratio for Women in India's Prosperous Regions

1. **Smaller Family Norms Coupled with Son Preference:** In wealthier and more urbanized regions, families often opt for fewer children. Within a patriarchal framework, this intensifies the preference for male offspring, leading to gender-biased family planning.
2. **Access to Sex-Selection Technology:** Prosperous regions typically have greater access to advanced medical technologies such as ultrasound. When combined with existing son preference, this results in a higher incidence of sex-selective abortions.
3. **Cultural and Social Prejudices:** Deep-rooted gender biases continue to prevail, where women are often seen as a financial burden due to practices like dowry and are perceived as less valuable than sons in terms of social and familial roles.
4. **Patrilineal Inheritance Norms:** The belief that only sons can carry forward the family name and inherit property reinforces the preference for male children, particularly in traditional, male-dominated societies.

Another point of worry is with respect to the sex ratio at birth (SRB). The sex ratio at birth is the number of female children born per 1,000 male children born.

As per NFHS-5, the sex ratio at birth stands abysmally low at 929, though there has been an increase of 10 points since NFHS-4 (2015–2016). WHO estimates that the natural sex ratio at birth is 952. It clearly indicates sex selection at birth, patriarchal mindset and gender-based inequality in society (Table 3.2).

An unfortunate pattern that has been noticed is that such parochial practice has spread even in those states that traditionally had a better sex ratio, such as the tribal states of Chhattisgarh, Jharkhand and southern states like Kerala and Tamil Nadu. On the brighter side, states with the worst sex ratio at birth such as Haryana, Punjab and Delhi showed significant progress.

Brief Analysis

In spite of the decline in SRB in some of the states, the overall sex ratio of the country has improved. It is most likely because of the improvement in female life expectancy across states and the improvement in SRB in many of the large states.

State	NFHS-5	NFHS-4	Increase
India	929	919	10
Delhi	923	812	111
Uttarakhand	984	888	96
Karnataka	978	910	68
Haryana	893	836	57
Jammu and Kashmir	976	923	53
Gujarat	955	906	49
Punjab	904	860	44
Uttar Pradesh	941	903	38
Assam	964	929	35
Madhya Pradesh	956	927	29
Telangana	894	872	22
Andhra Pradesh	934	914	20
West Bengal	973	960	13
Rajasthan	891	887	4
Maharashtra	913	924	-11
Chhattisgarh	960	977	-17
Jharkhand	899	919	-20
Bihar	908	934	-26
Odisha	894	932	-38
Himachal	875	937	-62
Tamil Nadu	878	954	-76
Kerala	951	1,047	-96

Table 3.2 Sex Ratio at Birth (Last Five Years)

Source: National Family Health Survey (NFHS-5) Report 2019–21

2. Demographic Dividend and Its Prospects for India

The United Nations Population Fund (UNFPA) defines a demographic dividend as 'is the economic growth potential that can result from shifts in a population's age structure, mainly when the share of the working-age population (15 to 64 age group) is larger than the non-working-age share of the population (14 and younger, and 65 and older)'.

This favourable situation emerges mainly when there is a decline in Total Fertility Rate (TFR) and increase in the life expectancy gets stabilised. This is because with the decline in TFR, the younger population, i.e. dependent ones, declines and the working-age population grows relatively more.

In the case of India, the year 2018 was considered to be the starting point when the working-age population exceeded the dependent population. This window of opportunity is expected to last until 2055, i.e. for 37 years. As per the Economic Survey of India 2018–2019, India's demographic dividend will peak around 2041, when the share of the working-age population is expected to hit 59%. Moreover, India is expected to add around 183 million people to the working age group of 15–64 years between 2020 and 2050.

2.1 Brief Analysis

1. It is to be understood that simply having potential or a *window of opportunity* does not simply result in economic growth in a society. Rather, it all depends on how India makes the right policies for its population in terms of health, school and higher education, skill development, employment opportunities and infrastructural progress.

2. The above discussion is with respect to the country as a whole. The window of opportunity varies across states depending on their fertility rate and life expectancy. Thus, a few states will start transitioning to an ageing society by the 2030s.

3. As can be seen from Fig. 3.10, many countries, e.g. Japan, Italy, etc., have been witnessing ageing of the population and the period of demographic dividend for these countries has already passed. This situation provides an opportunity for India to export skilled manpower, generate foreign exchange, build trade relations, etc.

4. As per a report by the Confederation of Indian Industry (CII) titled *'Harnessing India's Demographic Dividend for Boosting Growth,'* published in 2022, if India does not create enough jobs and its workers are not adequately prepared for those jobs, its demographic dividend may turn into a liability. It asserted that education and skill development will be the biggest enablers for reaping this dividend.

Apart from government initiatives with respect to skill education, corporate investment in employee education and training can play a critical role in creating highly skilled workers.

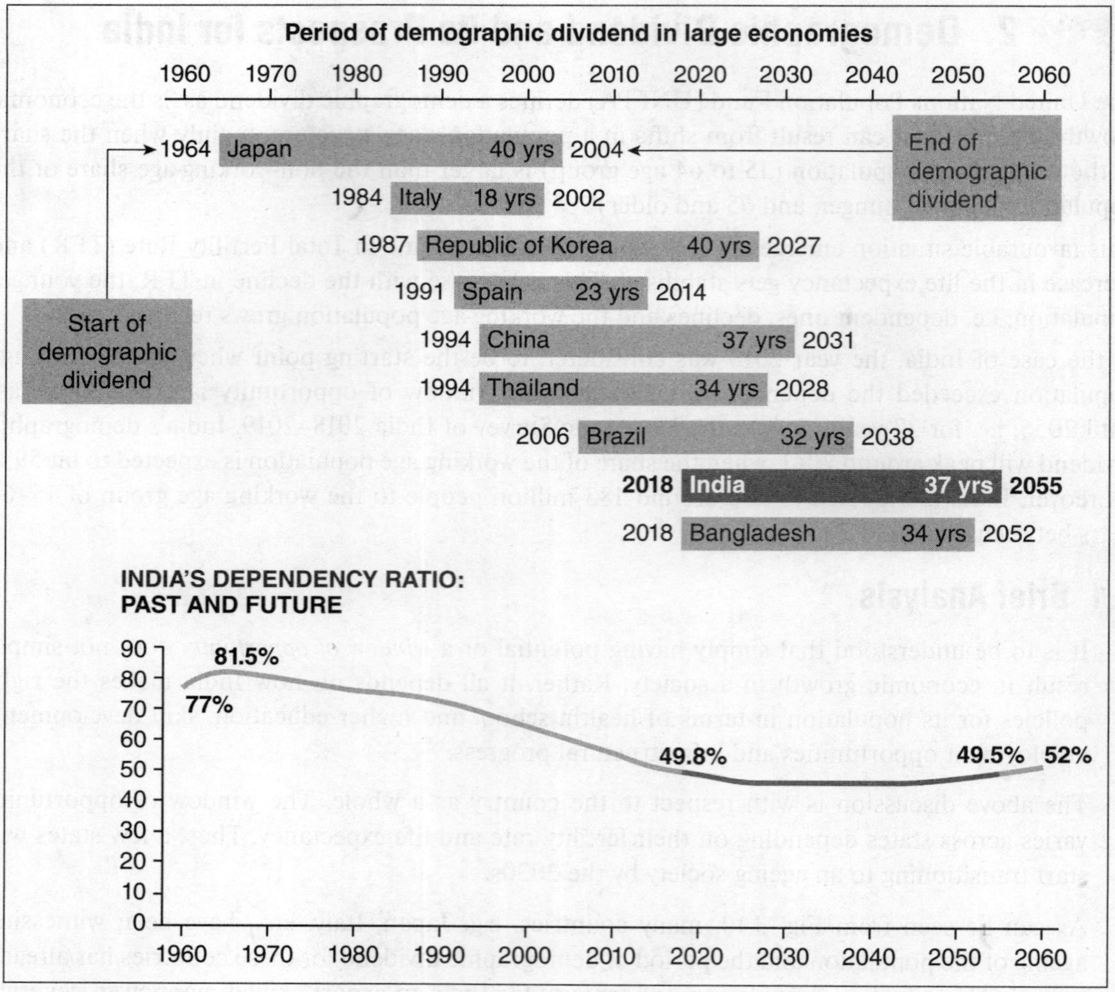

Fig. 3.10 Period of Demographic Dividend in India: 2018–2055

3 Theories of Population Growth

3.1 Malthusian Theory of Population Growth

Political economist Robert Malthus argued that the human population growth rate will always be greater than the rate at which means of human subsistence, such as food, clothing and other agricultural-based products, etc., can grow. He believed that human population grows in geometric progression (i.e. 2, 4, 8, 16,...) while agricultural production grows in arithmetic progression (i.e. 2,

4, 6, 8,...). Thus, humans are condemned to live a miserable life. The only way to overcome this crisis is to control population growth.

In order to control population growth, Malthus has suggested some *'preventive checks'* to control population growth, which includes delayed marriage, birth control by using contraception and practicing celibacy. As per Malthus, humans have a very limited ability to reduce population through these mechanisms. Hence, he believed there are some inevitable factors, such as famine, war, diseases, etc., that will ultimately control the population. These factors were termed *'positive checks'* by Malthus. However, this theory proved false as the world witnessed a simultaneous rise in food production and standard of living along with rapid population growth.

3.2 Demographic Transition Theory

This theory suggests that population growth is related to economic development. It says that with economic development, birth and death rates change, ultimately affecting the population growth rate. Population growth takes place in three stages, as per this theory:

First Stage	Second Stage	Third Stage
Both birth and death rates are high, and the difference between them is low. Thus, population growth rate is low.	Death rates are low. But birth rates are still high. Thus, there is a significant increase in population at this stage.	Birth and death rates are reduced to a great extent. The difference between them is small. Thus, the population growth rate is low.
Under-developed and technologically backward society	Society in transition: from an underdeveloped to an advanced society	Technologically advanced and developed society

4 Causes and Effects of Over Population

It is now a common understanding among the policymakers and governments across the world that overpopulation or population explosion creates innumerable issues, including environmental, economic, social and political. Hence, governments, in their own way, are trying their best to control population growth to make it more sustainable for the larger society.

4.1 Causes of Over Population in India

1. *Mismatch between birth and death rates:* As per the SRS survey, in 2020, the birth rate for the country was estimated at 19.5, whereas the death rate was estimated at 6.0. Thus, the death rate has been controlled, but the birth rate is still on the higher side. Keeping other factors constant, it is natural that the population will rise.

2. *Lack of family planning knowledge:* Family planning is not considered an important topic of discussion in Indian families in general and particularly in rural areas. Family members feel shy, and such discussions are normally avoided within families.
3. *Cultural norms and beliefs:* In India, there is still a large populace with a specific preference for male child. This is because they believe that only male children can carry forward their lineage. Apart from this, there is also a cultural belief that sons are the primary breadwinners for the family. In order to achieve this, couples keep giving birth to children until they give birth to a male child. Consequently, the family size becomes large. Economic Survey 2018-19 called this phenomena as Son Meta-Preference.
4. *Lack of knowledge and awareness about oral contraceptive pills and other birth control measures:* It results in the unplanned conception of a child. Even though pills have been made available, but there is still a shyness about using them by the majority of the population despite oral contraception being safe and effective option for women, its usage in India is only ~4% (Fig. 3.11).
5. *Religious reasons:* Some orthodox and conservative religious people believe that using the family planning method is against their religious beliefs. Also, there is a belief that children are God's will, and no one should interfere with this.

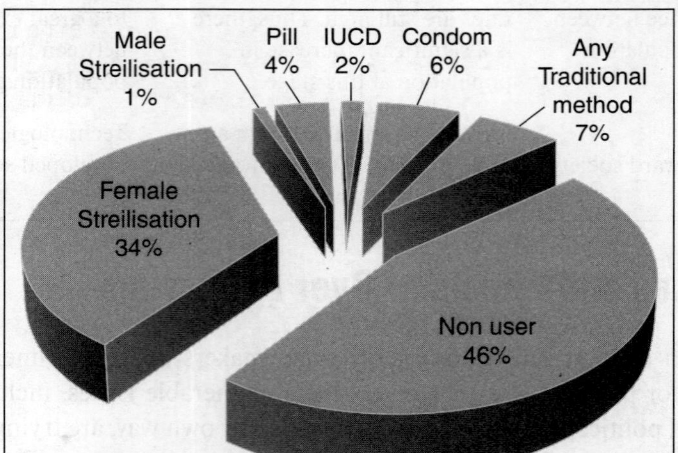

Fig. 3.11 Oral Pill Usage

6. *Child marriage:* Estimates suggest that every year, at least 1.5 million girls under 18 get married in India. Fertility rates are directly impacted by the age of marriage. It increases as the age of marriage decreases. Young brides have less knowledge about family planning.
7. *Poverty:* It also results in population increase. Poor families believe that having more hands means more income. Hence, they produce more children so that their income increases.

Landmark Judgements

In a landmark judgment in *Society for Enlightenment and Voluntary Action & Anr. v. Union of India & Ors.*, delivered in October 2024, the Supreme Court of India declared child marriage a serious violation of children's fundamental rights under Article 21 of the Constitution. The petition, filed by the NGO Society for Enlightenment and Voluntary Action, sought comprehensive measures to curb the widespread practice of child marriage in India. Chief Justice D.Y. Chandrachud, delivering the judgment, underscored the harmful consequences of child marriage on the rights of children – including their autonomy, health, education, and sexual and reproductive rights. The Court stressed that child marriage robs children of their dignity and agency, denying them a free and meaningful childhood.

4.2 Effects of Over Population in India

Economic issues

1. *Issue of unemployment:* An unrestricted increase in population is accompanied by an increase in the labour force, which is seeking employment from the market. However, in the current situation in India, not all who enters the market get absorbed. According to the CMIE (Centre for Monitoring Indian Economy) data, India's unemployment rate in May 2023 was 7.7%.

2. *Issue of poverty:* Overpopulation creates a vicious cycle of illiteracy, unemployment and poverty. Lack of proper education results in a decrease in unemployability, which results in low earning capacity and ultimately leads to poverty.

3. *Economic inequality:* Overpopulation results in an unequal distribution of wealth. Over time, it results in a widening gap in terms of income, thus causing inequality.

Social issues

1. *Migration of population:* Due to unequal resource distribution, people migrate from poor regions to better and more developed regions in search of food, shelter and employment opportunities.

2. *Pressure on cities and the development of slums:* Since cities provide better opportunities, more and more people migrate there, causing immense pressure on cities. However, the city may not be able to accommodate everyone. It results in the haphazard growth of settlements in cities and the development of slums in cities, e.g. Dharavi in Mumbai

3. *Burden on physical infrastructure:* Overpopulation results in increasing health issues such as infectious diseases and epidemics. As a result, there is immense pressure on the health infrastructure.

4. *Family issues:* Overpopulation, coupled with a rise in life expectancy, results in an increasing old-aged population as well. Old-aged population faces issues of neglect and discrimination from family members, financial issues, among others.

Environmental issues

1. *Pressure on natural resources:* To cater to the increased population, new development in terms of infrastructure is required. It causes over-exploitation of natural resources.

2. *Issue of pollution:* More people means more waste generation. Lack of a waste disposal system results in generating huge amount of solid, semi-solid and liquid wastes.

4.3 How Can We Tackle the Issue of Over-Population

Controlling over-population is important because resources are limited, and available resources might not be able to cater to all the needs of people. Moreover, over-population results in various issues such as increased crimes, inequality, poverty, etc. In a way, it becomes difficult for policymakers to provide a quality life to all the people. A few measures that can be adopted include:

1. *Family planning:* First of all, it is of utmost importance that family planning become part of our general discourse. Family members should plan children and give birth accordingly. If needed, members should not shy away from using modern methods.

2. *Eliminating child marriage:* It should be done through both awareness mechanisms and legal steps. Child marriage often results in severe health issues as well as an increase in the birth rate.
3. *Improving health infrastructure:* This is necessary to make families confident that their children will survive after birth and that they will not lose children due to a lack of health infrastructure.
4. *Empowering women:* It is to be done both by means of education and financial empowerment. An empowered and educated woman is more likely to understand the importance of a small family size.

5. *Reducing poverty:* This can be done through a relatively fair distribution of resources and better employment conditions and opportunities for the deprived ones.
6. *Government policies:* The government is a key player in promoting the value of small families size, spreading awareness and knowledge about contraceptive and other birth control mechanisms. It is important to highlight that few States have mandated two child norm for Government service and local elections.

Apart from this, if the government is able to promote balanced regional development, it can reduce forced migration to developed cities.

5 Elderly Population in India - Emerging Issue of Ageing

5.1 Growth of Elderly Population in India

According to the 2011 Census, there were nearly 104 million elderly persons (aged 60 years or above) in India: 53 million females and 51 million males. It is important to note that in India, both the share and size of the elderly population are increasing with time. From 5.6% in 1961, the proportion of the elderly has increased to 8.6% in 2011.

Report of the Technical Group of Population Projection July 2020 (2011–2036)

As per this report, there were nearly 138 *million* elderly persons in India in 2021: 67 million males and 71 million females.

It is expected to increase to 194 *million* by 2031 (93 million males and 101 million females), a rise of 41% over a decade.

This trend of increasing elderly populations is likely to continue for several decades in India. As per a 2017 report by the United Nations Population Fund (UNFPA), the share of older people will be around 12.5% of India's population by 2030. This will increase to nearly 20% in 2050. Figure 3.12 below clearly shows an increasing pattern until the end of this century.

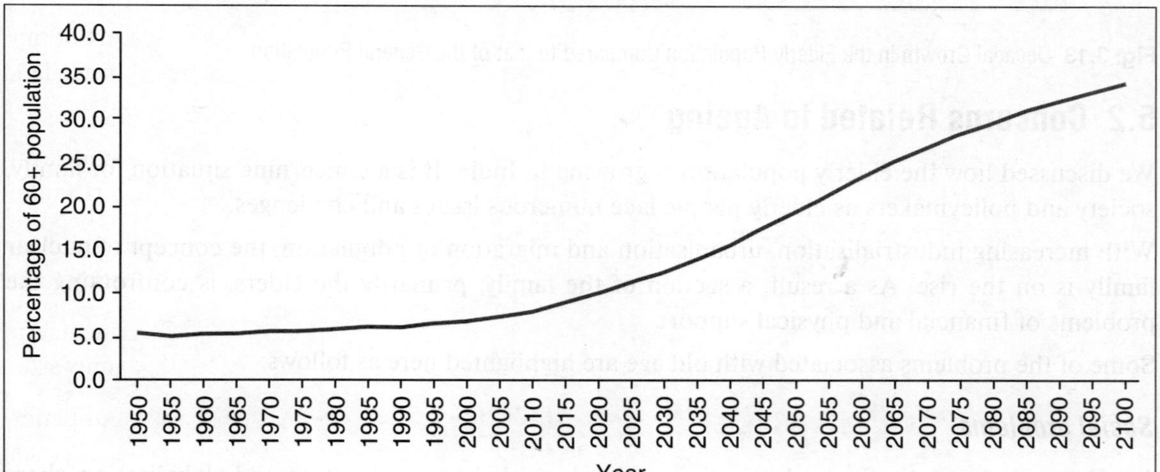

Fig. 3.12 Percentage of 60-plus Persons in Total Population (1950–2100)

Here, it is also important to highlight that the elderly population is growing at a faster rate than the rate at which the general population is growing in India. Thus, it will be correct to say that our population is 'ageing'. Figure 3.13 clearly highlights the difference in growth rate.

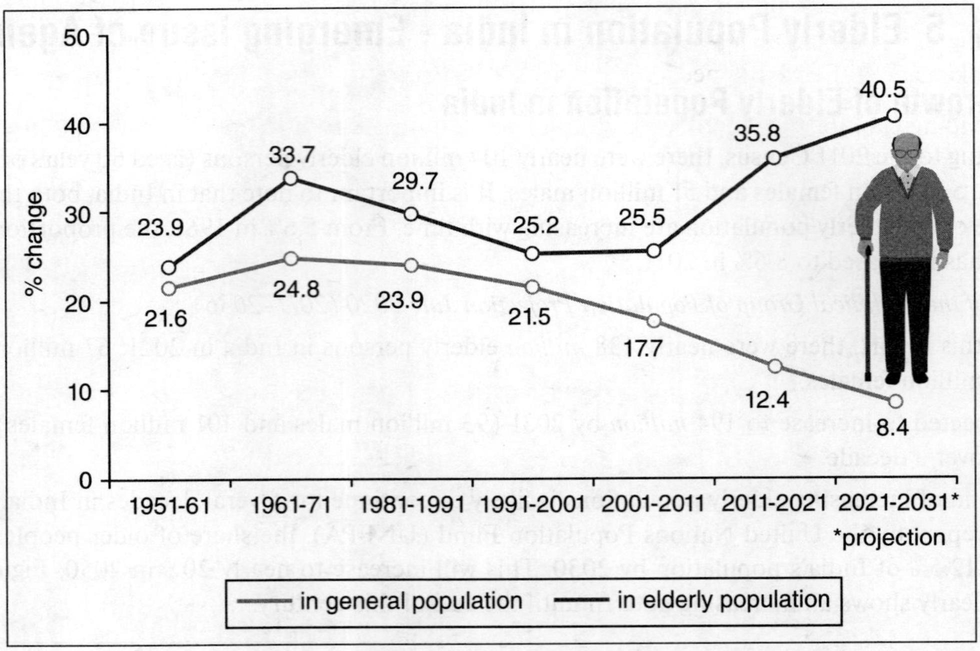

Fig. 3.13 Decadal Growth in the Elderly Population Compared to that of the General Population

5.2 Concerns Related to Ageing

We discussed how the elderly population is growing in India. It is a concerning situation for family, society and policymakers as elderly people face numerous issues and challenges.

With increasing industrialisation, urbanisation and migration of population, the concept of nuclear family is on the rise. As a result, a section of the family, primarily the elders, is confronting the problems of financial and physical support.

Some of the problems associated with old age are highlighted here as follows:

Social problems

1. Due to industrialisation, urbanisation, technological change, education and globalisation, there is rapid transformation in Indian society. As a result, traditional values and institutions are in the process of erosion and adaptation, resulting in the weakening of intergenerational ties. Thus, elderly people face neglect, abuse, discrimination and ignored both within the family and outside.
2. Since elderly people have retired from their professions in most cases, they feel disillusioned and unwanted in society. If the elderly people are economically dependent on the children, the problem is likely to become even worse.

3. Economic pressure, opportunities and the rise of modern communication push younger people to migrate to urban areas from rural areas. Thus, the elderly ones are left alone without anyone to take care of their basic needs.

   Providing care for the elderly was never an issue in the value-based joint family system in India. However, with the growing trend of nuclear families, the vulnerability of the elderly has increased manifold.

4. Earlier, in an agriculture-based traditional society, children used to follow their parents occupation. Thus, the elderly ones played a crucial role in transmitting the knowledge to the next generation.

But, in the modern set-up, new job opportunities and roles have emerged. The younger ones rarely take the advice of the elderly members. This realisation often results in feelings of loss of status, worthlessness and loneliness.

Financial concerns

1. Due to retirement from formal jobs or due to declining ability to work because of decreased physical and mental abilities, the elderly become dependent on their children for basic needs.
2. As ageing progresses, they have to face various health issues. This results in increased out-of-pocket expenditures.
3. Since they are less preferred for any job at this age, they seldom get any scope for employing themselves. In many cases, the elderly couple faces issues of poverty and distress.
4. Elderly people also face economic dependence when management responsibilities relating to finances and other business matters shift to children. Thus, they become dependent on children.

Health and psychological issues

1. Ageing is predominantly a women's problems, i.e there is *feminisation of ageing*. Not only do women live longer, but most of them are widows. As a result, they face severe discrimination. This affects their health, nutrition and mental well-being. They feel emotionally void. Many times, they move to old-age homes for food and shelter.
2. The *Longitudinal Aging Study in India (LASI),* commissioned by the Ministry of Health and Family Welfare (MoHFW), found that 75% of the elderly people suffer from one or the other chronic disease. 40% of the elderly people have one or the other disability, and 20% have issues related to mental health.
3. Typical psychological challenges encountered by older individuals encompass sensations of powerlessness, inferiority, and depression, among several others. These issues, coupled with the challenges of widowhood and societal biases, intensify the distress experienced by the elderly.

Insight Box

Empty Nest Syndrome

Parents undergo a range of emotions when their children leave home, either for education or for employment. They feel empty and hollow in their heart. This feeling of emptiness and immense sorrow that one experiences when their kids leave home is called Empty Nest Syndrome. It may result in depression, alcoholism, identity crisis and stress.

Well, there might be multiple other concerns about ageing. Many elderly people live below the poverty line suffers from multiple other psychological and physical issues. To alleviate these concerns, the government has adopted various measures that are discussed further.

Insight Box

Potential of The Elderly Population

The traditional economic perspective regarding ageing perceives elderly as financial and physical burden. It is captured in concepts such as demographic dividend and dependency ratio whereby a younger population is seen as more conducive to economic growth. While a young and skilled populace is undoubtedly an asset for any economy, the potential of elderly population is also being recognised now. Concepts like 'Longevity Dividend' capture this emerging perspective. Longevity dividend states that older workers have better experience and skills and can contribute to better output. Societies must enable participation of this elderly population so that they can continue contributing to economic growth even in retirement years.

5.3 Important Schemes for the Welfare of Senior Citizens in India

1. *Integrated Programme for Older Persons (IPOP):* The main objective is to improve the quality of life by providing basic amenities like food, shelter, entertainment, etc.
2. *Rashtriya Vayoshri Yojana (RVY):* Under this, aids and assistive devices are being provided to senior citizens belonging to the BPL category who suffer from age-related disabilities such as low vision, hearing impairment, loss of teeth and locomotor disabilities.
3. *Varishtha Pension Bima Yojana (VPBY):* It aims to provide social security during old age and protect elderly persons against a future fall in their interest income due to uncertain market conditions. It will provide an assured pension based on a guaranteed rate of return of 8% per annum for ten years, with the option to opt for a pension on a monthly, quarterly, half-yearly and annual basis.

4. *Vayoshreshtha Samman:* It is conferred as a national award, and given to eminent senior citizens and institutions in recognition for their service to elderly persons, especially indigent senior citizens.
5. *Atal Vayo Abhyuday Yojana (AVYAY):* It is an umbrella scheme by the Ministry of Social Justice and Empowerment that encompasses the following schemes within its domain:
   a. National Action Plan for Senior Citizens: Shelter and Health for Senior Citizens
   b. Rashtriya Vayoshri Yojana' (RVY)
   c. Health and Nutrition: Poshan Abhiyan for Elderly
   d. Livelihood and Skilling Initiatives for Senior Citizens
      - Senior Able Citizens for Re-Employment in Dignity (SACRED)
      - Action Groups Aimed at Social Reconstruction (AGRASR Groups): Elderly Self-Help groups
   e. Promoting the silver economy: equity participation in the startup for elderly care
   f. Initiative for channelling corporate social responsibility (CSR) funds for elderly care
   g. Awareness generation and capacity building for welfare of senior citizens

Thus, with the growing elderly population, the challenges associated with them are bound to increase both in intensity and magnitude. The focus of policymakers should be to include these specific issues while making welfare policies. More focus should be placed on the elderly women population as they live longer compared to their male counterparts and face various forms of discrimination after widowhood. It is important that they become an integral part, remain in good physical and mental health and continue their involvement in family and community throughout the ageing process.

6 Migration and Associate Concerns

6.1 Overview of Migration

Migration means the movement of people away from their usual place of residence. It can be both internal (within a country) and international (across countries). Census 2011 highlighted that there were 45.6 crore migrants in 2011 (38% of the population) compared to 31.5 crore migrants in 2001 (31% of the population). Thus, between 2001 and 2011, while the population grew by 18%, the number of migrants increased by 45%. Also, 99% of the total migration was internal migration and immigrants (i.e. international migrants) comprised only 1%.

Definition of migrants

Migrants have been defined as those for whom the last usual place of residence (UPR), any time in the past, is different from the present place of enumeration. The UPR of a person is the place (village/town) where the person has been staying continuously for at least six months.

As per the *Migration of India Report:* 2020–2021, published by the Ministry of Statistics and Programme Implementation, the migration rate in India was 28.9%. The migration rate for any category of person (say, for rural or urban, male or female) is the percentage of migrants belonging to that category of person (Fig. 3.14).

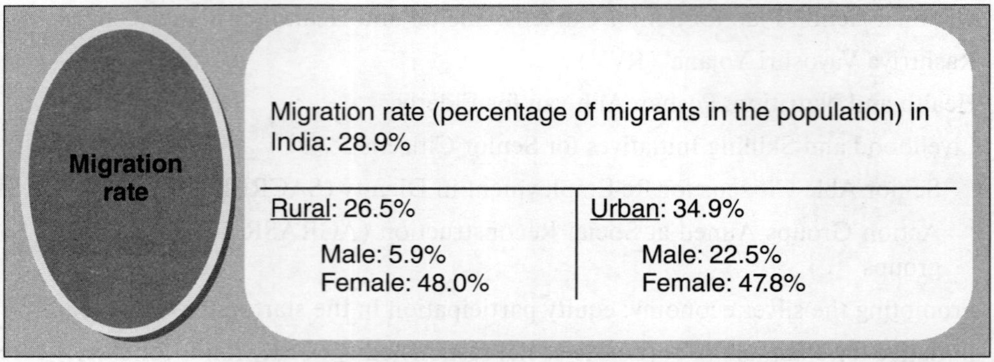

Fig. 3.14 Migration Rate in India

6.2 Pattern of Internal Migration

Internal migration in India can be classified on the basis of origin and destination: (1) Rural-rural, (2) Rural-urban, (3) Urban-rural and (4) Urban-urban.

From Fig. 3.15, it is clear that out of the total migrants to rural areas, 84% (approx.) migrated from rural areas and only 16% (approx.) migrated from urban areas.

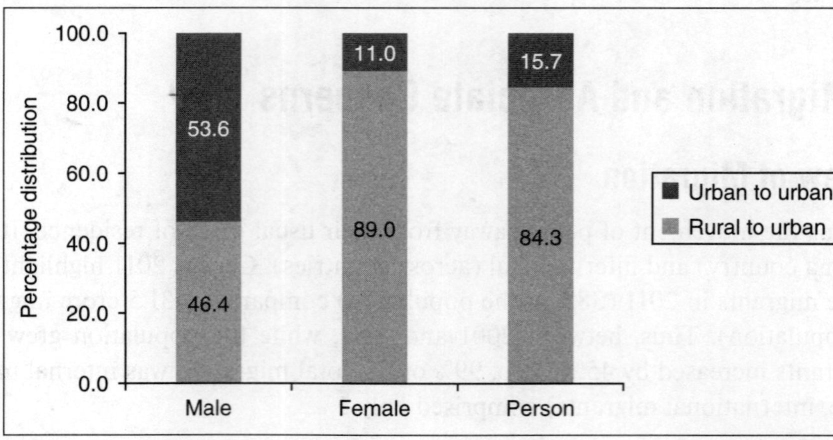

Fig. 3.15 Percentage Distribution of Internal Migrants in Rural Areas

Thus, out of total migrants to urban areas, 54% (approx.) migrated from rural areas, while 46% (approx.) migrated from urban areas (Fig. 3.16).

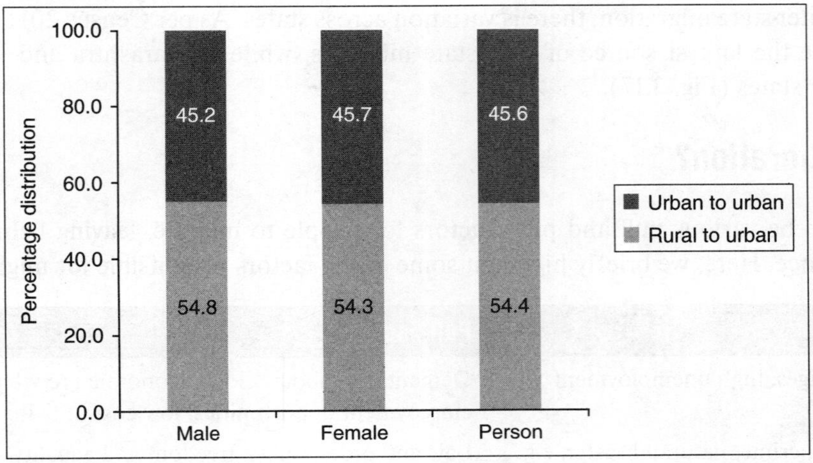

Fig. 3.16 Percentage Distribution of Internal Migrants in Urban Areas

When it comes to migration to urban areas, there are certain states or regions that are favoured by the migrants. This is because of the greater economic opportunities available in these pockets. In fact, there are 25 districts in India, which make up for more than 30% of the migrants from rural areas. Out of which, six districts have more than a million migrants who made the rural-to-urban move: Mumbai Suburban, Surat, Thane, Pune, Bengaluru and Ahmedabad.

Apart from the above classification, there is another way to classify migration: *(1) Intra-state and (2) Inter-state.*

As per the 2021 *National Statistical Office (NSO)* report on migration in India, 87.5% of all internal migration was intra-state and females were the major intra-state migrant population. The inter-state migration comprised only 11.8%.

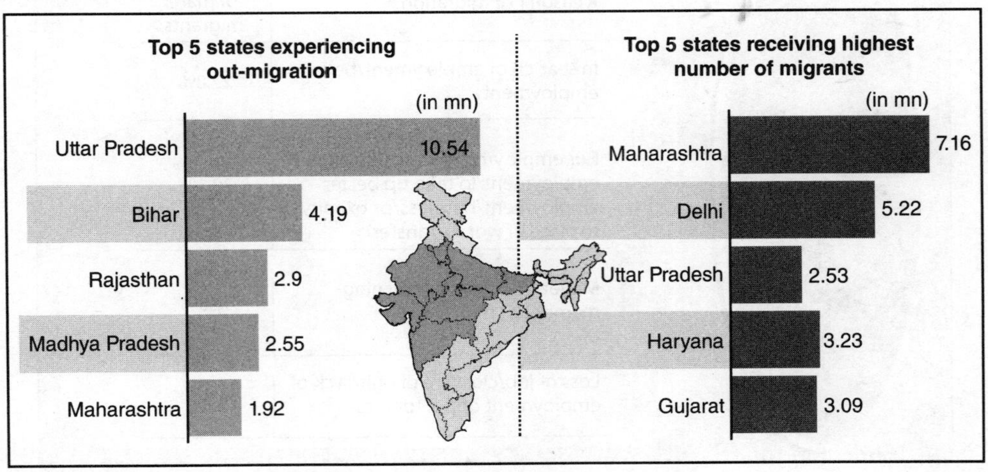

Fig. 3.17 States with Largest Out-Migration and In-Migration
Source: Inter-State Migration India (Census 2011)

If we discuss inter-state migration, there is variation across states. As per Census 2011, Uttar Pradesh and Bihar were the largest source of inter-state migrants, while Maharashtra and Delhi were the largest receiver states (Fig. 3.17).

6.3 Why Migration?

Well, there can be various pull and push factors for people to migrate, leaving behind their usual place of residence. Here, we briefly highlight some of the factors responsible for migration:

Push Factors	Pull Factors
Poverty, low wages, high unemployment	Demand for labour, Good economic growth and employment opportunities, low cost of living and education
Discrimination, crime, natural disaster, e.g. flood, famine	Law and order, safety, freedom and equality

Some of the push factors, in a way, are responsible for what is known as *Distressed Migration* from rural areas. Especially due to the collapse of millions of livelihoods in agriculture and allied activities on account of globalised agricultural practices, distress migration has increased particularly among landless farmers, agricultural labourers and marginal farmers, who are victims of poverty.

The Migration Report 2020–2021 has highlighted some of the key reasons for migration. Reasons vary for male and female migrants, as shown in Fig. 3.18 and Fig. 3.19.

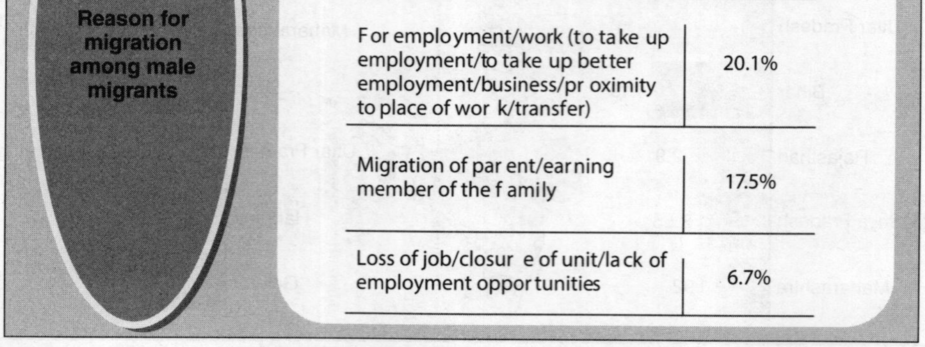

Some main reasons for migration among male migrants

Reason for migration	Percentage of male migrants
In search of employment/better employment	22.8%
For employment/work (to take up employment/to take up better employment/business/proximity to place of work/transfer)	20.1%
Migration of parent/earning member of the family	17.5%
Loss of job/closure of unit/lack of employment opportunities	6.7%

Fig. 3.18 Some Important Reasons for Migration Among Male Migrants

Reason for migration among female migrants

Some main reasons for migration among female migrants

Reason for migration	Percentage of female migrants
Marriage	86.8%
Migration of parent/earning member of the family	7.3%
Housing problem	0.8%
For employment/work (to take up employment/to take up better employment/business/proximity to place of work/transfer)	0.7%

Fig. 3.19 Some Important Reasons for Migration Among Female Migrants

Insight Box

Migration in India and Gig Economy

The gig economy broadly refers to a labour market system where individuals engage in short-term, flexible, and often freelance or contractual work, typically facilitated through digital platforms that connect workers with employers or clients.

According to a NITI Aayog study, around 7.7 million workers were engaged in the gig economy in 2020. This number is expected to expand to 23.5 million by 2029-30. Although there is no official data yet, it is estimated that migrants constitute a significant proportion of gig economy workers, particularly in urban areas.

During COVID-19, the issue of migrants involved in the gig economy was highlighted. Many migrants faced immense challenges in the absence of any support from their organisation or any legal backing.

Even today, migrant workers in the gig economy face challenges such as inconsistent income, lack of social networks, absence of social security, and lack of formal contracts - all of which increase their vulnerability to exploitation.

In the future, the following steps are essential:

- Conducting an official estimation of the number of migrants involved in the gig economy;
- Ensuring proper implementation of the Code on Social Security, 2020 to provide legal and social protections;
- Establishing minimum wage standards specifically for migrant gig workers.

Source: India's *Booming Gig and Platform Economy - Perspectives and Recommendations on the Future of Work (NITI Aayog: June 2022)*

6.4 Concerns Related to Migration

1. *Absence of legislation for intra-state migrants:* Most of the migrants in India are intra-state migrants, i.e. short-distance migrants. They engage in seasonal movements, are employed temporarily and belong to marginalised sections of society. However, there is no legislation for their welfare. The labour laws that exist in the country need to adopt a migrant lens and address the problems of migrant labourers.

2. *Inadequacy of correct data:* Short-term seasonal movements, which form a large component of the migration, remain unaccounted for. Inadequacies in the data remain the biggest challenge as far as correct information and policymaking are concerned.

3. *Loss of democratic rights:* Short-term internal migrants are unable to participate in the democratic process of voting. They are not residents of the place where they are temporarily placed and may not be at their native place of residence at the time of voting. Thus, they lose political voice. Hence, issues of the migrant population may get neglected at the institutional and policy levels.

4. *Poor implementation of protections under the Inter-State Migrant Workmen Act, 1979 (ISMW Act):* The ISMW Act provides for certain protections for inter-state workers. Labour contractors recruiting migrants are required to: (i) be licensed, (ii) register migrant workers with the government authorities and (iii) arrange for the worker to be issued a passbook recording their identity.

   However, a Standing Committee on Labour, 2011, found that implementation of this Act was poor and the central government has not made significant efforts to implement the Act in its true spirit.

5. *Lack of affordable housing and basic amenities in urban areas:* The Ministry of Housing and Urban Affairs (MoHUA) in 2015 identified migrants in urban areas as the largest population needing housing in cities. There is an inadequate supply of low-cost housing. This results in the generation of informal settlements and slums in cities.

6. *Instances of assault and abuse on migrants:* There have been various instances and movements in the past in various states against the migrant population. The recent case in Tamil Nadu is an example in which a man was reportedly seen abusing and assaulting three migrant workers on a moving train in Tamil Nadu.
7. *Issue of Distressed Reverse Migration:* This was witnessed during COVID-19. Due to the loss of their sources of livelihood and shelter in urban areas during such times, migrant workers have no option except to go back to their native state. It was a situation of human crisis that affected children and women as well.

Insight Box

Distressed Migration: A Case Study of KBK Districts in Odisha

It is a form of migration that is undertaken in conditions where individuals have no other options but to migrate in order to survive with dignity. It can be due to extreme economic deprivation, caste discrimination, ethnic or religious violence, or environmental disaster.

The former districts of Koraput, Balangir and Kalahandi, also known as the KBK districts, were reorganised into eight districts in 1992. The area suffers from significant underdevelopment due to prevalent high poverty levels, inadequate literacy rates, poorly established agriculture, and insufficient infrastructure and transportation. Within these districts reside indigenous tribal communities such as the Gonds, Koyas, Kotias, etc., whose livelihoods rely on forest resources and subsistence farming. The arid nature of the region contributes to agricultural challenges, including crop failures, severe natural disasters, limited irrigated land, and reduced government investment, thereby plunging these workers into extreme poverty.

Consequently, seeking alternative livelihoods, these individuals migrate seasonally to rural or urban areas for employment opportunities during agricultural downturns–a prevalent trend in these districts. However, their dependence on non-timber forest resources faces obstacles due to rapid deforestation caused by development projects and mining activities.

It is important to highlight that the government has been recognising the issues faced by the migrant population, particularly after the human crisis witnessed during the COVID lockdown. The government is making an effort to create a credible real-time database of inter-state migrant workers, providing housing at an affordable rent to migrants near their workplace.

The government has also come up with the idea of the *One Nation One Ration Card Scheme (ONORC)*. ONORC seeks to provide universal access to Public Distribution System (PDS) food grains for migrant workers. Thus, migrants would not have to apply for a new ration card after they migrate to a different state.

NITI Aayog has also prepared a draft *National Migrant Labour Policy*. It recommended that migration should be acknowledged as an integral part of development and that government policies should not hinder but seek to facilitate internal migration.

7 India's Population Policy

India is one of the developing nations in the world. In India, there is a significant chunk of the population that is still facing the evils of poverty. The goal of realising equitable distribution of resources through the much-touted top-down approach has faced several challenges. Consequently, there is huge inequality in Indian society. Thus, it is very important that along with economic development, the growth of the population remains manageable so that the government is able to provide at least a decent quality of life to its citizens. In this respect, population policy assumes critical importance.

Even before independence, efforts were undertaken to bring the growing population under control. After independence, in 1952, India was the first country in the world to launch a national programme emphasising family planning to the extent necessary for reducing birth rates 'to stabilise the population at a level consistent with the requirements of the national economy'. After 1952, India witnessed sharp declines in the death rate. But it was not accompanied by a similar drop in birth rates.

The government then announced its first **National Population Policy in 1976**. The population policy covered multiple issues related to population growth prevention.

- The legal age of marriage was increased. The minimum age for marriage was twenty-one for boys and eighteen for girls.
- Particular emphasis was laid on the development and spread of literacy among women.
- Emphasis was placed on spreading family welfare programmes among the masses through various media.
- The new focus was on research on reproductive physiology and birth control issues.
- Make the sterilisation program more popular; cash will be provided to those who perform sterilisation.

This policy was formulated while the emergency was in force. The implementation of the mass sterilisation program to reduce population growth invited the wrath of citizens. It discredited the entire family planning programme of the government. Later, the government decided not to use force in family planning programmes. Also, family planning programmes were to be renamed family welfare programmes.

After this experiment, the Government of India formed an expert group under the chairmanship of *Dr. M.S. Swaminathan* to draft India's population policy. Accordingly, the latest National Population Policy finally came into force in 2000.

The **National Population Policy (NPP) 2000** focussed on the voluntary and informed choice and consent of citizens while availing of reproductive health care services and the continuation of the target-free approach to administering family planning services. The approach is centered on addressing child survival, maternal health, and contraception concurrently, aiming to expand the reach and coverage of a comprehensive package of reproductive and child health services. This involves collaborative efforts between the government, industry, and voluntary non-governmental organisations working in partnership to enhance outreach and accessibility to these services.

Immediate objective of NPP 2000

a. Tackle the deficiencies in access to contraception, healthcare infrastructure, and medical professionals.

b. Deliver comprehensive and integrated services for fundamental reproductive and child healthcare needs.

Medium-term objective of NPP 2000

a. To bring the TFR to replacement levels by 2010

Long-term objective of NPP 2000

a. To achieve a stable population by 2045, at a level consistent with the requirements of sustainable economic growth, social development, and environmental protection.

In order to fulfill these objectives, the NPP 2000 has highlighted the following goals to be achieved by 2010.

7.1 Goals of NPP 2000

1. Address the unmet needs for basic reproductive and child health services, supplies and infrastructure.
2. Make school education up to age 14 free and compulsory, and reduce dropouts at primary and secondary school levels to below 20% for both boys and girls.
3. Reduce Infant Mortality Rate (IMR) to below 30 per 1000 live births.
4. Reduce Maternal Mortality Ratio (MMR) to below 100 per 100,000 live births.
5. Achieve universal immunisation of children against all vaccine-preventable diseases.
6. Promote delayed marriage for girls, not earlier than age 18 and preferably after 20 years of age.
7. Achieve 80% institutional deliveries and 100% deliveries by trained personnel.
8. Ensure universal availability of information, counseling, and services pertaining to fertility regulation and contraception, offering a diverse range of options to choose from.

9. Achieve 100% registration of births, deaths, marriage and pregnancy.
10. Contain the spread of Acquired Immunodeficiency Syndrome (AIDS) and promote greater integration between the management of reproductive tract infections (RTI) and sexually transmitted infections (STI) and the National AIDS Control Organisation.
11. Prevent and control communicable diseases.
12. Incorporate Indian Systems of Medicine (ISM) into the delivery of reproductive and child health services, as well as in outreach initiatives aimed at households.
13. Promote vigorously the small family norm to achieve replacement levels of TFR.
14. Achieve alignment and coordination in executing interconnected social sector initiatives, thereby transforming family welfare into a people-centric programme.

7.2 Critical evaluation of India's NPP 2000

As of today, India has made significant progress in terms of reductions in IMR, MMR, universal immunisation, AIDS control. Even India has achieved a replacement level of TFR. In fact, southern states such as Kerala and a few in the north, such as Himachal Pradesh, have achieved significant success in ensuring education and public health and, at the same time, have been able to reduce birth rates.

However, in terms of population control, India still has to make significant progress. A recent report suggests India has crossed China to become the world's most populous country.

Experts believe that our national policy places exclusive emphasis on family planning programs to reduce the population growth rate in India. They believe that family planning might not work if we don't focus on reducing *poverty and illiteracy*. Poor people do not show interest in reducing the birth rate, mainly due to economic reasons. Poverty and illiteracy are major causes of the growing population. This is especially true for less developed regions such as Bihar, UP, parts of Madhya Pradesh and, Jharkhand. In these states, TFR is still above the national average or the replacement level.

Also, education programmes are yet to create enough awareness, particularly in the rural set-up, so that family planning and use of contraceptives become part of daily discourse. Still, people are not upfront about discussing such issues with others.

Moreover, many argue that India lacks trained manpower and health infrastructure to cater to the needs of India's population. The quality and reach of health infrastructure in the hinterland are also matters of concern. As a result, in India, still around 4.5% of child delivery is home-based delivery, i.e. not institutional. It affects MMR as well as child health.

Nonetheless, there is progress in family welfare programmes in India. With time, the less developed states are also expected to perform better, and India will be able to reduce its population both in absolute terms and in terms of rate of growth. As of now, India also has an opportunity to utilise its younger population for India's progress when most of the developed regions of the world are ageing.

Additional Readings

1. A. Thakur, India enters 37-year period of demographic dividend. *Times of India.*
2. E. Roy and A. Mascarenhas, India's population 142.8 crore in 2023, crosses China's: UN population report. *Indian Express.*
3. E. Roy, India's population growth rate on a steady decline since '90s. *Indian Express.*
4. Census of India 2011 : Population Projections for India and States 2011–2036.
5. India's demography at 2040: Planning public good provision for the 21st century. *Economic Survey 2018-19.*
6. Can India's demographic dividend turn into liability? *Livemint.*
7. National Family Health Survey (NFHS-5) 2019–2021.
8. SRS Bulletin 2022, Volume 57 (June 2025)
9. N. Lal, India's infant mortality rate improves, but still lags behind much of Asia. *The Diplomat.*
10. Registrar General of India (RGI), Special Bulletin on Maternal Mortality in India 2018–2020.
11. V. Manocha, India's child sex ratio has reached 'emergency proportions': UN study. *Down to Earth.*
12. Ministry of Health and Family Welfare (MoHFW), Reference *Manual for Oral Contraceptive Pills.*
13. S.C. Shettar, Problems of Aged in Changing Indian Scenario (1 August 2013).
14. Ministry of Health and Family Welfare (MoHFW), Longitudinal Ageing Study of India (LASI) Wave-1, India Report 2021.
15. Ministry of Social Justice and Empowerment, Atal Vayo Abhyuday Yojana (AVYAY).
16. P. Mujrai and L. T. Rao, A Critical Analysis and Evaluation of National Population Policy (February 2022).
17. K. Bajeli-Datt, Institutional deliveries in India on the rise, but home deliveries still a norm: Govt data. *The New Indian Express.*
18. Ministry of Health and Family Welfare, National Population Policy 2000.
19. M. Iyer, Migration in India and the impact of the lockdown on migrants. *PRS* (10 June 2020).
20. Ministry of Statistics and Programme Implementation, Migration in India 2020-2021.
21. S.I. Rajan, India's soul: From rural to urban. *Deccan Herald* (15 August 2022).

Previous Years' Questions

1. Critically examine whether growing population is the cause of poverty OR poverty is the main cause of population increase in India. (2015)

2. "Empowering women is the key to control the population growth." Discuss. (2019)

3. Discuss the main objectives of Population Education and point out the measures to achieve them in India in detail. (2021)

UPSC CSE 2024

1. Why do large cities tend to attract more migrants than smaller towns? Discuss in the light of conditions in developing countries. (150 words | 10 Marks)

Model Answer

In developing countries, internal migration is largely driven by rural distress and the aspiration for better livelihoods. Large metropolitan cities attract more migrants than smaller towns due to a mix of economic, infrastructural, and social factors. For eg, 6 large cities have more than a million migrants who made the rural-to-urban move: Mumbai Suburban, Surat, Thane, Pune, Bengaluru and Ahmedabad.

Reasons for Migration to Large Cities:

1. **Economic Opportunities:**
   - Cities like Mumbai and Bengaluru offer diverse opportunities in industries, IT and services -options rarely available in smaller towns.
   - Moreover, the *informal sector, like construction work*, in large cities also provides better opportunities and scope for higher wages.
2. **Better Infrastructure & Services in Healthcare and Education:**
   - Access to quality healthcare and education is higher in cities like Chennai and Hyderabad compared to tier-III towns.
3. **Urban Amenities & Lifestyle:**
   - Large cities offer a modern lifestyle characterised by greater social freedom, recreation and mobility.
   - Cities, such as Mexico and New Delhi, have better access to *transportation facilities* like metro rail, buses, railways and airports.
4. **Social Networks & Chain Migration:**
   - Migrant communities in cities like Ahmedabad and Kolkata facilitate easier integration for new arrivals. 5. Neglect of Smaller Towns:

5. **Neglect of Smaller Towns:**
   - Towns like Gaya or Bhagalpur lack economic dynamism, pushing people toward metros.

Large cities act as magnets for migrants due to concentrated development, better socio-economic opportunities and quality infrastructure. However, this trend exacerbates urban challenges like inadequate housing, pollution and rising crime. Therefore, policymakers need to focus on balanced regional development.

2. What is the concept of a 'Demographic Winter'? Is the world moving towards such a situation? Elaborate.

(150 words | 10 Marks)

Model Answer

The concept of 'Demographic Winter' means sustained decline in fertility rates below replacement level of 2.1, resulting in an ageing population, decline in overall population and ultimately a shrinking workforce. This phenomenon poses significant socio-economic challenges.

Current Trends Indicating Demographic Winter:

1. **Declining Fertility Rates:**
   - As of 2024, the global fertility rate stands at 2.25 births per woman, down from 3.31 in 1990.
   - Countries like Italy (1.2), South Korea (0.68) and China (1.2) have fertility rates well below the replacement level of 2.1.
   - India's fertility rate has declined to 2.0, indicating a future demographic shift towards an ageing population
2. **Ageing Populations:**
   - Japan has ~30% of its population aged 65 or older, the highest globally.
   - Southern Europe is the oldest region, with 22% of its population aged 65 and above.
   - In India too, the share of population aged 60 or above is expected to increase from 8.6% in 2011 to around 20% by 2050.

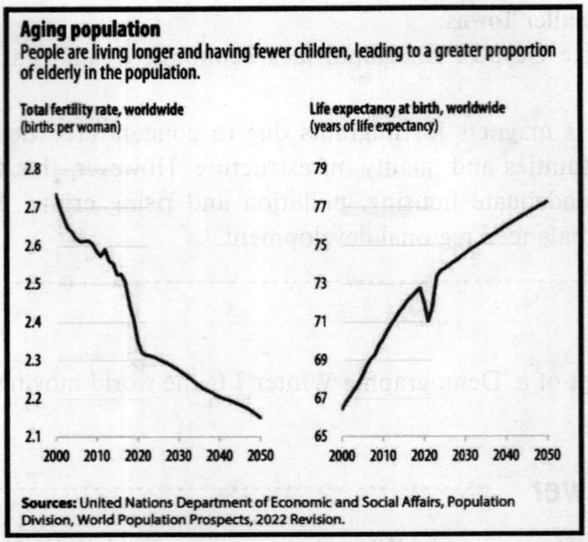

3. **Economic Implications:**
   - Dependency ratio at global level is also expected to increase, putting pressure on the economic system of a nation.
   - Ageing of population leads to shrinking workforce, increased healthcare costs and pension burdens.
   - IMF projects a global average age rise from the mid-30s now to the mid-40s by century's end, potentially slowing economic growth.

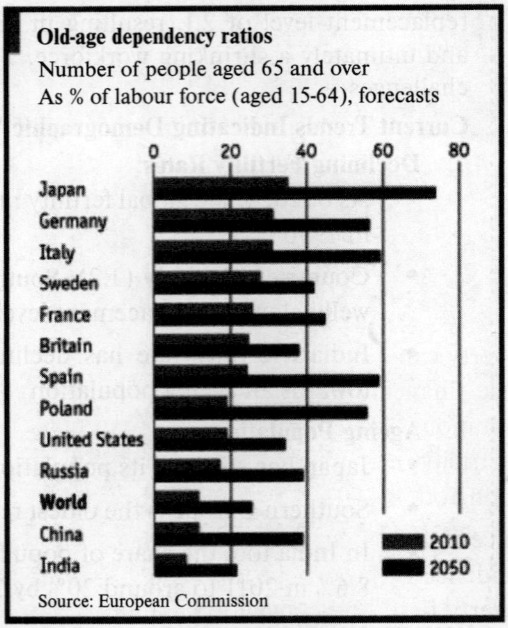

Clearly, several regions of the world are heading towards a demographic winter. However, there are countries in sub-Saharan Africa -Somalia, Nigeria, Uganda -where the fertility rate of 5 is still well above the replacement rate. In future, making suitable population policy will be needed to overcome the associated challenges with 'demographic winter'.

Source: 1. The troubling decline in the global fertility rate (Financial Times: Feb 2024) 2. AGING IS THE REAL POPULATION BOMB (IMF: July 2023) 3. Old-age dependency ratios (The Economist: May 2009)

4 Poverty and Developmental Issues

1 Concept of Poverty

Poverty can be understood as a situation in which an individual or household does not possess the basic financial resources to afford a basic minimum standard of living. They suffer from various limitations, including low wages, poor quality housing facilities, a lack of access to clean water and electricity, extreme gender inequality in the participation of gainful employment and education, among others.

Since independence, there have been discussions and deliberations at various levels to lessen the incidence of poverty in the country. However, in order to achieve this, it is important to measure poverty first. The conventional approach to measure poverty is to specify a minimum expenditure (or income) required to purchase a basket of goods and services necessary to satisfy basic human needs. This expenditure is called the *poverty line*. The basket of goods and services necessary to satisfy basic human needs is the Poverty Line Basket (PLB). It is important to highlight here that the basic understanding of what constitutes poverty varies across regions and time.

1.1 Measurement of the Poverty Line in India

Planning Commission was the nodal agency in India to estimate poverty based on the poverty line. Post-independence, various committees and expert groups were set up by the Planning Commission to study and decide upon the poverty line in India.

1. *Working Group (1962)*: In India, for the first time, the poverty line was quantified by this group in terms of the minimum requirements (food and non-food) of individuals for healthy living. It formulated separate poverty lines for rural and urban areas: ₹20 and ₹25 per capita per month respectively in terms of 1960–61 prices. This was widely used in the 1960s and 1970s to estimate the poverty ratio at the national and state levels.
2. *Study by V.M. Dandekar and N Rath (1971)*: This study was not commissioned by the Planning Commission. These economists derived poverty line based on expenditure adequate to provide 2250 calories per day in both rural and urban areas. They found poverty lines to be: Rs. 15 and Rs 22.5 per capita per month for rural and urban households respectively.
3. *Task Force on 'Projections of Minimum Needs and Effective Consumption Demand' headed by Dr. Y. K. Alagh (1979)*: This task force defined the poverty line as the per capita consumption expenditure level to meet the average per capita daily calorie requirement of 2400 kcal and 2100 kcal per capita per day in rural and urban areas, respectively. It set poverty lines at Rs. 49.09 and Rs. 56.64 per capita per month in 1973–1974 prices for rural and urban areas, respectively.
4. *Lakdawala Expert Group (1993)*: It was constituted by the Planning Commission to 'look into the methodology for estimation of poverty and to re-define the poverty line, if necessary'. It, however, did not re-define the poverty line. It retained the poverty lines as defined by the Alagh Committee based on minimum nutritional requirements.

   However, it came up with the idea of state-specific poverty lines in order to reflect the price differences across states.
5. *Tendulkar Expert Group (2009)*: One of the significant recommendations of the Tendulkar group was to shift the calculation of poverty lines from the calorie norms used in all poverty estimations since 1979 to nutritional outcomes. Apart from this, it recommended taking into account private expenditure on health and education while estimating poverty. As per the expert group, the national poverty line for 2011–2012 was estimated at Rs. 816 per capita per month for rural areas and Rs. 1,000 per capita per month for urban areas.
6. *Rangrajan Committee (2014)*: The Tendulkar group was severely criticised for its recommendation on the national poverty line data. Hence, this committee was set up. It recommended separate consumption baskets for rural and urban areas, which include food items that ensure recommended calorie, protein and fat intake and non-food items like clothing, education, health, housing and transport. It set the poverty line at Rs. 972 per month per capita consumption expenditure in rural areas and Rs. 1407 in urban areas. Thus, it was seen as an improvement from the Tendulkar Group recommendation. However, the government did not take a call on the report of the Rangarajan Committee.

Insight Box

Why Consumption Expenditure, and Not Income Levels, has been Favoured for calculation of Poverty Line?

The estimation of the poverty line in India has traditionally relied on measuring consumption expenditure rather than income levels. This approach is taken because assessing the incomes of self-employed individuals, daily wage laborers, and others poses challenges. Additionally, there are significant income fluctuations due to seasonal factors, supplementary incomes, and data collection difficulties, especially in the predominantly rural and informal economy of India. Given that households can access credit markets or use their savings to stabilise their consumption patterns to some extent, consumption expenditure provides a more reliable basis for determining a household's actual standard of living. Consequently, many Poverty Estimation Committees have recommended using per capita consumption expenditure or household expenses as the appropriate statistical measure for calculating poverty in India.

1.2 Limitations of 'Below Poverty Line (BPL)' Approach

As we discussed above, various committees and expert groups have set specific poverty lines and used them to decide the number of poor people in the country. It is also clear that the exercise to arrive at a golden 'poverty line' has been in constant flux.

It is to be noted that there have been several criticisms of the methodology used by the committees and also of the data with respect to the poverty line. Subject experts argue against the use of the minimum adequate norm of nutrition as a key criterion to determine the poverty line. They also argue that the expenditure levels of households decided by the committees are inadequate to meet the minimum standard of living.

Also, it is understood that poverty lines should vary across regions, considering tastes and preferences and price differences across regions. Therefore, identifying the components of the Poverty Line Basket (PLB) presents another hurdle in poverty line estimation in India. This challenge arises because the prices of items within the basket differ across states and fluctuate over time. Moreover, consumption patterns, nutritional needs, and the prices of these items constantly change in response to the dynamics of the macroeconomy and demography.

As a result, it has also been seen that a significant number of households above the expenditure-based poverty line were not able to fulfill their basic minimum calorie requirements. Thus, the practice of defining the poverty line solely on the basis of per capita monthly expenditure has been questioned.

The next question that arose based on the above criticisms is:

Insight Box

Is poverty only about consumption?

In short, the answer is No. Rather, poverty encompasses various factors such as limited access to education, lack of clean water and electricity, poor quality of work, poor health or malnutrition, among others. However, the deprivation faced by the poor in various fields such as health, education, social life, geographical isolation, sanitation, etc. is not accounted for in the Below Poverty Line (BPL) approach. No committee or task group could capture this multi-dimensional aspect of poverty.

1.3 Socio-Economic Caste Census Survey (SECC) 2011

On the basis of the recommendation of an expert committee chaired by Dr. N. C. Saxena to propose a new methodology for identifying BPL households, the Ministry of Rural Development (MoRD) launched the Socio Economic and Caste Census (SECC). SECC was a door-to-door enumeration across both rural and urban India, collecting household-level socio-economic data.

The objective of the SECC was not to replace the poverty line. Rather, it was to provide '*information regarding the socio-economic condition and education status of various castes and sections of the population*' and '*enable households to be ranked on their socio-economic status*' to identify households that live below the poverty line.

The SECC 2011, which completed its survey in March 2016, ranked households in three categories:

a. *Automatically excluded:* Households meeting exclusion criteria - any of the 13 assets and income-based parameters - are automatically excluded from welfare benefits;

b. *Automatically included:* Households satisfying inclusion criteria: any one of the five acute social destitution parameters is automatically included for welfare benefits;

c. *Others:* 'Others' are ranked on the basis of seven indicators of deprivation and would, resources permitting, be eligible for welfare benefits.

SECC did a survey on socio-economic status of 17.97 crore rural households. It resulted in the automatic exclusion of 7.07 crore (39.36%) of households as not poor. 0.16 crore (0.91%) households were automatically included as they were found to be the poorest of the poor, and 8.72 crore (48.54%) of rural households were found to be in the 'others' category (Fig. 4.1). (Note: 1.41 crore rural households had raised objections to the findings about their socio-economic status.)

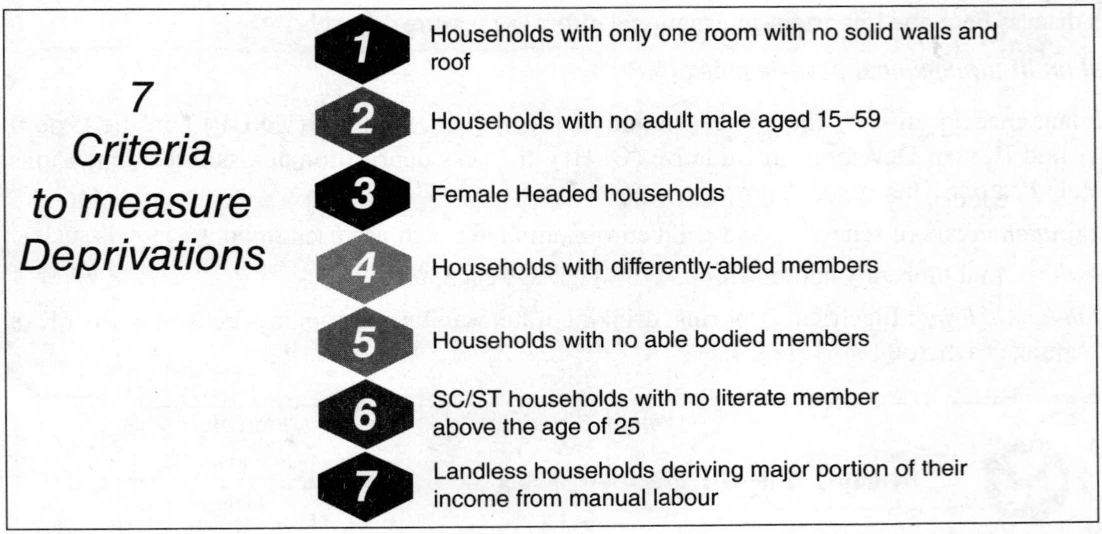

Fig. 4.1 SECC's Seven Criteria to Measure Deprivations

Thus, it was for the first time that deprivation factors were considered with a focus on multi-dimensional poverty. Hence, this data was much more useful for beneficiary identification. The Sumit Bose Committee (2017), thus, recommended using SECC data for identifying beneficiaries for all centrally sponsored, central and state government schemes as far as possible.

SECC data provides evidence-based developmental interventions. Hence, the government has used SECC data for the identification of beneficiary households in the implementation of its social welfare programmes, including Deendayal Antyodaya Yojana-National Rural Livelihood Mission (NRLM), Pradhan Mantri Aawas Yojana-Gramin, Pradhan Mantri Jan Arogya Yojana-Ayushman Bharat, Pradhan Mantri Sahaj Bijli Har Ghar Yojana and Pradhan Mantri Ujjwala Yojana. It is also being used by several state governments to implement the National Food Security Act.

In these programmes, Gram Sabhas validate the selection of beneficiaries. In order to establish identity, Aadhar is being used wherever legally allowed. This results in the selection of the right beneficiaries and minimisation of duplication. This process has led to an improvement in the effectiveness of government initiatives aimed at addressing multi-dimensional poverty, extending beyond measures solely based on income or expenditure.

1.4 International Indices to Measure Poverty

As per the World Bank, poverty is defined as deprivation of well-being in many dimensions. It includes low incomes and a lack of ability to acquire the basic goods and services necessary to survive with dignity. As far as India is concerned, in recent years, international research institutions have suggested that India has made substantial progress in reducing poverty.

Let us discuss here one important international effort to measure poverty:

Global multi-dimensional poverty index (MPI)

It was launched in 2010 by the United Nations Development Program (UNDP) and the Oxford Poverty and Human Development Initiative (OPHI). It tracks deprivation across three dimensions and ten indicators. They are as follows:

1. *Education*: Years of schooling and child enrolment (1/6 weightage each, total 2/6)
2. *Health*: Child mortality and nutrition (1/6 weightage each, total 2/6)
3. *Standard of living*: Electricity, flooring, drinking water, sanitation, cooking fuel and assets (1/18 weightage each, total 2/6) (Fig. 4.2)

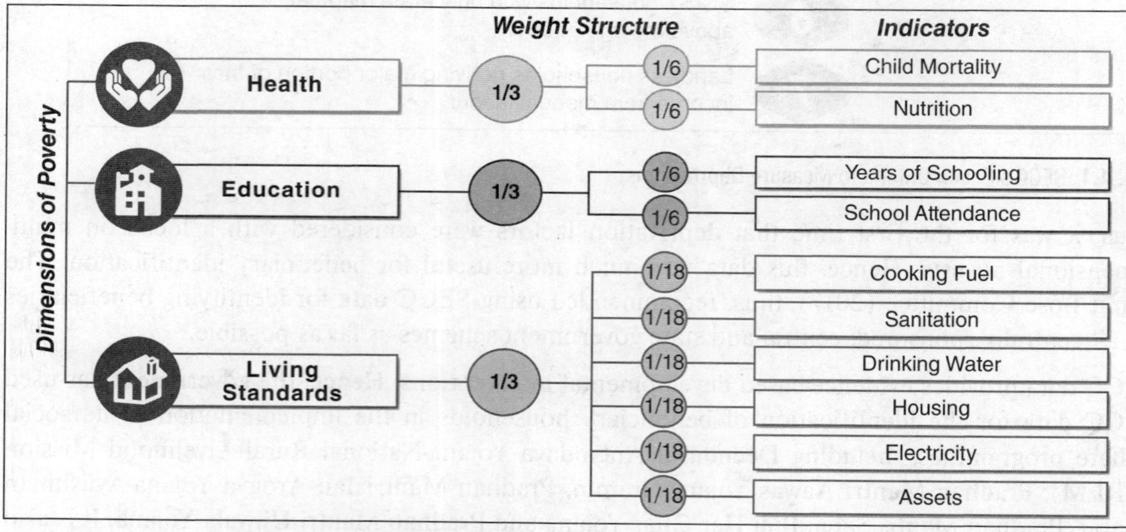

Fig. 4.2 Global MPI: Dimensions, Indicators and Weights

It is one of the most comprehensive methodologies to measure multidimensional poverty as it includes various deprivation factors. Unlike the conventional approach, it does not measure poverty only in income or monetary terms.

Based on calculation, if a person is deprived in one third or more (means 33% or more) of the weighted ten indicators, he is considered multi-dimensionally poor. If the person is deprived in one half or more of the weighted indicators, then he is considered living in extreme multidimensional poverty.

The Global Multidimensional Poverty Index (MPI) 2024 report highlights a significant decline in India's poverty rate–from 55.1% in 2005-06 to 16.4% in 2019-21. Despite this progress, India has the highest number of people living in multidimensional poverty, with around 23.4 crore (234 million) individuals classified as poor. India, along with Pakistan (93 million), Ethiopia (86 million), Nigeria (74 million), and the Democratic Republic of the Congo (66 million), ranks among the top five countries with the highest number of poor individuals. Together, these five countries account for nearly half of the global population living in poverty.

> **Debate Corner**
> Does the Multidimensional Poverty Index truly capture the realities of poverty in India, or does it risk oversimplifying complex socio-economic deprivations into quantifiable indicators?

World Bank poverty line

The World Bank defines extreme poverty as living on less than **$2.15 per person per day**, based on 2017 purchasing power parity (PPP). According to the **Poverty and Equity Brief** released in April 2025 by the World Bank, India has made remarkable progress in reducing extreme poverty. The proportion of people living in extreme poverty declined sharply from **16.2% in 2011–12 to just 2.3% in 2022–23**. During this period, 171 million people were lifted out of extreme poverty.

Key highlights from the report include:

1 In urban areas, the poverty rate fell from **10.7% in 2011-12 to 1.1%** in 2022-23.

2 In rural areas, it dropped from **18.4% to 2.8%** during the same period.

3 In 2011–12, Uttar Pradesh, Maharashtra, Bihar, West Bengal, and Madhya Pradesh accounted for **65% of India's extreme poor**. By 2022–23, these states contributed to two-thirds of the national reduction in poverty.

Note: In June 2025, the World Bank revised the international poverty line to $3 per person per day, based on 2021 purchasing power parity (PPP) prices. This means that anyone living on less than $3 a day is considered to be living in extreme poverty. Current estimates suggest that approximately one in ten people worldwide fall below this threshold, with a large proportion residing in Sub-Saharan Africa or in regions affected by fragility and conflict.

1.5 Current Level of Poverty in India

Last time, the official estimate of poverty was released by the Planning Commission in 2011–2012. Poverty was estimated at 21.92%, which was calculated using the Tendulkar Committee approach. After that, no official estimates of poverty have been released.

Recent development: Report by NITI Aayog

Recently, NITI Aayog released a Discussion Paper titled 'Multidimensional Poverty in India since 2005-06'. The National Multidimensional Poverty Index (MPI) measures simultaneous deprivations across the three equally weighted dimensions of health, education and standard of living that are represented by 12 SDG-aligned indicators (Fig. 4.3).

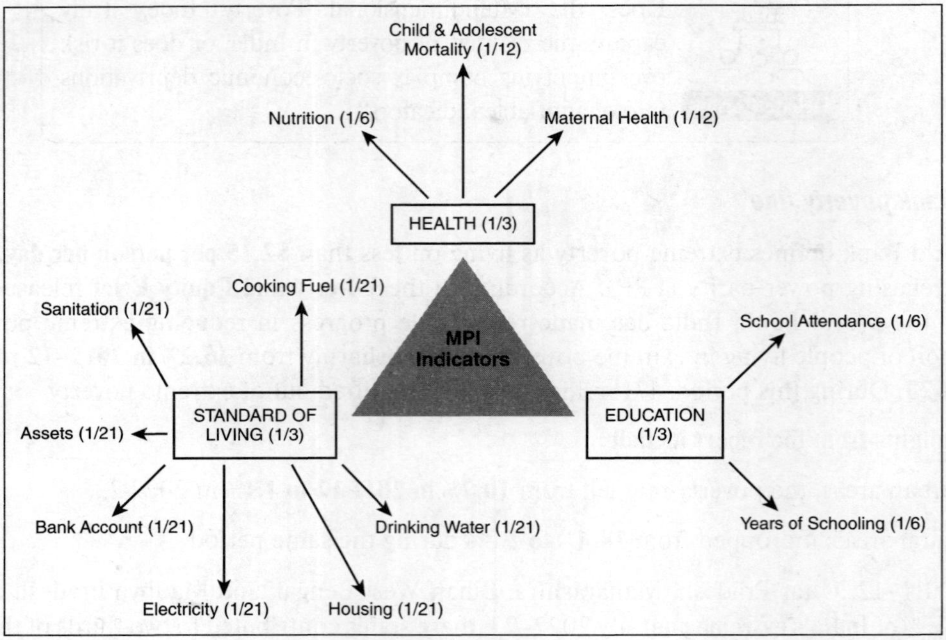

Fig. 4.3 Indicators for Measuring MPI and their Respective Weights

Few important highlights from the Discussion Paper

- India has seen a notable reduction in multidimensional poverty, dropping from 29.17% in 2013-14 to 11.28% in 2022-23 - a decline of 17.89 percentage points.
- Over the past nine years, approximately 24.82 crore people have moved out of multidimensional poverty.
- All 12 indicators used to measure the MPI have shown marked improvement during this period.
- India is on track to achieve its Sustainable Development Goal (SDG) of halving multidimensional poverty well ahead of the 2030 deadline.

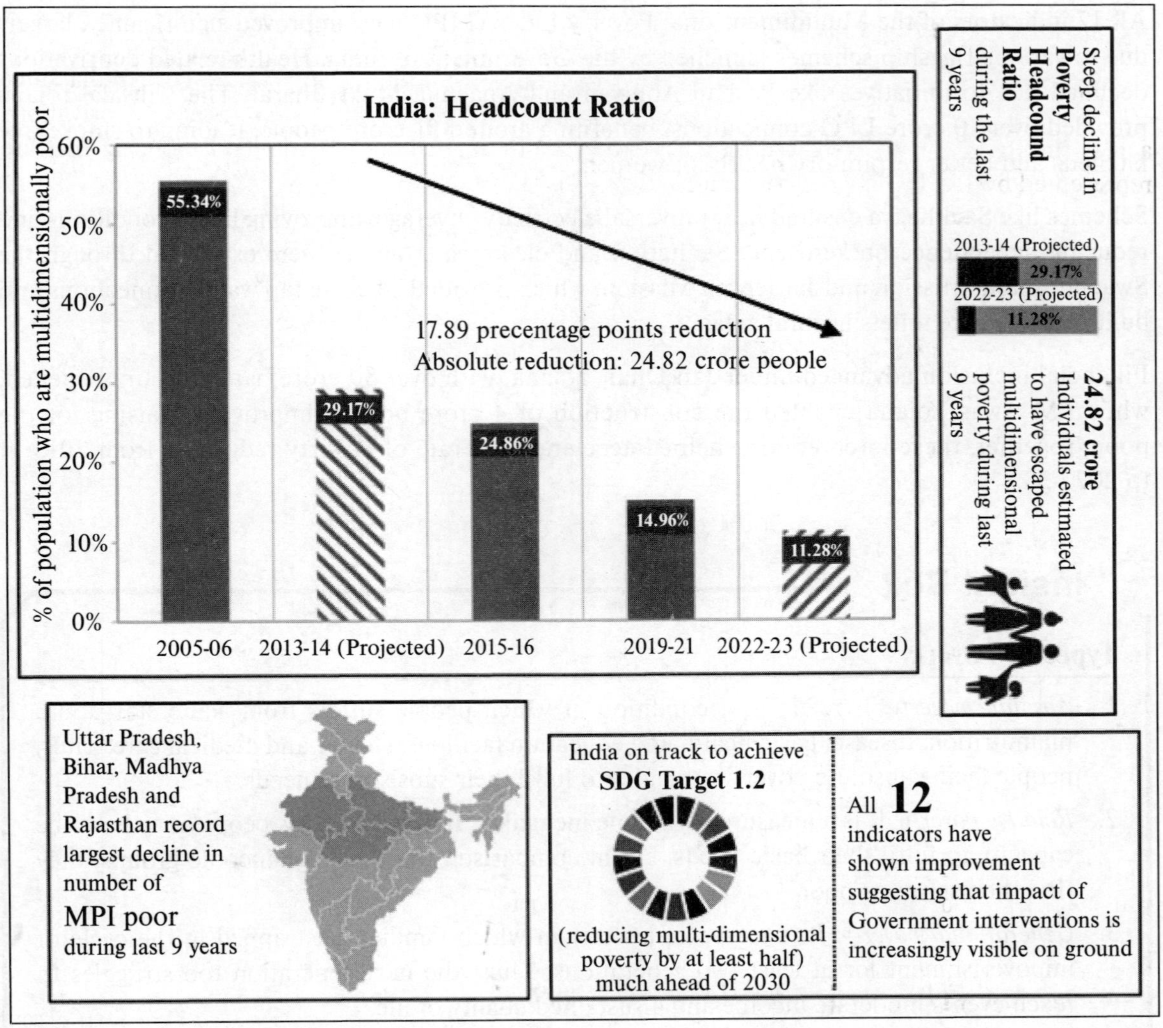

Fig. 4.4 Highlights from the NITI Aayog Discussion Paper

- Among the states, Uttar Pradesh recorded the largest reduction, with 5.94 crore people escaping poverty, followed by Bihar (3.77 crore), Madhya Pradesh (2.30 crore) and Rajasthan (1.87 crore).

All 12 indicators of the Multidimensional Poverty Index (MPI) have improved significantly, largely due to various flagship schemes launched by the Government of India. Health-related deprivations declined due to initiatives like Poshan Abhiyan and Anaemia Mukt Bharat. The Ujjwala Yojana provided over 10 crore LPG connections, benefiting around 31 crore people, leading to smoke-free kitchens and better respiratory health for women.

Schemes like Saubhagya ensured near-universal electricity coverage, improving living conditions and reducing dependence on kerosene. Sanitation and clean water access were expanded through the Swachh Bharat Mission and Jal Jeevan Mission, which provided 14 crore tap water connections and built over 11 crore toilets in rural areas.

Financial inclusion advanced under Jan Dhan Yojana, with over 50 crore bank accounts opened, while PM Awas Yojana enabled the construction of 4 crore homes, improving housing for the poor. Together, these interventions helped accelerate the rate of poverty reduction from 2013-14 to 2022-23.

Insight Box

Types of Poverty

1. *Absolute poverty*: It refers to a condition in which people suffers from acute starvation, malnutrition, disease, basic health and education facilities, shelter and medical care. Thus, people facing absolute poverty struggles to fulfil their subsistence needs.
2. *Relative poverty*: It is a measure of income inequality. In this category, people may have the capacity to fulfil their basic needs, but in comparison to other high-income groups, they find themselves as poor.
3. *Generational poverty*: It is a type of poverty in which families get trapped in the cycle of impoverishment for at least two generations. Thus, the next generation too struggles to reach even a moderate income and a sustained quality of life.
4. *Situational poverty*: It is a temporary situation with results from some life-changing events such as death of family members, illness, divorce, environmental disaster.

   It is to be noted that there can be various other kinds of poverty such as Natural and Artificial (Social) Poverty, Primary and Secondary Poverty, Subjective Poverty, Rural and Urban Poverty.

2 What Has Caused Poverty in India?

A number of factors are responsible for widespread poverty in India. Some of the factors are as follows:

1. One of the reasons is the low level of economic development during the British administration. The British policies ruined traditional handicrafts and discouraged the development of industries like textiles. Such low economic growth persisted until the 1980s. As a result, there were less job opportunities and low income growth. Simultaneously, this period was marked by high growth of population. These two factors, i.e. high population growth and low economic growth, perpetuate the cycle of poverty.
2. Income inequality, due to the unequal distribution of land and other resources, is another reason for the high poverty rates in India. Policy initiatives like land reforms, aiming at the redistribution of assets in rural areas, could not be implemented effectively across states. Proper implementation of land reforms could have positively improved the lives of millions of rural poor.
3. Most of rural India depends on agriculture for their subsistence. Due to many irrigation projects and the much-appreciable Green Revolution, many job opportunities were created in the agriculture sector. However, the benefits of these projects were concentrated only in limited regions of India. Thus, in other parts, agriculture continued with its traditional methods. The growth rate in agriculture was unable to pull people out of poverty.
4. Due to low growth in rural areas, people migrated to urban areas in search of job opportunities. In urban areas, industries did come up both in the public and private sectors. However, they were not enough to absorb all the job seekers. As a result, many people started working as construction workers, informal vendors, etc. They had irregular and meagre income in such professions, which was not enough to lead a quality life in cities. Thus, they were forced to live in slums. Consequently, the problem of poverty, largely a rural phenomenon, became a noted feature of urban areas as well.
5. Subject experts also say that even socio-cultural factors are responsible for poverty in India. In India, people have many socio-cultural obligations, such as *marriage, upanayana, shraddha*, among others. In all these religious ceremonies, people in India, including the very poor, spend a lot of money. In fact, it has been observed that people even take out debt to carry out these social events. Due to their low income, they are unable to pay their debt and become victim of indebtedness. This further perpetuates poverty.

Debate Corner

Is poverty in India primarily a legacy of historical factors like colonial rule and early policy failures, or is it now being perpetuated by present-day structural and socio-economic challenges?

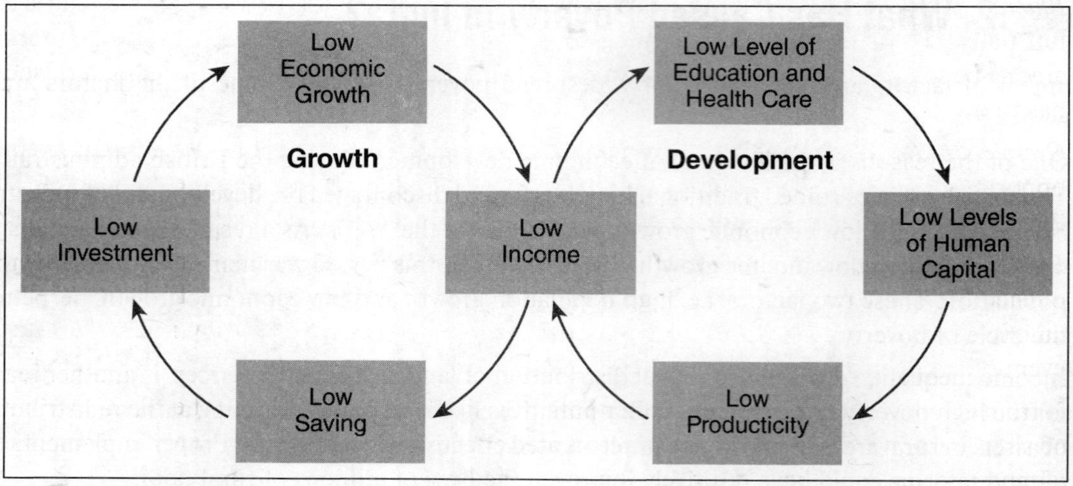

Fig. 4.5 Poverty Trap

6. Poverty leads to poverty. A poor person does not have enough resources to get a quality education and acquire the skills necessary for employment. They suffer from poor physical health, which further impedes their progress. Overall, this results in lower productivity and, hence, low income. This is called the '*Poverty Trap*'. Figure 4.5 explains the situation.

3 Poverty in India: Social or Economic?

In the discussion related to poverty, generally, it is understood that poverty is an economic-related phenomenon. It is concerned with a lack of income and employment opportunities. As a result, people fail to have a 'reasonable' standard of living. Definitely, this is one aspect of poverty. However, many scholars believe that poverty should not only be seen through the lens of economics. Rather, there are social aspects too, which have the potential to cause poverty. Let us discuss some of the social causes here:

1. *Social inequality*: Due to social inequality, the available opportunities cannot be availed equitably in a society, especially among the weaker sections of the society.

2. *Social exclusion*: It is a grave form of inequality in which a community or group is socially excluded from mainstream society. They fail to participate in social and economic affairs.

3. *Social evils*: Evils, such as untouchability, limit the ability of people from certain castes to participate in general employment opportunities and are forced to do meagre jobs. Thus, they are shunned from society and pushed towards poverty.

4. *Illiteracy*: It is one of the major causes of poverty. Due to illiteracy, they are unable to realise their full potential. As a result, their earning sources are limited. Also, illiteracy caused ignorance among people. Thus, they remain unaware of all the possible opportunities our modern society has to offer.
5. *Overpopulation*: It means that more people are waiting and competing for limited available opportunities. Hence, it is quite natural that many will not be absorbed in the job market. Thus, they are forced to work in informal jobs with low and uncertain incomes.
6. *Patriarchy*: In a strictly patriarchal set-up, women are rarely allowed or encouraged to work outside. Also, the properties are seldom registered in the name of women. This causes poverty among the women of such a society, i.e. *feminisation of poverty*, especially in the unfortunate event of the death of the husband.

Apart from the above causes, there are other potential causes of poverty. It is not easy to link poverty to one single reason. Rather, a variety of factors are responsible for the same. Here, let us enumerate a few important ones.

Insight Box

Other Potential Causes of Poverty

Economic Factors

1. *Slow and imbalanced economic development*: People from low development region suffers from poverty due to less income generating opportunities. It also results in income inequality across regions.
2. *Low agricultural output*: It causes serious distress among farmers dependent on agriculture for subsistence. These farmers fall in the poverty trap as well in case they fail to return loan, if any.
3. *Inadequate industrialisation*: People from low industrialised areas suffers from *forced migration* to other developed and industrialised areas. Due to huge competition, many do not get good opportunities and end up in informal jobs with low and erratic wages.

Geographical and Environmental Factors

1. *Fertility of land*: Fertility of land varies across regions. It is one of the factors which determine agricultural production. People in regions having infertile lands may get pushed towards poverty naturally.
2. *Floods and droughts*: Natural calamities destroy farmlands and adversely affects farm produce. Such situation can cause poverty among the people of the particular regions.
3. *Lack of seasonal rainfall*: Lack of optimum rainfall too affects farm produce of various agricultural products. It results in price rise of various agricultural products. It can cause inflation related poverty.

4 Issues Related to Poverty

A few important issues that are associated with poverty include:

1. *Homelessness*: Poverty and homelessness are directly linked to each other. The majority of poor people in India are landless and homeless. According to the 2011 Census, India has more than 1.7 million homeless people. However, independent estimates place the number of homeless people in India at about 2.3 million.

Landmark Judgements

Chameli Singh v. State of Uttar Pradesh (1996)

Issue: Forced eviction and the right to shelter.

Judgment: The Court ruled that the Right to Shelter is an essential part of Right to Life, including the right to live with dignity. It emphasised that poverty cannot justify denial of basic housing.

2. *Unemployment*: People suffering from poverty fail to acquire skills necessary for the market. Hence, they do not get absorbed in the job market and remain unemployed.
3. *Size of families*: Generally, there is a tendency to have a larger family size among the poor. They believe that with more hands, they will have more income. However, due to poverty, families are unable to provide good education, nutrition and many other essential facilities to their children.
4. *Illiteracy*: Poor people seldom get the opportunity to acquire a good education. Also, children from poor families start working at an early age, and hence, they are unable to complete even their schooling.
5. *Poor health/malnutrition*: Poverty also results in families not getting proper health facilities. They cannot afford costly treatment in hospitals. Moreover, they have a lack of knowledge about nutrition. Hence, children suffer from malnutrition too in poor families.
6. *Child labour*: According to Census 2011, the number of working children in India in the age group 5–14 years is 10.1 million (3.9% of the total child population), of which 5.6 million are boys and 4.5 million are girls. It results in denial of education and weakened physical and mental health.
7. *Inequality and exclusion*: Poor people also suffer from social and economic inequality. Because of this, they are unable to participate in social activity, i.e. they face exclusion from mainstream society.

8. *Helplessness*: Poor people become so helpless with their condition that they take up any work available for them just to survive. It often results in the exploitation of the poor.
9. *Continuation of the vicious cycle*: Since poverty does not allow people to get the required social and economic support, they indulge themselves in menial tasks, which further pushes them into poverty. They get trapped in this cycle of poverty.

5 India: Urban Poverty

India's urban population has increased rapidly over the last century from 25 million in 1901 to 377 million in 2011. As per the 2011 Census, the urban population constituted 31.2% of the total population. Even though the urban population has grown significantly, the required infrastructure and essential services cannot grow enough to sustain this burgeoning population.

The urban areas face deprivation of basic services such as housing, drinking water, health facilities, regular electricity connections, transportation, etc. As a result, there is a rise in slums in urban areas. Moreover, most people are forced to indulge in informal jobs where there is erratic income, a constant threat of eviction or removal and almost non-existent social security cover.

As per the 2011 Census, 17.7% of the urban population comprising 65 million people, lives in slums. Further, it is estimated that by 2030, another 250 million people would be added to Indian cities. If basic infrastructure is not created for them, it will give rise to more slums and, consequently, increase in urban poverty.

5.1 India: Urban Poverty Report 2009

It was India's first-of-its-kind report on the nature and dynamics of urban poverty in the country. The report was launched by the Ministry of Housing and Urban Poverty Alleviation (MoHUPA), Government of India, with the support of the United Nations Development Programme (UNDP).

Key findings from the Report

1. *The urban population of India is increasing, but not as fast as in other Asian countries*: Researchers, however, expect that the rate of urbanisation will increase in the coming years. It expects that India will have 41% of its population living in cities and towns by 2030.
2. *Increasing urbanisation has been accompanied by poverty*: Urban poverty in India remains high, at over 25%. Over 80 million poor people live in the cities and towns of India.
3. '*Urbanisation of poverty*': The ratio of urban poverty in some of the larger states is higher than that of rural poverty, leading to the phenomenon of '*Urbanisation of Poverty*'.
4. *Increase in slum population*: While the slum population has grown, the actual number of slums has decreased, leading to a higher population density within existing slums. This trend is particularly notable in major urban centres, where the slum population is more concentrated.

5. *Poor people in slums do not have access to basic services like sanitation or water*: Poor people reside in overcrowded slums, characterised by pollution and a lack of essential civic amenities such as clean drinking water, sanitation, and healthcare facilities.

Proposed solutions to urban poverty

1. Greater equity in the provision of basic services as interstate and intercity disparity has acquired alarming proportions.
2. Special assistance from the government to small and medium towns, particularly in backward states, as their economic bases are not strong enough to generate adequate resources.
3. Identifying a select number of towns in each state with significant development potential and work towards connecting them to national and international markets.
4. Promote the use of solar, bio-gas, and other non-conventional energy sources for street lighting and household energy needs wherever viable. It is crucial to ensure every slum household has access to electricity connections for comprehensive coverage.
5. To improve sanitation standards, community toilets may be constructed where individual toilets are not possible.
6. In slums, the report recommends organising slum communities. There is also the need to extend sewerage networks to slum areas and to manage toilets in common places.

5.2 Government Initiatives to Tackle Urban Poverty

The Ministry of Housing and Urban Affairs (MoHUA) has been instrumental in assisting the states to implement various schemes in urban areas. These include:

1. *Atal Mission for Rejuvenation and Urban Transformation 2.0 (AMRUT 2.0)*: It aims to make cities 'water secure' and provide functional water tap connections to all households in all statutory towns across the country. It also targets universal coverage of sewerage and septage management in 500 AMRUT cities. The Mission, through the provision of tap connections, is to mitigate the hardships and reduce the burden on the poor. Improved sewerage facilities reduce the disease load and health risks, thus enhancing the quality of their lives.

2. *Smart Cities Mission*: The objective is to promote cities that provide core infrastructure and give a decent quality of life to their citizens, a clean and sustainable environment and application of 'Smart' solutions.

   The core infrastructure elements of a smart city would include:

   - adequate water supply
   - assured electricity supply
   - sanitation, including solid waste management
   - efficient urban mobility and public transport
   - affordable housing, especially for the poor

- robust IT connectivity and digitalisation
- good governance, especially e-Governance and citizen participation, a sustainable environment
- safety and security of citizens, particularly women, children and the elderly
- health and education

3. *Swachh Bharat Mission-Urban 2.0 (SBM-U 2.0)*: It was launched on 2 October 2014 and continued till 30 September 2021 with the objectives of –
   i. achieving 100% Open Defecation Free (ODF) status in all states and Urban Local Bodies (ULBs)
   ii. 100% scientific processing of all the municipal waste in the country and
   iii. behaviour change through *Jan Andolan* in all statutory towns.

   Under SBM-U, the individual households not having access to toilets were identified, and 62,79,304 units of Individual House Hold Latrines (IHHL) were completed against the target of 58,99,637 IHHL units.

4. *Pradhan Mantri Awas Yojana-Urban (PMAY-U)*: The Mission addresses the urban housing shortage among the EWS/Low Income Groups (LIG) and Middle Income Groups (MIG) categories, including slum dwellers, by ensuring a pucca house for all eligible urban households by the year 2022. In August 2022, the Union Cabinet approved continuation of PMAY-U up to 31 December 2024 (Fig. 4.6).

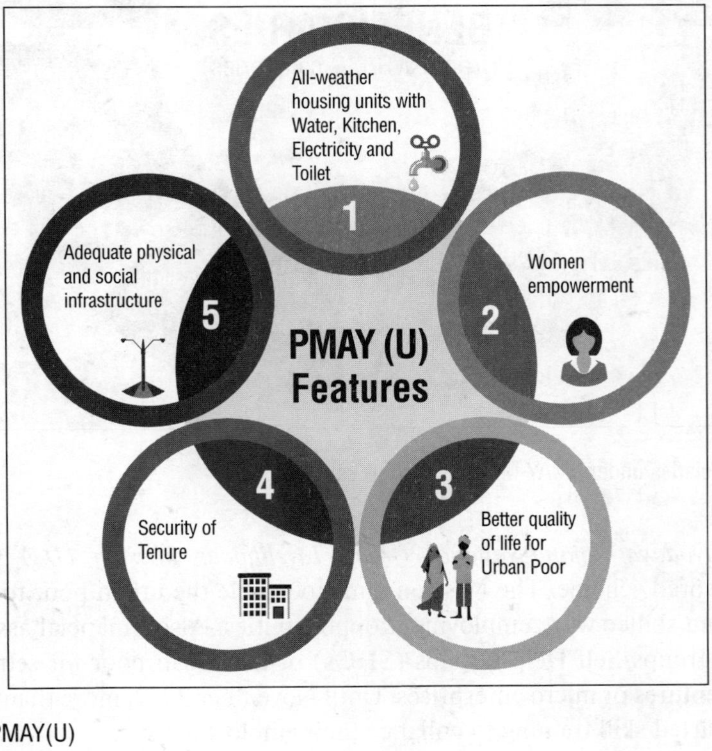

Fig. 4.6 Features of PMAY(U)

The mission fosters women's empowerment by granting house ownership in the name of female members or jointly. Priority is also given to differently-abled individuals, senior citizens, Scheduled Castes (SCs), Scheduled Tribes (STs), Other Backward Classes (OBCs), minorities, single women, transgender individuals, and other marginalised and vulnerable sections of society.

The Ministry of Housing and Urban Affairs has launched Affordable Rental Housing Complexes (ARHCs), a sub-scheme under *Pradhan Mantri Awas Yojana - Urban* (PMAY-U). This initiative aims to improve the quality of life for urban migrants and the economically disadvantaged in both the industrial sector and the informal urban economy. It provides them with access to decent, affordable rental housing situated near their workplaces, enhancing their overall living conditions.

Fig. 4.7 Target Beneficiaries under PMAY-U from EWS/LIG categories

5. *Deendayal Antyodaya Yojana-National Urban Livelihoods Mission (DAY-NULM)*: This is a centrally sponsored scheme. The Mission aims to enable the urban poor to access gainful self-employment and skilled-wage employment opportunities. Also, financial assistance is provided to individuals/groups/Self Help Groups (SHGs) of the urban poor for setting up gainful self-employment ventures or micro-enterprises. Until November 2022, more than 13 lakh urban poor have been imparted skill training to enhance their employability.

6. *PM Street Vendor's AtmaNirbhar Nidhi (PM SVANidhi)*: The aim of this initiative is to facilitate micro-credit for street vendors in urban areas so that they can restart their businesses that were adversely affected during the COVID-19 pandemic. Under this scheme, street vendors may avail of a working capital loan of up to Rs. 10,000, followed by loans of Rs 20,000 and Rs. 50,000 in the second and third tranches, respectively, on repayment of the earlier tranche (Fig. 4.7).

> **Debate Corner**
> Urban areas are considered engines of economic growth. Yet, a significant portion of India's urban population continues to live in poverty. Is urban poverty in India primarily a consequence of flawed urban planning and governance, or is it driven more by structural socio-economic inequalities and migration pressures?

6 Policies and Programmes for Poverty Alleviation

We have already listed out the poverty alleviation programmes carried out by the government in urban regions. Apart from the above, there are various other schemes and programmes run by the government to tackle poverty in India. Apart from addressing poverty, these programmes are being implemented to increase livelihood opportunities, empower rural women, skill rural youth, and develop infrastructure, among others.

1. *Mahatma Gandhi National Rural Employment Guarantee Scheme (MGNREGS)*: It aims to promote rural development and reduce rural poverty. It provides for at least 100 days of guaranteed wage employment every financial year for each family whose adult members volunteer to perform unskilled manual work.

   In 2023-24, a total of 5.99 crore households have availed of employment under MGNREGS, and a total of 308.9 crore person-days of employment have been generated.

2. *Deendayal Antyodaya Yojana - National Rural Livelihoods Mission (DAY-NRLM)*: It is a flagship poverty alleviation program implemented by the Ministry of Rural Development. It aims to reduce poverty by enabling poor households to access gainful self-employment and skilled-wage employment opportunities.

   The Mission seeks to achieve its objective through investing in four core components:

   a. social mobilisation and promotion and strengthening of self-managed and financially sustainable community institutions of the rural poor;

   b. financial inclusion of the rural poor;

   c. sustainable livelihoods; and

   d. social inclusion, social development and convergence.

   As of October 2024, 10.05 crore women from rural households have been mobilised into 90.87 lakh Self Help Groups (SHGs) under this mission.

3. *Deen Dayal Upadhyay - Gramin Kaushalya Yojana (DDU-GKY):* The Ministry of Rural Development (MoRD) has revamped the placement-linked skill development programme under the National Rural Livelihood Mission as DDU-GKY. It focuses on skill training and placement of rural poor youth in the age group 15–35. It is being implemented in Public–Private Partnership (PPP) mode. Under this yojana, two special programmes are being implemented:
   a. **Roshni:** It is being implemented in 27 left-wing extremist-affected areas of nine states. It provides for a mandatory residential course with 40% coverage for female candidates.
   b. **Himayat**: All youth of the UT of Jammu & Kashmir and Ladakh are covered under this scheme with 100% central funding.

   Since the inception of DDU-GKY, a total of 16.9 lakh candidates have been trained, and 10.97 lakh candidates have been placed until November 2024.
4. *Pradhan Mantri Awaas Yojana - Gramin (PMAY-G)*: The Ministry of Rural Development has been implementing the Pradhan Mantri Awaas Yojana–Gramin (PMAY-G) since 1st April 2016 with the objective of providing assistance to eligible rural households for the construction of pucca houses with basic amenities, thereby fulfilling the vision of "Housing for All" in rural areas.

   Initially, the scheme targeted the construction of 2.95 crore houses during FY 2016-17 to 2023-24. Subsequently, the Government of India approved its continuation for the period FY 2024-25 to 2028-29 with a provision to construct 2 crore additional houses.

   As of 4th August 2025, the Ministry has allocated a cumulative target of 4.12 crore houses to States and Union Territories. Against this, 3.84 crore houses have been sanctioned, and 2.81 crore houses have already been completed.
5. *Shyama Prasad Mukherjee National RuRBAN Mission (SPMRM)*: Several rural areas in the country are organised into clusters of settlements that are geographically close to each other. Some of these clusters exhibit growth potential and possess a competitive economic advantage because of their strategic locations. The mission aims to develop these areas through the provision of economic, social and physical infrastructure facilities. These clusters, once developed, can then be classified as 'Rurban'.

   The vision of this mission is 'Development of a cluster of villages that preserve and nurture the essence of rural community life with focus on equity and inclusiveness without compromising with the facilities perceived to be essentially urban in nature, thus creating a cluster of "Rurban Villages"'. It was launched in 2016 in mission mode to develop 300 such clusters in the country.

   Presently, there are 109 tribal clusters and 191 non-tribal clusters under different stages of development across 28 States and 6 Union Territories (UTs) of the country.
6. *National Social Assistance Programme (NSAP)*: It offers essential financial support to elderly individuals, widows, and disabled persons, as well as to families who have lost their primary breadwinner and fall below the poverty line (BPL). Till date, more than 3 crore beneficiaries have been covered by the NSAP.

7 Poverty and Human Development

7.1 Growth, Development and Poverty

It is a general understanding that economic growth and development are useful and effective instruments to reduce poverty in developing countries. Growth and development have the potential to create a cycle of opportunity and prosperity. An increase in opportunity can allow job seekers to get absorbed in the economic market. As a result, there might be an increase in income for people. This can improve the purchasing power of people and provide a further boost to the economy.

Moreover, an increase in employment opportunities encourages parents to invest in the education of their children with the hope of getting better economic returns in the future. Educating children can also result in the birth of entrepreneurs, who can contribute significantly to the economy. Thus, the cycle of growth and development continues. This cycle ensures that many people move out of poverty.

However, the relationship between economic development and poverty reduction need not always be directly proportional. Even similar rates of economic development can have different impacts on poverty and the scope of employment. It depends on how much participation the poor have in the development process. Thus, it is not only growth but also the pattern and inclusiveness of growth that determine the level of poverty reduction.

Case of India

Economic Survey 2020-21 stated: 'Given India's stage of development, India must continue to focus on economic growth to lift the poor out of poverty by expanding the overall pie'. It highlighted that in a developing country like India, redistribution is possible only if the size of the economic pie grows. Also, the growth story of India has suggested a significant reduction in poverty due to high economic growth.

The World Bank, in its report 'India Development Update: India's Growth Story' said that in the past 50 years, India's economic growth has accelerated slowly but steadily across all sectors - agriculture, industry and services - and become more stable.

According to this report, India has seen an average growth rate of 4.4% between 1970 and 1980. It increased by 1% to 5.4% between 1990 and 2000. The opening of the Indian market in the 1990s has improved the average economic growth to 8.8% between 2000 and 2010. After the global financial crisis of 2008, there was a slowdown. Thus, between 2010 and 2018, India's average growth rate was 7.1%.

Over the years, India has also witnessed a significant decline in poverty. As per the latest update of the global Multidimensional Poverty Index (MPI), released by the United Nations Development Programme (UNDP) and the Oxford Poverty and Human Development

> **Debate Corner**
> Can genuine human development occur without first eradicating poverty, or is poverty itself a symptom of insufficient investment in human development?

Initiative (OPHI), in India, 415 million people have moved out of poverty within a span of just 15 years from 2005–2006 to 2019–2021.

It is to be understood that the reduction in poverty in India over the years, apart from economic growth, is also due to increasing expenditure on financial inclusion, self-employment programmes and skill development, among others.

7.2 Developmental Issues due to Poverty?

Poverty causes various issues as far as human and societal development is concerned. Let's enumerate a few issues below:

1. *Child Development*: Parents living below the poverty line often lack knowledge and understanding of nutrition of their children. Hence, children from such families are at increased risk of becoming malnourished.

   Apart from physical development, children from poor families are less likely to receive a good education, not only due to financial incapacity but also due to social exclusion. This restricts their cognitive development as well.

2. *Access to quality healthcare*: In India, over 75% of health infrastructure is concentrated in metropolises, whereas these cities have around 27% of population. The remaining 73% of the population lacks even basic medical facilities. People, especially from rural India, cannot afford to come to metropolises to receive quality treatment.

   Apart from this, in India, Out-of-Pocket (OOP) health expenditures account for around 63% of the total health expenditure, which is one of the highest in the world. The Economic Survey 2020–2021 observed that such a high OOP for health increases the risk of vulnerable groups slipping into poverty.

3. *Economic issues*: Poor people often fail to get the required skill-set necessary for the job market. As a result, many people remain unemployed or work in the informal system. As a result, there is a loss of human potential and the economy suffers in the long run.

   Moreover, if the poverty rate is high, the government has to provide subsidies and other financial support to the poor. Such expenditures do not create any sustainable infrastructure or revenue-generating assets in the economy. This also affects economic development.

4. *Effects on society*: Poverty affects societal health as well. This is because poverty leads to various issues, such as violence and crimes. Due to poverty and unemployment, poor people resort to criminal activities to earn money. Moreover, among the poor, there is some form of discontent, which can also translate into violent activities.

   Apart from this, there are issues of homelessness, child labour, over-population and stress among poor people.

8 Feminisation of Poverty

The term 'Feminisation of poverty' was coined by Diana Pearce in the late 1970s following her observation of women in the USA. Since then, there have been many studies to find out how economic status is affected by gender. The United Nations Development Programme (UNDP) defines 'feminisation of poverty' as a condition wherein the change in poverty levels is biased against women or female-headed households. It has been observed that women face a much higher intensity of poverty than men in all nations. India is no exception.

Insight Box

Pandemic-Induced Poverty Surge Among Women

According to the UN Women report *From Insights to Action: Gender Equality in the Wake of COVID-19* (2020), the COVID-19 pandemic was projected to push a staggering number of women into extreme poverty, particularly in low- and middle-income countries like India. The report estimated that around **87 million women and girls in India** were living in extreme poverty (defined as surviving on less than $1.90 per day) in 2020. This number was expected to rise to **100 million by 2021** due to the socio-economic disruptions caused by the pandemic.

The report further highlighted a **widening gender gap in poverty:** the **pre-pandemic poverty rate** stood at **13.3% for females** and **12.1% for males**, but was projected to rise to 14.7% for females and 13.7% for males by 2021. These projections underscored the **disproportionate impact of global crises on women**, particularly in terms of job losses, increased unpaid care burdens, and restricted access to resources and services.

8.1 Causes of 'Feminisation of Poverty'

There are many reasons responsible for causing poverty among women. The United Nations Development Fund for Women (UNWOMEN) has identified a few reasons that can potentially explain the higher rate of poverty among women.

1. Women, especially in developing nations, are primarily involved in family care and household activities, for which they do not receive any wages. With these responsibilities, women have less time to devote to paid employment.
2. Mostly, women are engaged in informal employment, which is not protected by any government regulation. These include private teaching, domestic services, elderly care, etc. These jobs lack stability and security, and even wages are too low.
3. In places where employment opportunities are limited, women may have to migrate to other areas to find work. If a woman has children, she cannot work far from her usual residence. This also reduces opportunities for women.

Moreover, children from such women fail to get a good education and adequate nourishment, which deprives them of better opportunities in the future. Thus, a cycle of poverty is perpetuated.

4. Due to societal barriers such as patriarchy and early marriage, women do not get the proper education and skill-set necessary to participate in the market economy. Thus, upward mobility in society through higher-skilled employment has become almost impossible for women.
5. Another reason is the higher life expectancy of women. Due to this, many women, after the death of husband, live alone without much family or financial support. They suffer from extreme poverty.
6. One of the most important reasons for the feminisation of poverty is the *gender-bias* present in society. This results in inequality in wages, benefits, property rights among others. It is commonly observed that even for the same amount of work, women are paid less.

Landmark Judgements

State of Maharashtra v. Chandrabhan Tale (1983)

Issue: Denial of pension benefits to a poor widow.

Judgment: The Court ruled in favor of the widow, stating that social justice and economic support to the vulnerable are constitutional duties under the Directive Principles of State Policy.

Additional Readings

1. Dr. Seema Gaur & Dr. N Srinivasa Rao - Poverty Measurement in India: A Status Update.
2. NITI Aayog, *National Multidimensional Poverty Index: A Progress Review* 2023.
3. Economics NCERT: Textbook for Class IX, Chapter 03.
4. Economics NCERT: Textbook for Class XI, Chapter 04.
5. Ministry of Housing and Urban Poverty Alleviation, India: Urban Poverty Report 2009.
6. Strategy for Poverty Alleviation in Rural Areas: PIB 17 December 2024.
7. Financial Support for Rural Women PIB (14 March 2023).
8. Shyama Prasad Mukherji Rurban Mission: Ministry of Rural Development.
9. SPMRM growth clusters are playing a role reducing urban migration: PIB (7 December 2021).
10. Year-End Review - 2022: Ministry of Rural Development: PIB (30 December 2022).

11. Key Highlights of Economic Survey 2020-21: PIB (29 January 2021).

12. P. Srivastava,India's economic growth story remarkable since 1990s, never mind quarterly fluctuations: World Bank. *Financial Express.*

13. 415 million Indians came out of multidimensional poverty in 15 years, says UNDP study. *The Hindu.*

14. P. Roy, *Effects of Poverty on Education in India* (West Bengal State University, Barasat, August 2018).

15. Varun Sheth, 5 reasons India's 'Missing Middle' is struggling to access quality healthcare. *Times of India* (14 August 2022).

16. Ambika Pandit, COVID may leave 100 million women in extreme poverty by 2021: UN. *Times of India* (15 September 2020).

Previous Years' Questions

1. An essential condition to eradicate poverty is to liberate the poor from the process of deprivation." Substantiate this statement with suitable examples. (2016)
2. Despite implementation of various programmes for eradication of poverty by the government in India, poverty is still existing'. Explain by giving reasons. (2018)
3. COVID-19 pandemic accelerated class inequalities and poverty in India. Comment. (2020)
4. Why did human development fail to keep pace with economic development in India? (2023)

UPSC CSE 2025

1. Achieving sustainable growth with emphasis on environmental protection could come into conflict with poor people's needs in a country like India -Comment (250 Words | 15 Marks)

Model Answer

India faces the twin challenge of pursuing sustainable growth while meeting the needs of over 230 million people below the multidimensional poverty line. The Supreme Court in *MC Mehta vs. Union of India* (1987) underlined that poverty cannot justify ecological degradation. The Brundtland Commission (1987) too stressed balancing present needs with future sustainability, highlighting the tension between livelihoods and the environment.

Why Conflicts Arise:

1. **Immediate vs. Long-Term Needs:** Poor households depend on firewood, fishing, and subsistence farming, prioritising survival over ecology.
2. **Displacement:** Projects like tiger reserves or dams displace tribals and forest dwellers, breaking socio-cultural bonds.

3. **Regulatory Restrictions:** Bans on tanneries, brick kilns, or plastics hurt informal workers lacking alternatives.
4. **Urban Redevelopment:** Evictions along Yamuna floodplains or Mumbai mangroves worsen homelessness and inequality.

How Degradation Harms the Poor:

1. **Resource Loss:** Deforestation and polluted rivers reduce access to fuel, fodder, and clean water.
2. **Health Inequalities:** Delhi's air pollution and Yamuna's contaminated water hit slum communities hardest.
3. **Climate Vulnerability:** Assam floods and Bundelkhand droughts devastate small farmers, forcing distress migration.

Way Forward:

1. **Inclusive Policies:** Strengthen the Forest Rights Act (2006), promote eco-tourism, and involve locals in conservation.
2. **Green Jobs:** Create livelihoods in renewable energy, waste management, and afforestation.
3. **Resettlement & Safety Nets:** Provide rehabilitation, skill training, and cash transfers for displaced groups.
4. **Global & National Guidance:** The Gadgil Committee suggested region-specific participatory models; India's LiFE Mission (2021) promotes sustainable lifestyles through citizen action.

India's growth path must integrate ecology with social justice. By combining regulation, tradition, and initiatives like LiFE, environmental protection can support poverty reduction rather than obstruct it.

2. How does Smart City in India address the issues of Urban Poverty and Distributive Justice?

(150 Words | 10 Marks)

Model Answer

The Smart Cities Mission (2015) seeks to make Indian cities sustainable, inclusive, and technologically advanced, with equity in access to services, housing, and livelihoods. In doing so, it directly addresses the challenges of urban poverty and distributive justice.

Key Initiatives for Urban Poverty Reduction

1. **Service Equity:** GIS mapping and smart meters extend water, sanitation, and lighting to slum households (e.g., Bhubaneswar's universal piped water supply).
2. **Inclusive Mobility:** Affordable transport such as Bus Rapid Transit Systems, cycle tracks, and last-mile e-autos ease mobility for the poor (e.g., Ahmedabad BRTS).

3. **Housing Security:** Linkages with *Pradhan Mantri Awas Yojana*-Urban and digital property records strengthen tenure rights (e.g., Chennai's digital records pilot).
4. **Livelihood Creation:** Digital kiosks and *Deendayal Antyodaya Yojana-National Urban Livelihood Mission* connect Self-Help Groups to e-markets (e.g., Lucknow livelihood centres).

Governance and Distributive Justice

1. **Targeted Welfare Delivery:** Integrated Command and Control Centres and grievance portals improve access to health, welfare, and crisis relief (e.g., Indore and Surat during COVID-19).
2. Citizen Participation: Mobile apps, consultations, and e-governance platforms enhance transparency and inclusiveness.

While often critiqued for creating elite enclaves, the Mission's shift toward affordable housing, livelihood security, and participatory governance embeds distributive justice in urban planning. If inclusively scaled, Smart Cities can become a vehicle for poverty reduction and equitable urban growth.

5 Urbanisation – Problems and Remedies

1. Urbanisation in India

India is now rapidly urbanising. As per the 2011 Census, 377 million people lived in urban areas, but this number is expected to reach 600 million by 2031, implying that at least 40% of Indians will be residing in urban areas in less than a decade's time. By 2047, the urban population is expected to be 53% of the total population, implying that urbanisation is a critical determinant of country's growth and future.

2. Definition

Urbanisation can be defined as a socio-economic and demographic transformation whereby people migrate to cities and urban settlements. In the economic sense, urbanisation is associated with a shift from agrarian employment to industrial and services-based employment.

There is no universal definition of 'urban'. As per the 2011 Census, following could be termed 'urban units':

a. All administrative units that have been defined by statute as urban, like Municipal Corporation, Municipality, Cantonment Board, Notified Town Area Committee, Town Panchayat, Nagar Palika, etc., are known as *statutory towns*. All statutory towns with a population of more than 100,000 are classified as cities.

b. All other places that satisfied the following criteria:
   i. A minimum population of 5000 persons;
   ii. 75% and above of the male main working population engaged in non-agricultural pursuits; and
   iii. A density of population of at least 400 persons per sq. km.

As per the Office of the Registrar General (Ministry of Home Affairs) circular, it is proposed to continue with the same definition of urban unit for the 2021 Census so as to maintain compatibility of data and to analyse urbanisation trends.

Insight Box

Urban Agglomerations

The term 'urban agglomeration' defines urbanisation beyond administrative boundaries. Urban agglomeration refers to cities and surrounding towns and areas which are economically and socially integrated with the main city. An agglomeration is a geographically contiguous area which creates benefits of agglomeration while easing land and resource pressure of main city. The Delhi National Capital Region (NCR) is a prime example of Urban agglomeration wherein satellite towns and outgrowths have come up in surrounding areas. Similarly, in Maharashtra, the Mumbai Metropolitan Region is an example of urban agglomeration around the city of Mumbai.

3 Potential of Urbanisation in India

In the immediate post-independence years, urbanisation didn't occupy much space in public and policy debate as rural India and its development were at the heart of most economic thinking. It is natural that in a majorly agrarian economy like India, urbanisation and the idea of cities as growth poles were recognised much later as compared to the rest of the world. It was the Eleventh Five-Year Plan that first recognised urbanisation as a positive trend and cities as major contributors to GDP (Gross Domestic Product) growth.

Post-liberalisation reforms, the potential of urbanisation as a poverty reduction tool has been well recognised. As the *UN Habitat's World Cities Report (2022)* notes, cities generate wealth. In the case of India, cities generate 60% of GDP growth while occupying only 3% of the country's land. Cities concentrate on employment opportunities, infrastructure and investment. This phenomenon can be explained using the concept of the *economics of agglomeration*. It states that cities are an advantageous form of social and physical organisation because they bring together individuals, ideas and resources.

India's economic structure and growth trajectory also mean that cities are crucial for the economic development of the country. Services sector contributes over 50% to India's GDP (Economic Survey 2021-2022). The services sector has been a major driver of growth in the country, while agriculture, which is a major economic activity in rural India, has seen slow growth in last two decades. Services sector-driven job opportunities in sectors like information technology, retail, and marketing are mostly concentrated in cities.

Cities in India have also been enablers of innovation and have nurtured start-up cultures. Metropolitan cities like Mumbai and Bengaluru are prime examples of cities that could attract investments and talent to build an innovation culture. The prospects of urbanisation in India seem very promising, if supported by foresighted planning and adequate infrastructure.

4 Trends and Pattern of Urbanisation

4.1 Gradual and Consistent Urbanisation

Table 5.1 indicates the pace of urbanisation in the country.

Census Year	Urban Population (in millions)	Percentage of Urban Population in Total Population
1961	78.94	17.97
1971	109.11	19.91
1981	159.46	23.34
1991	217.18	25.72
2001	286.12	27.86
2011	377.1	31.16

Table 5.1 Trends of Urbanisation in India (Census of India 2011)

Some scholars have been of the view that urbanisation in India has been slow. This argument is usually backed up by comparison with China, which crossed the 50% urbanisation mark even before 2011. But, as noted in the Economic Survey (2017-2018), the general trend of urbanisation in India is nothing unusual. India broadly adheres to the trend whereby the level of urbanisation has increased with an increase in Gross Domestic Product (GDP).

4.2 Diversity in Urbanisation across States

There is much diversity across states in the level and pace of urbanisation. Generally, the economically advanced states of southern and western India have shown a higher pace of urbanisation. Maharashtra has the largest share of urban population in India at 13.5% (Census 2011). At 45.2%, the level of urbanisation in Maharashtra is much higher than the national average of 31.1%. Alongside Maharashtra, states like Tamil Nadu, Kerala and Gujarat crossed the 40% urbanisation mark in 2011.

Goa emerged as the most urbanised state with 62.2% of the population living in urban areas (Census 2011). Among the Union Territories, Delhi and Chandigarh reported the highest level of urbanisation. Bihar, Assam and Odisha are some of the states that reported the lowest levels of urbanisation.

As highlighted in the Economic Survey 2017-2018, the patterns of urbanisation in India do not adhere to *Zipf's law,* which has been shown to be true for many countries. The law states that the largest city of a country is twice as large as the next biggest, three times as large as the third largest city and so on. In India, this pattern does not hold, as million-plus cities like Mumbai, Delhi, Bengaluru and Kolkata do not have such a huge difference in population.

4.3 Top Heavy Urbanisation

The pattern of urbanisation in India is top heavy, whereby most of the population is concentrated in metropolitan areas and Class I Urban Areas/towns. Tier 2 and 3 cities and towns have proportionately much less population. As per the 2011 Census, nearly 70% of urban population was concentrated in Class I Urban Areas/towns.

4.4 Unplanned Urbanisation and Lack of Spatial Planning

Urban planning in India has focused mostly on financial planning without giving due importance to spatial planning. With the rare exception of planned cities like Chandigarh and Naya Raipur, urbanisation has happened in a haphazard manner.

4.5 Challenges of Urban Service Delivery and Quality of Life

The direct consequence of unplanned urbanisation is weak service delivery by Urban Local Bodies (ULBs) and poor quality of life for urban citizens. Urban settlements crop first, and basic service delivery like water, sewage treatment plant, etc., is provided years later. Quality of life is also hampered by challenges of air, water and soil pollution, which become inevitable when urbanisation happens without due planning.

Insight Box

Urban Heat Island

An Urban Heat Island (UHI) develops when construction, transport mediums and crowding creates excess heat in urban areas. It is observed in densely populated and high building concentration areas. Heat generated in such packed urban areas is not dissipated easily and thus the average temperature of the urban pocket rises. UHI is one of the side effects of unplanned urbanisation wherein cities grow without adequate green and open spaces.

5 Urban Planning in India

Ensuring equitable distribution through Five-Year Plans had been a key development strategy in India. But the traditional planning approach has focused mostly on economic and financial planning without much discussion of spatial planning. When speaking of urban planning, it is essential to think of spatial planning, transport and communication planning, urban infrastructure and service delivery planning. Such comprehensive planning is essential for the following reasons:

1. Resource management in cities and optimum utilisation of assets are possible only with planning. For example, a metro-/rail-based public transport network has to be planned to discourage private vehicles and road congestion.
2. Managing infrastructure costs is possible only with planning. With proper planning, cities can explore avenues of self-finance and avoid duplication of investment.
3. Quality of life for citizens cannot be ensured without planning. Extreme road congestion, shortage of water and other natural resources and law and order issues are challenges that may arise due to a lack of planning.
4. The sustainability of cities is a huge challenge that absolutely mandates planning. The environmental costs of agglomeration must be offset through planning for cities to be liveable and sustainable. Delhi's annual winter air pollution crisis is a perfect example of how a lack of sustainability can bring cities to a halt.

The 74th Constitution Amendment Act of 1992 is foundational in the scheme of urbanisation in India as it gave constitutional recognition to Urban Local Bodies and mandated decentralisation of finances and responsibilities to them. The Amendment inserted Part IX-A titled 'Municipalities' and detailed 18 core functions of all urban local bodies in the Twelfth Schedule of the Indian Constitution.

The 74th Constitution Amendment provided a broad framework for urban development. However, Urban Governance and Development are part of the State list as per the 7th Schedule of the Indian Constitution. Most states have separate departments responsible for Urban Development. States also have legislation to guide planning activities in urban areas.

For example, the Gujarat Town Planning and Urban Development Act 1976 mandates a development plan for the entire city and then Town Planning Scheme for smaller pockets in the city. The Maharashtra Regional and Town Planning Act has provisions for development plans with various zones like settlement zone, green zone and the like.

To cope with the challenge of unplanned urbanisation, cities also make slum redevelopment plans. Similarly, when planning for urban agglomerations, states have built institutions to plan beyond administrative boundaries. For example, the Mumbai Metropolitan Region Development Authority (MMRDA) works with a regional plan for the entire area, covering many districts. Similarly, the Bengaluru Development Authority works to plan and regulate urbanisation in the entire region around Bengaluru.

The Government of India's revised **Urban and Regional Development Plans Formulation and Implementation (URDPFI) Guidelines 2015** has provided a broad framework for planning activities undertaken by various states. Despite elaborate administrative and legal structures, urban planning and implementation face many infirmities in India. Following are the main challenges hampering future-oriented urban planning and implementation:

- The Ministry of Housing and Urban Affairs' **National Urban Policy Framework Document** acknowledges that traditional planning approaches led to rigid plans that couldn't be completed despite years of effort. These plans failed to integrate functional, spatial and financial planning.
- Critics claim that the uniform set of 18 functions mandated to Urban Local Bodies by the Twelfth Schedule is unsuitable as the country has diverse forms of urban local bodies with varying financial capacities. Thus, there is a need for differentiation in functions as per the size and financial capacity of ULBs.
- Most urban local bodies have responsibilities and functions without funds. It has been noted that smaller urban local bodies struggle to implement their plans due to a lack of finance and investments.
- The smaller ULBs also struggle with making and approving master plans. As per NITI Aayog's report titled **'Reforms in Urban Planning Capacity in India'** (2021), 65% of the 7933 urban settlements in the country do not have any master plan to guide development. This leads to piecemeal interventions, haphazard constructions, urban sprawl, and environmental pollution.
- As pointed out by NITI Aayog, development control regulations in states are either outdated or are updated without sufficient data-based evidence.
- As the Economic Survey (2017–2018) highlighted, cities do not have a single city government, leading to functional overlap. Multiple planning authorities and overlapping jurisdictions are also hurdles in urban planning. Many of the functions performed by ULBs have various central and state schemes. Cooperative Federalism is much needed for the success of urban planning.
- Lack of skilled manpower and town planners is also a major reason why urban planning in India is not very viable. To encourage states to hire skilled manpower, the Government of India launched a 15,000 crore incentive scheme for states in July 2023. The scheme gives financial incentives to cities that hire urban planners in proportion to their population.

Debate Corner

Despite having policies, institutions, and frameworks for urban planning, Indian cities continue to grapple with issues like traffic congestion, pollution, and the growth of slums. Is the core problem a lack of coordination and skilled personnel, or are there deeper structural flaws in the very design and execution of our urban planning system?

To address the above-discussed issues, there is a need for comprehensive urban governance reforms, which will be discussed later. NITI Aayog has also recommended that the participation of the private sector in problem solving and innovation in urban spaces be encouraged. One such example is seen in Delhi, where private companies are providing services for bio-mining and the rehabilitation of landfills.

The National Urban Policy Framework has suggested the following division of functions between local, state and central governments to ensure effective planning.

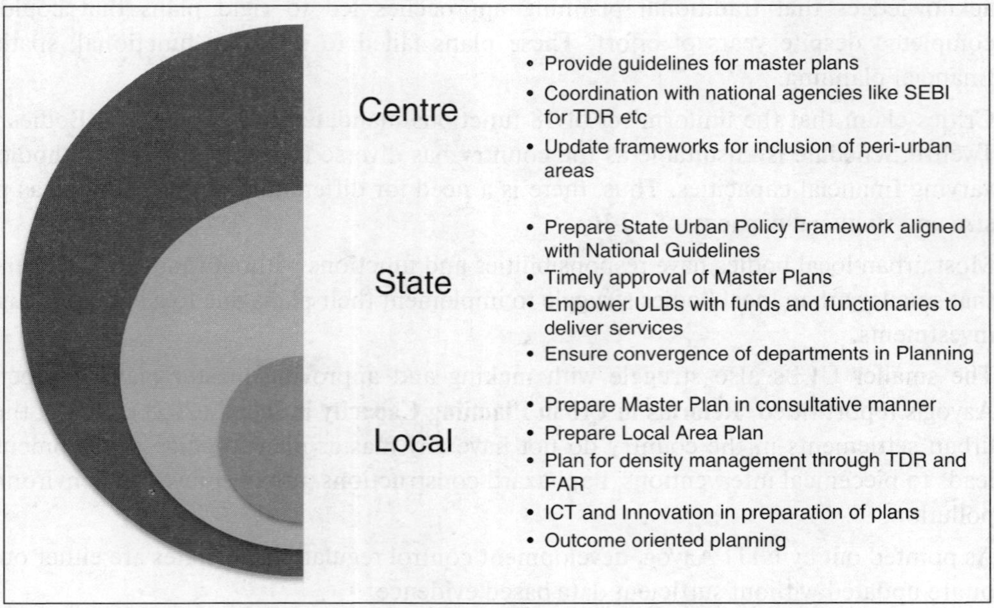

6 Financing the Urban Transformation

Finance and investments in urban infrastructure are two of the key challenges facing governments and ULBs. Almost a decade ago, the **High Powered Empowered Committee (2011)** estimated that nearly 39 lakh crores (2009–2010 prices) were required to finance urban infrastructure. The majority of this infrastructure funding was required for roads, water supply schemes, sewerage networks and other basic amenities.

Urban Local Bodies (ULBs) have two broad sources of revenue:

First, ULBs get devolved funds through various finance commissions.

The second source of revenue, which ideally should be the main source, is self-finance through the collection of taxes, user charges, public-private partnership and innovative investment mechanisms. Apart from the economic rationale, even democratic norms demand that cities raise their own revenue and spend it in a responsive manner. The Economic Survey (2017–2018) showed that the per capita expenditure of cities is much lower than that of the state's per capita expenditure, creating a paradoxical situation where the local governance body is spending the least on citizen needs.

- There is much diversity in the devolution of funds and functions to Urban Local Bodies (ULBs) across India. As noted in the Economic Survey (2017-2018), some states have not even delegated the right to levy property tax to ULBs.
- Even when there is delegation of financial and taxation powers, ULBs struggle to mobilise funds. The collection of taxes and user charges is hobbled by inefficiencies, poor coverage and leakage in the system. At times, ULBs are unwilling to tax more due to populist pressures. Citizens may be dissatisfied with gaps in service delivery and hence resist any tax hikes.
- There is a lack of updated land and property records that can be utilised for monetisation by ULBs. This lack is also responsible for the high prevalence of urban property disputes and court matters.
- Property tax is one of the most dynamic and strong potential sources that cities can harness for revenue generation. But surveys have shown that this source remains severely underassessed and underutilised. As per the World Bank Report, India collects only 0.2% of its GDP from property taxes, while the average for OECD countries is at least 1.1% of GDP. In an analysis done for the Economic Survey (2017-2018), it came to light that Bengaluru and Jaipur cities were only collecting 5-20% of their total property tax potential. Issues of property rate indexation, low coverage and out-dated rates limit property tax collection even in metropolitan cities.
- Another reason why powers to impose taxes don't translate into greater revenue mobilisation is the lack of skilled manpower and limited use of technology, which causes leakages and inefficiencies in the system.
- There had been some hesitance in experimenting with newer modes of fund raising, like municipal bonds, but now more and more ULBs are exploring such options.

6.1 Improving the Self-finance of ULBs

1. The first and foremost priority should be the delegation of funds and functions to ULBs by states. Even the 15th Finance Commission has emphasised the importance of delegation of funds for improving the fiscal health of ULBs. States need to not just decentralise funds but also grant adequate decision-making powers to ULBs.

2. A better and broader collection of property tax is critical for the self-finance of ULBs. ULBs must use satellite technology, train manpower and work on updating of the property register to realise the potential of property tax.

   For smaller ULBs, it has been suggested that a Revenue Board at the state level could be constituted for decisions on re-evaluation of property, use of ICT and capacity building. Model Municipal Act could also be circulated so that states could simplify tax and user charge collection.

   Municipal bonds are a way- Issuance of municipal bonds by pooling municipal bodies in the case of small and medium ULBs as has been done in Karnataka and Tamil Nadu.

3. Resource generation through Public Private Partnership and Value Capture Finance is also essential for infrastructure development in cities. An example of Gurugram in Haryana is relevant to understanding how private investment can bring rapid development to an area. Truly global cities like Singapore have benefitted greatly from private investment, and there should be no hesitance in tapping private players for urban India too.
4. NITI Aayog has strongly recommended that states and ULBs adapt outcome-based budgeting in urban space.
5. Administrative reforms and capacity building of manpower are naturally essential for improving the financial capacities of ULBs. This issue has been discussed in detail in the next section.
6. Transparency and citizen participation are absolutely essential for the good fiscal health of ULBs. Citizen participation can improve the quality of the expenditures being made and improve trust in ULBs. Improvement in trust and public perception is essential for the collection of tax and user charges.

7 Towards Sustainable and Inclusive Urbanisation

Making urbanisation inclusive and sustainable is perhaps the single biggest responsibility of governments and ULBs. This is a core government function that no other stakeholder is likely to perform. Certainly, governments may seek the help of NGOs and private partners towards this goal.

Land is a very scarce commodity in urban India. Consequently, affordable urban housing options that are practical in terms of commute and other services are few and far. The result is the mushrooming of slums and mega-slums in urban India. Slums are perhaps the biggest indicator of inequitable urbanisation in India. The Census defines slums as 'residential areas where dwellings are unfit for human habitation' because they are cramped and unhygienic. *Nearly 1.37 crore households and 17% of urban India, lives in slums (Census 2011).*

Different states use different definition of a slum depending on socio-economic status. But the main features and issues faced by slum residents are common across states. Following are the main challenges and issues posed by urban slums:

- Dilapidated or makeshift houses;
- Cramped and congested dwelling;
- Common toilets and inadequate systems of disposal of solid and liquid waste;
- Lack of minimum civic amenities like safe drinking water and street lighting;
- Many slum habitations are located in hazardous areas, *viz.,* edge of a landfill or in flood-prone area;
- Poor hygiene and living conditions make slum residents more susceptible to poor health and social burdens;
- Lastly, because most slums come up as encroachments, there is hesitation among ULBs in providing basic services to slums.

Landmark Judgements

The case of Almitra H. Patel v. Union of India (2000) was a landmark judgment in the domain of urban environmental governance in India. Environmental activist Almitra Patel filed a Public Interest Litigation (PIL) highlighting the poor state of solid waste management in Indian cities. The Supreme Court took serious note of the deteriorating urban sanitation and sharply criticized municipal authorities for neglecting their duties to maintain cleanliness and public hygiene.

The Court underscored that the right to a clean and healthy environment is intrinsic to the right to life under Article 21 of the Constitution. As a result of this judgment, the Municipal Solid Wastes (Management and Handling) Rules, 2000 were framed, laying out comprehensive guidelines for waste collection, segregation, transportation, and disposal.

This case became a turning point in urban environmental management, reinforcing the need for accountable governance, better infrastructure, and long-term urban planning in India's growing cities.

It is an often repeated but painfully relevant comparison of the posh-gated communities and the severely deprived slum residents which shows why urbanisation in India must be inclusive. It is important that urbanisation provides equal opportunities and basic amenities to all so that the economic growth potential of cities is captured. Otherwise, urbanisation may simply mean shift in locus of poverty from rural to urban areas.

The central government had schemes like the **Jawaharlal Nehru National Urban Renewal Mission (JNNURM)** - Basic Services to the Urban Poor (BSUP) and Integrated Housing and Slum Development Programme (IHSDP) for addressing infrastructure and service gaps in slums. States also have various mechanisms for slum improvement. Maharashtra has the Slum Rehabilitation Authority (SRA) while Karnataka has the Slum Development Board, which plans slum improvement and rehabilitation projects.

The flagship schemes of the Government of India are critical for infrastructure gap filling and providing basic services to all, including urban poor and slum residents. The **Pradhan Mantri Awas Yojana (PMAY-Urban)** aims at providing affordable and dignified housing to all urban poor. The scheme covers all urban areas of the country and has four main components:

- Beneficiary Led Construction/ Enhancement (BLC)
- Affordable Housing in Partnership (AHP)
- *In-Situ* Slum Redevelopment (ISSR)
- Credit-Linked Subsidy Scheme (CLSS).

PMAY houses have all basic facilities like kitchen and toilet and preference is given to women and differently abled beneficiaries. MoHUA has also initiated a **Global Housing Technology Challenges** to explore innovative and cost-effective construction technologies. Recently, **Affordable Rental Housing Complexes** scheme has also been initiated to provide affordable and decent housing to urban migrants and poor.

Recognising that livelihood opportunities for all are essential for sustainable urbanisation, the **Deen Dayal Antyodaya Yojana (DAY-NULM)** has been introduced to ensure livelihood for the urban poor. The scheme aims to provide the following:

- Gainful and skilled-wage employment for the urban poor
- Shelter with essential services for homeless persons
- Institutional credit and social security to urban street vendors
- Improvement in livelihood opportunities for the urban poor.

The Atal Mission for Urban Rejuvenation and Urban Transformation (AMRUT) is another flagship scheme that is making India ready for sustainable urbanisation. The scheme aims to build infrastructure like tap connections and assured water supply, sewerage connection and green spaces in cities. The scheme, covering 500 cities across the country, also seeks to promote public transport and reduce air pollution in cities.

The AMRUT scheme is encouraging Tier 2 and Tier 3 cities to build urban infrastructure. This is critical for a sustainable future because India must shift away from a top-heavy pattern of urbanisation as metropolitan cities are already under severe anthropogenic stress. The scheme will improve service delivery and ease of living in urban areas.

Ease of Living Index

The Ease of Living Index, developed by the Ministry of Housing and Urban Affairs, assesses the liveability of 114 Indian cities across 3 pillars and 50 parameters. The framework not only evaluates urban policies but also captures citizen satisfaction and perception, making it a valuable tool for participatory urban development. Since 2020, its scope has been expanded through the inclusion of a Citizen Perception Survey, which carries a weightage of 30% in the overall index.

QUALITY OF LIFE	ECONOMIC ABILITY	SUSTAINABILITY
Education Health Housing and shelter WASH and SWM Mobility Safety recreation	Level of Development Economic Opportunities Gini Coefficient	Environment Green spaces and Building Energy Consumption City Resilience

Source: Ministry of Housing and Urban Affairs, GOI

As pointed out by UN Habitat, the world's cities account for 75% of carbon emissions, even though they account for just 2% of land. Growing anthropogenic stress on cities and soil, air and water pollution are severely impacting the ease of living in cities. These ecological crises of various kinds have arisen due to unplanned urbanisation and legacy issues. The annual air pollution crisis in Delhi and the National Capital Region (NCR) is a much-discussed example in this regard. What is less recognised is how the solid waste management issue is worsening air pollution in this area.

With a growing population, managing solid waste has been a tough nut for Delhi. Three major landfill sites at Okhla, Bhalswa and Ghazipur have traditionally absorbed majority of solid waste from the region. Spread over 200 acres, these sites became increasingly unsustainable as they received unsegregated waste. Over time, this methane rich garbage dump became site of fire hazards, especially in the summer seasons. These further worsened the air quality and attracted strong remarks from the National Green Tribunal.

The ULBs of the NCR region have been using techniques like bio-mining to handle the legacy waste at the site. In October 2022, the National Green Tribunal imposed fine of 900 cores on Delhi government for inadequacy in managing of solid waste at these dump sites. This compensation amount will be utilised for remediation and rehabilitation of these sites. But, for any sustainable solution to waste management, implementation of the **Solid and Liquid Management Rules (2016)** is essential. Among other things, these rules mandate segregation at source so that only limited waste goes to landfills.

Insight Box

National Green Tribunal

This Tribunal has been established under the National Green Tribunal Act of 2010. The main objective of this Tribunal is effective and expeditious disposal of litigations and complaints regarding protection of environment. It may also reward relief and rehabilitation for persons and property impacted by environmental matters. As per the Act, the Tribunal shall not be bound by the procedure laid down under the Code of Civil Procedure, 1908, but shall be guided by principles of natural justice. The Tribunal has a Chairperson and some judicial as well as expert members.

Landmark Judgements

On September 3, 2015, the Principal Bench of the National Green Tribunal (NGT) at New Delhi delivered a landmark judgment that, for the first time, brought key principles of town planning within the scope and jurisdiction of the NGT. In its ruling in the case of *Sunil Kumar Chugh v. Secretary, Ministry of Environment and Forests*, the Tribunal held that open spaces, recreational grounds, and adequate parking facilities in buildings have a significant bearing on people's right to life.

While Delhi's example may have caught national attention, all mega cities are coping with one or the other ecological crises. The flash floods in Chennai (2015), Bellandur lake fire due to discharge of toxic waste and the growing natural resources shortage in almost all cities is a reminder that sustainability in urban planning is more of a necessity than a choice.

In this regard, it has become essential to mainstream the concept of **'circular economy'** in Urban planning (Fig. 5.1). This concept demands that sustainability be inbuilt into each stage of planning, production, use and reuse of goods. Circular economy demands that concept of waste to wealth be integrated in planning for waste management.

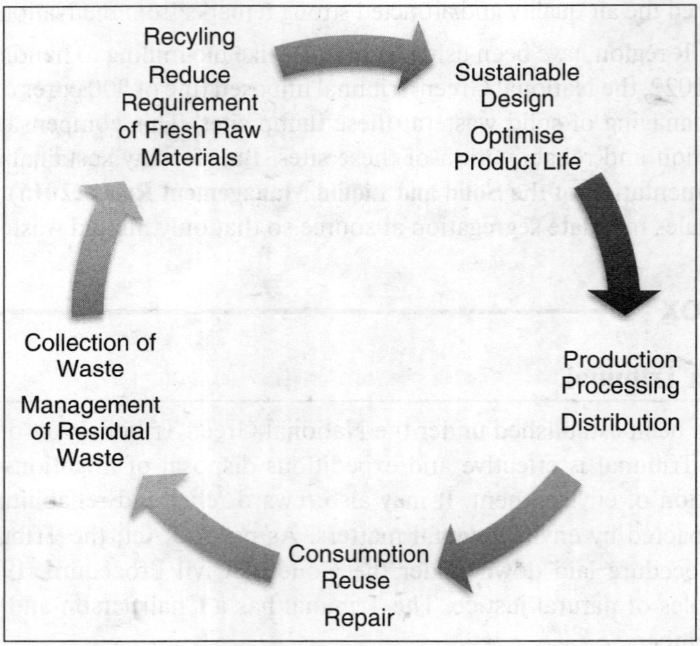

Fig. 5.1 Circular Economy: A Representation

Following are some points to guide planning for sustainable, inclusive and future ready cities:

- Preserve the natural and cultural heritage of cities and integrate them in urban planning. The HRIDAY (Heritage Development and Augmentation Yojana) scheme of GoI is a welcome measure to preserve legacy and original character of heritage cities while ensuring basic tourist conveniences in the city.
- Recent experiences suggest that mix use and mix income neighbourhoods are more advisable than planning for exclusively residential and commercial areas. The concept of the 15-minute city is a relevant guide here.

Insight Box

15-Minute City Concept

This is a new concept for guiding urban planning. It states that planners must conceive of mix use, pedestrian friendly cities where any need could be fulfilled with 15 minute travel on foot/ cycle or public transport. This concept considers citizens and their convenience as the key goal of any planning activities while not compromising on sustainability. It is also essential that this concept should account for mix income neighbourhoods and not become gated enclaves of wealthy alone.

- Planning for end-to-end connectivity through public transport is a non-negotiable for managing carbon footprint of cities. In addition, city streets and road furniture should be pedestrian and cyclist friendly. Innovative measures like car free Sunday as practiced in cities like Bogota and Jakarta can also be experimented with.
- Mandating energy efficient homes, planning for segregation at source and using pricing to ensure rational use of water and electricity are some of the other steps which must be taken for sustainable urban spaces.

Planning for disaster risk reduction and resilience in cities should now be an essential feature of urban planning. Concept of Build Back better and mainstreaming disaster preparedness is essential for inclusive urbanisation as it is often the poor and vulnerable who are most impacted in times of crisis. The migrant crisis cause in the wake of Covid'19 pandemic is a strong example of this.

Insight Box

Sponge Cities

Sponge cities is a recent urban regeneration and disaster adaptation technique. It recognises the fact that cities need to be structured in a water smart and disaster resistance manner. Cities should have abundant spaces which allow for water absorption and recharge of urban aquifers. This landscape and structure prevents flash flood and inundation in cities. In addition, the water retained is slowly released and helps address water demands of the city. It is a technique which integrates the water cycle into town planning and helps cities become disaster resilient.

8 Urban Governance Reforms

Almost all of the challenges plaguing Indian cities, like poor fiscal health, anthropogenic stress and gaps in service delivery, cannot be addressed without urban governance reforms. The challenges created by overlapping jurisdiction and a lack of planners in city administration have been discussed in previous sections. The following are the main reforms required to strengthen urban governance:

1. *Delegation of funds, functions and functionaries*: There is a need for more aggressive delegation of funds and responsibilities to ULBs. The principle of subsidiarity should be followed in the delegation of powers and responsibilities.
2. *Reduce fragmentation in governance*: As far as possible, a single authority should be empowered to take all decisions regarding land use and urban planning.
3. *Skill gap*: As already discussed, there is a severe shortage of trained planners and architects in city administration. This must be addressed so that financial and spatial planning can be coordinated.
4. *Rationalisation of laws*: Rationalisation of urban development codes and laws at the state level is necessary so that ULBs have reasonable freedom in planning and raising infrastructure finance.
5. *Transparency and public participation*: This is an often neglected but critical component as citizens are the ultimate beneficiaries of all urban policies and their feedback must be sought and acted upon.

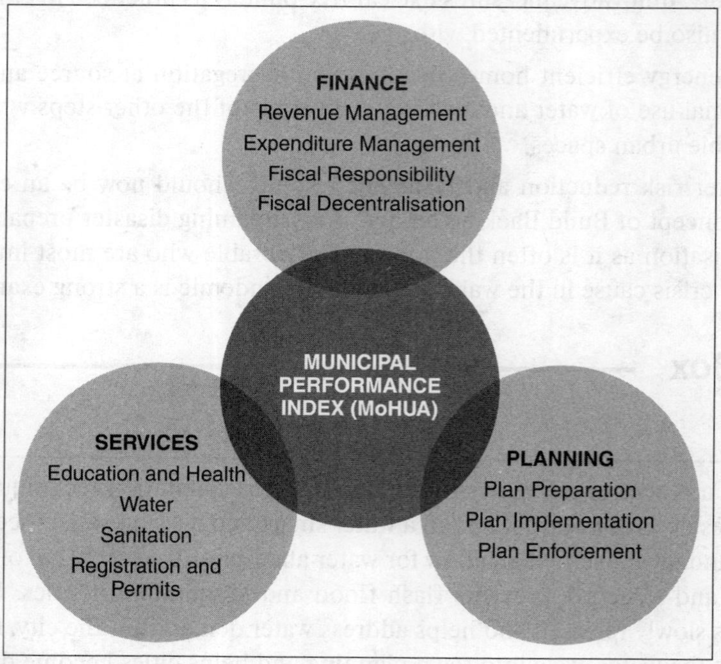

Fig. 5.2 Municipal Performance Index

9 Smart Cities

The Government of India launched the Smart Cities Mission in 2015 with the objective of promoting sustainable and inclusive cities. The goal is to equip smart cities with core infrastructure and provide a decent quality of life to all citizens. Following the principles of competitive federalism and co-operative federalism, the selection of cities for this scheme was done through a competitive screening process. The scheme is implemented through a Special Purpose Vehicle (SPV), which is constituted under the Companies Act, 2013.

Following are the main objectives of the scheme:

- City improvement through retrofitting works
- City renewal through redevelopment projects
- City extension through green filed development projects
- Pan-city initiatives like the use of smart solutions and e-governance.
- Special emphasis is placed on area-based development - for example, slum redevelopment to ensure basic services.

The Smart Cities mission has brought momentum to the use of technology in city administration. It has also encouraged innovation and start-ups in urban ecosystems. The use of ICT is likely to provide data that can be valuable for future city planning. Smart cities can ultimately enhance the ease of living and economic potential of a country.

The visionary Smart Cities initiative has faced some challenges in implementation due to vacancy and shortage of skilled manpower in Special Purpose Vehicles (SPV). A Parliamentary Committee has also noted that as many as 68 smart cities could not achieve their physical work targets by January 2023 due to local challenges of land and coordination among multiple departments. COVID-19 disruption is also one of the explanations offered for project delays.

Experts have also raised concerns regarding data safety and privacy while implementing the Smart Cities Mission. Due care for data protection and safeguarding individual privacy must be taken in building the digital infrastructure. It is also noted that the use of technology in Smart Cities must be accessible to all, practical, and inclusive so that smart cities offer opportunities for all.

Additional Readings

1. National Urban Policy Framework: Strategic Intent, Ministry of Housing and Urban Affairs, GoI.
2. Reforms in Urban Planning Capacity in India, NITI Aayog, September 2021.
3. UN Habitat's World Cities Report 2022.
4. Economic Survey 2017–2018.
5. Rajul Awasthi Mohan Nagarajan, Property Taxation in India: Issues Impacting Revenue Performance and Suggestions for Reform.
6. Slums in India Statistical Compendium 2011.

Previous Years' Questions

1. Discuss the various social problems which originated out of the speedy process of urbanisation in India. (2013)
2. How is the growth of Tier 2 Cities related to the rise of a new middle class with an emphasis on the culture of consumption? (2022)
3. Does urbanisation lead to more segregation and/or marginalisation of the poor in Indian metropolises? (2023)

6 Impact of Globalisation on Indian Society

1 Understanding Globalisation In Indian Context

Globalisation can simply be defined as the process of economic, financial and cultural integration of economies so that goods and services, as well as human capital, can flow freely across national boundaries. In the Indian context, the onset of globalisation coincided with the economic crisis of the early 1990s. Starting from the late 1980s, the liberalisation, privatisation and globalisation of the Indian economy proceeded in various phases.

The trio of the World Bank (WB), International Monetary Fund (IMF) and World Trade Organisation (WTO) provided much of the ideological leadership to the country in this decade. Structural Adjustment Policies were introduced in India as much as in the developing world. The Indian economy was opened to foreign goods and services, and a number of Transnational Corporations arrived with an interest in the huge potential market of the country.

While the Liberalisation, Privatisation and Globalisation (LPG) reforms were primarily economic in nature, these reforms integrated Indian society with the rest of the globe in an unprecedented manner. The economic reforms brought landmark changes to the Indian economy as for the first time ever, the agriculture sector became integrated with the global economy, and the fluctuations of the export-import market had major consequences for the agrarian economy. Secondly, with developments in Information and Communications Technology (ICT), new opportunities for urban white collar employment also arose. Multinational and Transnational Corporations (TNCs) also began to explore the country as a production site and supplier of labour. These economic and structural changes naturally spilled over into social and cultural domains, and Indian society transformed and adapted to the demands of the global economy. These changes are discussed in detail in the next section.

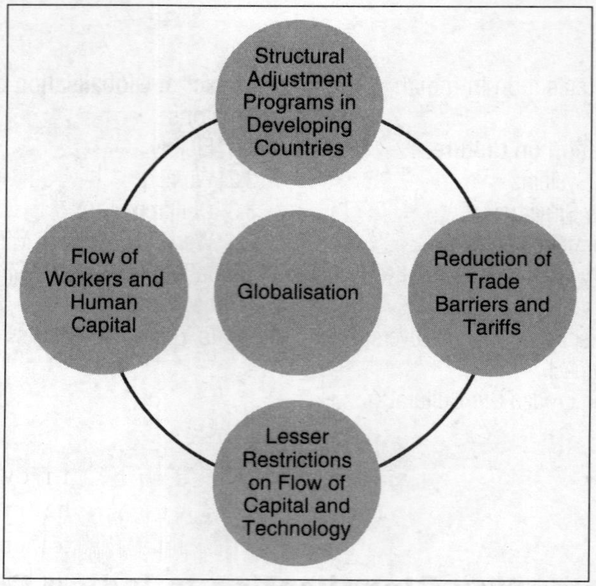

2 Impact of Globalisation on Culture

2.1 Change in Value Systems

Traditionally, traditional societies like Indian society were influenced by norms of cooperation, accommodation and harmony. There was much emphasis on maintaining familial and social ties. But due to modernisation and globalisation trends, individualism has seen a rise in Indian society. Decision-making and choices are now increasingly determined by individual needs rather than community considerations. In addition, there is greater recognition of individual privacy and autonomy in Indian society. Its positive impact is greater personal freedom for the individual, but it is also eroding cohesion and social-emotional integration in society.

2.2 Change in Family Structure

Traditional family structures have undergone change due to globalisation and urbanisation. There is a greater prevalence of nuclear families as this pattern is better adapted to the demands of the modern economy. Educational and employment opportunities have resulted in migration and the disintegration of traditional family structures. On the one hand, such changes have brought more income and growth opportunities for individuals, particularly women. On the other hand, individuals may find themselves deprived of the emotional and economic support that joint family structures had previously offered.

2.3 Change in Consumption Patterns

Perhaps the change in consumption patterns is the most visible. Indian society was traditionally seen as frugal and non-materialistic. But globalisation has brought a noticeable shift in consumption patterns due to the introduction of 'mall culture', international brands and now increasingly, online shopping, where one can be a consumer from the comfort of their homes.

As per Bain and Company Report, due to the growth of High Net worth Individuals (HNIs), penetration of e-commerce and strong burgeoning middle class, the Indian luxury goods market will triple in size to reach US$200 billion by 2030. It is only after the introduction of the New Economic Policy that terms like retail therapy (shopping to improve one's mood) have entered public discourse.

Insight Box

Revenge Shopping

Due to COVID-19 pandemic, nationwide lockdowns and curbs on movement were imposed so as to contain the spread of infection. Once the lockdown and other measures were relaxed, phenomenon of *revenge shopping* was observed. It means that customers were shopping and spending excessively after the pandemic. It also highlights dependence on shopping and marketing activities and possibilities of addiction to shopping.

2.4 Change in Dietary Habits

A shift in dietary practices away from locally grown and sourced products to imported and exotic items is one of the palpable consequences of globalisation. Greater access to processed foods and foreign food items has significantly changed dietary patterns. A very relevant example in this context is that of transnational food chains that relentlessly market burger, fizzy drinks and fried items like chips.

A shift to high-calorie, high-sodium and nutrient poor diets are also one of the reasons for the high prevalence of lifestyle diseases in the country. Another example is the sudden popularity of exotic fruits like avocado and dragon fruit, which caught the fancy of many Indians and were imported to satiate the curiosity-fuelled demand for these.

2.5 Entertainment

The options and modes of entertainment have changed vastly in the wake of the internet and globalisation. The popularity of the American TV series *Friends* is a relevant example of how many international and foreign language shows have gained popularity in India.

The more traditional modes of entertainment, like the circus and village fairs, have seen a gradual decline. OTT platforms, which allow one to be entertained anytime and anywhere, are fast becoming one of the most popular means of public entertainment.

2.6 Impact on Linguistic and Cultural Diversity

It is hard to argue against the fact that English is the *lingua franca* of globalisation. An English-medium education is seen as almost essential for good employability, and hence, there is a strong preference for English-medium education among middle-class parents.

Concerns have been expressed regarding the loss of linguistic diversity in the way of such 'homogenising' globalisation. Central Institute of Indian Languages (CIIL) has noted that globalisation is impacting languages in the sense that when speakers realise a language doesn't have global functionality, i.e. it is not spoken or understood in the global mainstream, then they shift to other languages.

A language dies when its speakers die. For example, a language of Andaman and Nicobar Islands, namely, Aka-Bo, has died recently when its last speaker died in 2010. The celebration of Friendship Day and Valentine's Day, which are basically western imports, is also an example of how globalisation has impacted culture.

2.7 Psychological Impact

A less recognised but nonetheless important effect of globalisation is its psychological impact. Researchers have now documented that increased competition and pressures of globalisation are giving rise to mental distress. The individualistic tendencies of globalisation also deprive individuals of necessary support in times of need.

Needless to say, the forces of globalisation are not unilateral. If western norms and cultural practices have influenced Indian society, Indian culture has also made its unique mark. The most famous symbol of Indian culture abroad is the **Bollywood film** industry. Bollywood movie stars act as ambassadors of Indian culture, and this industry has strengthened India's cultural diplomacy with nations across the globe.

India's other most renowned export to the world is its cuisine and spices. The example of **Chicken Tikka Masala** is enough to appreciate the popularity of Indian cuisine across the ocean. In 2001, the then United Kingdom's Foreign Secretary 'Robert Cook' termed *Chicken Tikka Masala,* a true British national dish. Though the dish has Indian origins, it was adapted to suit the British palette and is an example of how Indian curry now transcends borders.

Homogenisation	Polarisation	Hybridisation
• This hypothesis postulates that the world is converging towards common traits, values and consumption patterns. • This theory points to CoCa-colonisation or McDonladisation of world culture and economy. These terms point to the significance of Transnational Companies in the globalised world economy. • Proponents of this view also believe that Globalisation is nothing but Westernisation or Americanisation. While the popularity of Microsoft, Amazon and other US-based Transnational Corporations is high, it is hard to accept this point of view as completely valid. • There are cultural resistances, and not all American products and values have found acceptance in the Non-Western World. Little to no knowledge of American sport like baseball in Asian countries is an example of this. Similarly, Multi-national burger chains from the West have adapted to the Indian palette and do not sell beef so as to survive in the Indian market.	• This hypothesis claims that instead of becoming a global village, the world is moving towards greater ethno-nationalism and resilience in identity politics. • Proponents of this view draw from the Clash of Civilisation theory (Samuel P. Huntington) and claim that religious and cultural identities will be the main source of conflict in the Post-Cold war era. Huntington had theorised that the post-Cold war era world would see conflict between the Western and emerging Islamic-Confucian cultures. • Instead of converging towards common culture and values, the world is getting even more polarised due to cultural friction. • While there are undeniable elements of truth in this hypothesis, it is hard to ignore the many convergences in global culture that are happening due to the ICT Revolution, Transport and connectivity and the emergence of social media. • Another problem with this approach is that the imagined unity between all Non-Western Cultures against the Western Culture is issue-based only, and there is much diversity among the Non-Western nations that cannot be ignored.	• This hypothesis postulates that a hybrid culture is evolving in the wake of globalisation. • Proponents of this approach argue that a hybrid global culture with elements from all nations and civilisations is evolving. Such culture is evolving due to micro- and macro-interactions between cultures and is most visible in the areas of music, dance, cuisine and clothing. • Proponents also argue that cultures have become so intermixed that there is no authentic culture remaining in the world. • This evolving culture belongs to no specific nation or culture but rather draws from all to varying extents. • Individuals belonging to such a hybrid culture have a cosmopolitan outlook, wherein they may not identify with a specific country but rather identify as citizens of the world. Large-scale usage of 'hinglish' - mix of English and Hindi- in conversations and even in literature is a relevant example in this case.

Apart from food, **Indian festivals** and cultural practices have also been adapted and replicated across the globe. This has been made possible by the burgeoning Indian diaspora, which has created awareness about vibrant Indian festivals abroad. A fit example in this case is the Gujarati diaspora and the organisation of *Garba* and *Dandia* events in countries across the globe. India's cultural heritage, like the Taj Mahal, continues to attract global tourists, and the diversity of cultural heritage in the country is now globally recognised and respected.

Any discussion of India's cultural influence on the world shall remain incomplete without discussion of **Spirituality** and India's image as the abode of spiritualism. India's spiritual heritage sites, like cities of Varanasi and Bodh Gaya, are major attractions for spiritual seekers. More recently, there has been increased awareness about Yoga and Ayurveda. Yoga as an activity for physical and mental well-being has now gained global recognition. Similarly, the long-term benefits of Ayurveda-based practices are now well acknowledged, and there is demand for both of these in much of the Western world.

Concerns are often raised about **'monolithic globalisation'** and the erosion of indigenous cultures due to onslaughts of cultural globalisation. This is a very valid concern because, as seen in the previous section, globalisation has transformed not just material patterns of consumption but also value systems.

Insight Box

Monolithic Globalisation

The term '*Monolithic Globalisation*' is used to describe homogenising tendencies inbuilt among all agents of globalisation. Proponents argue that the forces of globalisation are pushing single 'hegemonic' culture across the world. Multinational Burger Chains, Fizzy drinks and Western values like Individualism and western clothing items like the jeans are seen as part of this hegemonic culture. Instead of representing all cultures and nations, globalisation is only forcing the Western values and institutions upon rest of the world and thus driving hegemony of the Western world. Thus, proponents argue that globalisation is essentially Western cultural imperialism and is destructive of the cultural diversity in non-western nations.

2.8 Has Globalisation Eroded Our Cultural values?

Globalisation, specifically cultural globalisation has impacted all nations of the world, and India is no exception. Often, concerns are raised about the loss or dilution of Indian culture in the wake of western products and values. There is an undeniable change in the lifestyle, values and preferences of the average Indian. Yet there is significant continuity in cultural values and traditions. This continuity and change can be observed in the following:

- *Family structure:* Due to the demands of the global economy, family structure has undergone a change whereby nuclear families are becoming more prevalent. Yet, the emotional and social connection with family remains. Family still forms the core of an individual's identity and self-image in India. The only difference is that instead of the traditional joint family, individuals are more connected with the nuclear family.

- *Religion and rituals:* Religion is widely regarded as an important pillar of Indian society. Yet, the hectic and travel-intensive nature of work for many has made it difficult to follow conservative religious norms. The practice of religion and rituals has adapted to the pressures of globalisation. The growing culture of *online darshan* and aarti is an example in this case. Religion still remains a significant part of private and public life in India. It still determines many choices, from food to marriage partner choices. But certain flexibility has been imbibed in the practice of religion.
- *Institution of marriage:* There are very few social practices that are considered as important as marriage ceremonies in India. Marriage is still a family decision rather than an individual decision for most. But influenced by Western norms of individual autonomy and freedom of choice, there is now greater respect for individual preference in the selection of a partner. The process of spouse selection is no longer dependent on informal networks alone. Matrimonial sites and dating apps are also being utilised in the search for the ideal partner. Similarly, due to consumerist pressures, wedding planners and grand weddings are becoming a feature even among the middle class.
- *Festivals:* India is well-known for its many and vibrant festivals. Festivals still serve to strengthen familial bonds as family members usually come together to celebrate festivals. Due to globalisation, apart from the traditional festivals, the country now also celebrates Valentine's Day, Friendship Day, Mother's Day and the like.
- *Value system:* There is a discernible shift in value systems in the wake of globalisation. There is more attention to individual needs and not just the demands of the community. Yet core Indian values like respect for elders and spirituality remain intact. There is both continuity and change in value systems.

3 Impact of Globalisation on Vulnerable Sections

3.1 Elderly

Ageing brings not just physiological but also financial and emotional changes. While India today is a young nation, this won't be true thirty years down the line. India's elderly population (60+ age) is likely to double from 10.5% in 2022 to 20.8% in 2050. Access to sophisticated healthcare for the elderly is an undeniable advantage in the wake of globalisation, but access to it is not equal for all. It is also true that the concept of '*active ageing*' is now being promoted, and many elderly people are finding opportunities even beyond the retirement age.

Globalisation has also created new challenges for this already vulnerable section of society. As per Census 2011, nearly 71% of India's elderly live in villages. Migration from rural to urban areas has led to loneliness and gaps in care for the elderly. Even in urban areas, hectic schedules and increasing individualist tendencies have given rise to **'old age homes'** where the elderly lead solitary and emotionally poor lives.

Migration for education and employment also leads to **'empty nest syndrome'** even in urban areas, whereby elderly parents run their own independent households and cope with loneliness. Such elderly-only households also face many security risks as they are easy targets for violence and crime.

Another issue specific to India is **'feminisation of ageing'**. Widowed elderly women are forced to survive with little income of their own and much functional morbidity. Such women are at great risk of abandonment and abuse. The vulnerability of India's female elderly population is likely to worsen with the weakening of the traditional family system and the dilution of the elderly care ethos in Indian society. The forces of globalisation and the ICT revolution have brought along many technologies, which the elderly may find hard to cope with. These elderly face many digital and technological barriers to accessing and enjoying the benefits of globalisation.

3.2 Women

Globalisation and the values of modernisation have had both an empowering and constraining impact on women in India. Globalisation brought many educational and employment opportunities for women and gave them recognition beyond the domestic sphere. Educated English speaking urban women could benefit from the IT sector boom and earn financial independence. Globalisation also brought along a shift in value systems, and women's autonomy and independence have come to be respected, at least to some extent.

At the same time, critics argue that socially disadvantaged and resource-poor women have suffered in the wake of globalisation. One issue is the quality of employment opportunities for women, which have come about in the wake of globalisation. Largely, women have found employment in competitive export-driven industries. Such employment, such as in the garments industry, is characterised by informality, poor remuneration and no non-wage benefits. In this contractual employment system, there are 'manufacturers without factories' as women work from households or small units and work is sub-contracted through many layers. Such monotonous work offers very little chance of upward mobility for women. This arrangement is not just cost-effective but also reduces labour law compliance for corporations. But it is severely disadvantageous for women as it is poorly paid and comes without basic social security like paid maternity leave.

Another issue is that though women are finding paid employment, enabling mechanisms like *access to crèche facilities* are limited. And women face a dual burden as their household work burden typically continues even after employment. The right social policies are needed to support working women and protect all sections of women from economic inequality in the age of globalisation.

3.3 Children

Globalisation has transformed the experience of childhood in both positive and negative ways. Children now have access to many digital tools of learning as well as quality English-medium education.

At the same time, unfiltered access to the Internet is rapidly depriving children of their innocence. Access to online pornography, violent games and other destructive materials like the *Blue Whale challenge,* which promoted teen suicide, is a huge risk for children. Instances of mobile phone and gaming addiction among children are fairly common now. In the urbanised set up, working parents struggle to devote adequate time for psycho-emotional support to children and thus mental disorders among children are on the rise.

Globalisation also has a massive impact on the dietary patterns of children. Rising disposable income, easy access to processed foods and relentless advertising have led to increased consumption of sugary and carbohydrate-rich diets.

3.4 Working Class and Migrant Workers

There has been much debate and discussion regarding the impact of globalisation on the working class in India.

One side of the debate takes a dim view of globalisation and points to the increased vulnerability of the working class. The reason cited for such vulnerability is the rise of *informality* as a strategy for passing labour laws and increasing the competitiveness of industries. This has led to insecure contractual employment that is devoid of social protection. Such informal employment also offers little to no chance of upward mobility or skill upgradation. Some examples of this kind of employment are *beedi making industry* and *domestic help-wage labour.*

Critics of globalisation also argue that globalisation and the opening of the Indian economy have severely diluted worker's organisations and *trade unions*. Due to rising informality and the resort to *contractual appointments*, organising and effective exercise of bargaining power by labour unions has become tedious.

Another issue has been the intense competition that Indian small and medium industries are facing due to the opening of the economy. One example in this context is that of handloom workers who struggle to survive in the face of power looms and mass-produced, cheap clothing items. When speaking of the working class, new types of wage labour, such as that done by food delivery agents, must be considered. Undoubtedly, globalisation and the rise of e-commerce have given rise to such new opportunities. But such employment is insecure, exhausting and repetitive work, which may not be sustainable.

In the context of developing countries like India, globalisation has also led to a demand for individuals with specific skill sets, and such demand usually works against unskilled and semi-skilled workers. Specific skill sets like speaking English and operating internet and digital devices are in demand, and those without these skills may find themselves deprived of the opportunities that have come in the wake of globalisation. An example is the hospitality sector, which has grown in the wake of greater tourist inflow but requires English fluency in most cases. Thus, many members of the working class are adversely positioned and cannot benefit from globalisation.

The above-noted issues and critical examination of globalisation only point to the need for adequate social security for the working class as well as the need for massive skilling of the workforce so that they may benefit from the opportunities offered by globalisation.

Debate Corner

Has globalisation exacerbated socio-economic inequalities in India, or has it empowered marginalised sections by opening up new avenues for growth and development?

4 Globalisation and the Middle Class

The term 'Middle Class' evades any definition as there is no specific income criterion that is used to identify this section of society. Yet it is globally recognised that India's strong middle class is fuelling consumption led growth in the country.

As per a survey (The Rise of India's Middle Class) by People Research on India's Consumer Economy (PRICE) and India's Citizen Environment, a not-for-profit think tank, India's middle class is currently 432 million strong and is expected to rise to 1.02 billion of India's projected population of 1.66 billion in 2047. The report uses income criteria to identify individuals belonging to the middle class and claims that one out of every three Indians belongs to the middle class today.

In one sense, the Middle class has been the biggest beneficiary of globalisation as reforms opened up many employment and educational opportunities for this segment. Globalisation also brought many lifestyle upgrades for this section of society as well as exposure to advanced technology and digital devices. Following are the main trends which can be observed in relation to Globalisation and the Indian Middle class:

1. Disposable incomes have risen due to increase in English-medium education, white collar employment and more earning hands.
2. The rise of consumerism and high demand for goods and services with a rise in disposable incomes is observed. An example in this context is the increasing use of airlines as a mode of transportation by the Middle Class.
3. There is a palpable shift from frugality towards consumerist and gratification-based mentality. Earlier, the emphasis was on consuming only what one could afford. An example in this context is prevalence of EMI (Equated Monthly Instalment) and credit cards, which allow the middle class to spend beyond their financial capacity.
4. The high consumption capacity of the Indian middle class has attracted Trans-national and Multi-national companies. The presence of malls, luxury retail outlets and penetration of e-commerce is relevant in this context.
5. Conspicuous consumption is now a quick way to gain status and social legitimacy in society.
6. Attractive advertising and the many choices have increased pressure on middle-class budgets.

The above points highlight how the middle class has been a major beneficiary due to the opening up of the Indian economy to the global world. Yet this section faces economic pressures due to the upward spiral of consumption.

Additional Readings

1. R. Bharucha, Politics of Culturalisms in an Age of Globalisation Discrimination, Discontent and Dialogue. *Economic and Political Weekly* 34(8), 477–489 (1999).
2. M.N. Panini, Trends in Cultural Globalisation from Agriculture to Agribusiness in Karnataka. *Economic and Political Weekly* 34(31): 2168-2173 (1999).
3. S. Ambirajan, Globalisation, Media and Culture. *Economic and Political Weekly* 35(25), 2141-2147 (2000).
4. M.H. Bala Subrahmanya, Small Industry and Globalisation Implications, Performance and Prospects. *Economic and Political Weekly* 39(18), 1826-1834 (2004).
5. P. Dodh, Globalisation and Human Rights in India. *World Affairs: The Journal of International Issues* 24(4), 44-57 (2020).
6. V.S. Vyas, Globalisation: Hopes, Realities and Coping Strategy. *Economic and Political Weekly* 37(12), 1109-1114 (2002).
7. A. Krishna and D. Bajpa, Layers in Globalising Society and the New Middle Class in India Trends, Distribution and Prospects. *Economic and Political Weekly* 50(5), 69-77 (2015).
8. Indian luxury market in 2023 and beyond, Retail News, ET Retail.
9. A.K. Joshi, Globalisation and Ageing in India. *The International Journal of Social Quality* 1(1), 33-44 (2011).

Previous Years' Questions

1. Critically examine the effect of globalisation on the aged population in India. (2013)
2. Discuss the positive and negative effects of globalisation on women in India. (2015)
3. Discuss the changes in the trends of labour migration within and outside India in the last four decades. (2015)
4. To what extent globalisation has influenced the core of cultural diversity in India? Explain. (2016)
5. 'Globalisation is generally said to promote cultural homogenisation but due to this cultural specificities appear to be strengthened in the Indian Society.' Elucidate. (2018)
6. Is diversity and pluralism in India under threat due to globalisation? Justify your answer. (2020)
7. Are we losing our local identity for the global identity? Discuss (2019)
8. Elucidate the relationship between globalisation and new technology in a world of scarce resources, with special reference to India. (2022)

UPSC CSE 2025

1. How do you account for the growing fast food industries given that there are increased health concerns in modern society? Illustrate your answer with the Indian experience.

(250 Words | 15 Marks)

Model Answer

The growing fast-food industry in India reflects a wider sociological and economic transformation. Driven by urbanisation, rising incomes, and aspirational lifestyles, the sector continues to expand despite increasing awareness of lifestyle diseases. India's food services market was valued at nearly ₹4.7 lakh crore in 2023, underscoring its scale and reach.

Reasons for Growth:

1. **Urbanisation & Lifestyle Changes:** Nuclear families and working couples rely on quick, convenient food options.
2. **Aspirational Middle Class:** Global brands like McDonald's and Domino's are viewed as symbols of modernity and status.
3. **Demographic Dividend:** With 65% of Indians under 35, youth see fast food as trendy, affordable, and suited to their fast-paced lives.
4. **Media & Marketing Influence:** Aggressive advertising associates fast food with cosmopolitanism and happiness.
5. **Technology & Consumerism:** Food delivery apps such as Zomato and Swiggy foster instant gratification and new consumption habits.

Concerns:

1. **Public Health:** India already has 101 million diabetics and rising obesity rates (24% of Indian women and 23% of Indian men are overweight or obese as per NFHS-5).
2. **Erosion of Traditional Diets:** Traditional staples like millets and pulses are being replaced by maida and sugary foods.
3. **Childhood Impact:** High consumption of sugary drinks and fast foods leads to obesity and dental problems among school children.
4. **Cultural Shifts:** Declining family meals weaken traditional bonds and food heritage.
5. **Mental Well-being:** Fast-food-linked diets worsen anxiety, concentration, and body image issues among youth.

Way Forward:

1. **Regulation:** Enforce clear labelling, sugar taxes, and bans on trans-fats.
2. **Cultural Revival:** Promote healthy traditional diets, as seen in the International Year of Millets (2023).
3. **Awareness & Behavioural Change:** Strengthen FSSAI's *Eat Right India* and integrate food literacy in schools.

The fast-food boom mirrors India's socio-economic transition but raises health and cultural challenges. A balanced strategy integrating regulation, tradition, and awareness is vital for sustainable food culture.

2. Do you think that globalisation results in only an aggressive consumer culture? Justify your answer. (250 Words | 15 Marks)

Model Answer

Globalisation has significantly influenced consumer behaviour, often intensifying materialistic tendencies through global brands, fast fashion, and e-commerce. However, its impact extends far beyond consumerism, shaping education, culture, technology, and collective action.

1. **Consumerist Impact**
   - **Materialism & Status Consumption:** Proliferation of global brands and lifestyle aspirations has driven conspicuous consumption, rising e-waste, obesity, and fastfashion waste.
   - **Economic Integration:** Digital platforms and e-commerce provide instant access to global products, deepening consumerist culture.
2. **Transformative Potential**
   - **Education & Healthcare:** Online courses (MOOCs), ed-tech platforms, and telemedicine democratise knowledge and healthcare.
   - **Cultural Exchange:** Globalisation promotes hybridity – e.g., Indian yoga and cinema gaining global reach, while K-pop and anime influence youth worldwide.
   - **Political & Environmental Movements:** Transnational campaigns like #MeToo, climate strikes, and democracy movements spread rapidly via global networks.
   - **Ethical Frameworks:** Corporate Social Responsibility (CSR), Environmental-Social-Governance (ESG) norms, and India's LiFE (Lifestyle for Environment) initiative counterbalance excessive consumerism.

Globalisation undoubtedly intensifies consumerism but is not confined to it. It also fosters education, cultural flows, and global solidarity. The task for states and societies is to channel it towards sustainable, equitable, and ethical development.

UPSC CSE 2024

1. Globalization has increased urban migration by skilled, young, unmarried women from various classes. How has this trend impacted upon their personal freedom and relationship with family? (250 words | 15 Marks)

Model Answer

The forces of globalisation have opened up new employment avenues in urban centres, especially in services like IT, healthcare, retail, and hospitality. This has led to a surge in internal migration of young, skilled, unmarried women from diverse socio-economic backgrounds.

Impact on Personal Freedom:

1. **Economic and Lifestyle Autonomy:** Urban migration provides financial independence, freedom over personal spending, and the option to live independently - experiences often unavailable in their hometowns.
2. **Social Assertion and Identity Formation:** Exposure to cosmopolitan cultures enables women to assert individuality, challenge patriarchal norms and make independent lifestyle choices.
3. **Access to Opportunities:** Many benefit from gender-inclusive HR practices in modern workplaces, gaining leadership roles and upward mobility.
4. **Sexual and Emotional Autonomy:** Urban life also offers women greater control over emotional and sexual autonomy, such as the choice to delay or forgo marriage.

> **Negative impact**
>
> Financial Exploitation: In informal sectors, women may face low wages, job insecurity, and limited opportunities for personal growth.

Impact on Family Relationships:

1. **Enhanced respect in family:** Financially independent women often gain greater respect and voice in family decisions.
2. **Inspiring Family Members:** Working women often motivate younger siblings to pursue education and jobs, becoming role models within the family.

However, urban migration can also strain familial relationships:

1. **Conflict in value system:** Conflicts may arise due to contrasting values - urban liberalism vs. traditional expectations - especially regarding marriage or lifestyle.
2. **Lack of emotional support from family:** Due to increased distance, emotional support from family members may suffer. Women may feel isolated and depressed, straining familial bonds.

> Women from Tier-2 towns working in IT or healthcare in Bengaluru or Pune often report increased autonomy, yet face pressures from both urban demands and conservative families.

In sum, this trend is reshaping gender roles and family dynamics - reflecting both empowerment and generational friction in a globalising India.

7 Social Empowerment

1 Meaning and Concept of Social Empowerment

'Empowerment' literally means to *equip your ability or supply with opportunity*. It can be understood as strengthening the capabilities of individuals or a group, particularly the vulnerable sections of society. This can be achieved through the full participation of people in the formulation, implementation and evaluation of decisions that determine the proper functioning and well-being of our societies. Strengthening capabilities requires the removal of disabilities or bondages, which have historically constrained the vulnerable sections from realising their full potential. For instance, disabilities are caused by the inequality built into the structure of Indian society based on caste and gender.

The basic idea behind empowerment is the social transformation of common people who are marginalised, unorganised and suffer from various disadvantages. The Indian Constitution has provided various rights to disadvantageous groups. However, all the rights have not been enforced. Empowerment is seen as a way of addressing the issues related to the rights that remain unenforced.

Empowering is considered a continuous process. Although, ideally, it should be initiated by the individual himself, there are individuals who are not in a position to empower themselves. For them, efforts from external agencies, such as government institutions, are required. These institutions are expected to provide ample opportunities to facilitate realisation of their goals.

2 Dimensions of Social Empowerment

The majority of people think that earning money makes them empowered. However, empowerment is a broader team that goes beyond this and includes various aspects such as social, political, technical, technological and cultural, among others. Various dimensions of social empowerment are shown in Fig. 7.1.

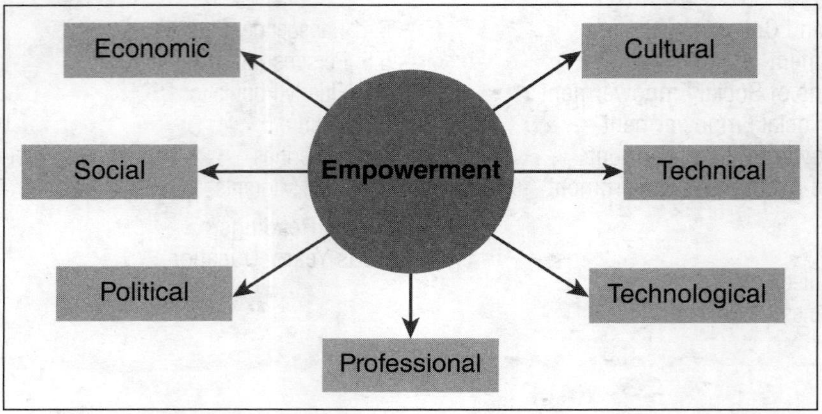

Fig. 7.1 Various Dimensions of Empowerment

1. *Social empowerment*: It means removing the socially induced inequalities, disparities and barriers so that there is transformation in the lives of weaker sections such as SC/ST, women, etc. For example, conferring property rights, particularly land titles, to women would ensure breaking the 'patriarchal' structure in society to some extent.
2. *Economic empowerment*: It means creating provisions for employment, self-income-generating activities that can help economically deprived sections alleviate poverty, generate assets and improve their standards of living. For example, Self Help Groups (SHGs) provide for self-employment.
3. *Cultural empowerment*: It means developing a sense of pride in one's own cultural values, heritage, customs and traditions. Moreover, assimilating the cultural practices of the weaker sections of mainstream culture can help in their cultural empowerment. For example, assimilating tribal cultural practices such as worshipping natural habitat can potentially benefit the overall society.
4. *Political empowerment*: It happens when the decision-making process about policies and developmental plans runs from 'bottom to top' and not the reverse. Thus, people, including the weaker sections, should have a say in decision-making and should decide the developmental initiatives best suited to them. For example, Panchayati Raj Institutions (PRIs) have the potential to empower people politically if implemented in true spirit.

5. *Technological empowerment*: The application of modern technology in the fields of education, health, etc., can result in empowering common people in ways beyond our comprehension. The Internet and technology have opened up various possibilities. For example, **Project Gurushala** was launched in September 2019 to provide online courses to school students and also provide a networking platform for teachers across India. It is a collaboration between Indus Towers Ltd., Vodafone Idea Foundation and Pratham Education Foundation.
6. *Professional empowerment*: It means allowing the professionals at the workplace to contribute to the decision-making process. The work culture should promote transparency and encourage professionals to share information freely, without any fear.
7. *Technical empowerment*: It means growth in skill in a particular subject or field. In the modern world of specialisation, it is important to develop specific skillsets to be more relevant and empowered.

3 Need for Social Empowerment

Social empowerment is needed for any society to ensure that natural or man-made obstacles are removed or reduced in the way people seek to achieve their goals. Especially in a society like India with caste barriers, gender-discrimination and economic challenges, the social empowerment of various groups becomes more important. Some of the factors for which social empowerment is needed include the following:

1. Addressing inequalities	Empowering women and the poor through various economic and political measures can help reduce inequalities.
2. Removing structural barriers	Legal measures, social measures against caste and gender-based oppression can help in removing structural barriers.
3. Economic growth and development	With the progress of vulnerable groups, there is high scope for overall economic progress and development
4. Progress of marginal communities	Marginal communities can progress as they have better access to opportunities and resources and acquisition can acquire new skills.
5. Equitable distribution of resources	Various developmental schemes for disadvantaged groups ensure that resources are devolved to them.
6. Increased participation of people	Various developmental schemes provide for 'social audit', thus ensuring the participation of people in the implementation of schemes

4 Barriers Towards Empowerment

There are few barriers to the process of empowering people. Such barriers are not universal in nature; rather, they vary from place to place and people to people. These are discussed as follows:

1. *Lack of correct information*: In today's age, having correct and timely information is crucial as far as making decisions for oneself is concerned. Many people do not have access to the requisite Information and Communication Technology (ICT) and, hence, access to information. This becomes one of the significant barriers. For example, not having information about the schemes run by the government might prevent individuals from getting the benefits.
2. *Social and cultural barriers*: For instance, in some parts of India, women are still not encouraged to work outside and even their education is not given as much priority. There is biasness in the way how society treat women, elderly, transgenders, etc.
3. *Lack of access to technology*: Access to technology empowers many as it opens a plethora of opportunities in terms of financial knowledge and business opportunities, among various know-how. The lack of access to technology prevents individuals from such benefits.
4. *Issue of co-operation*: In a society, there are ideological differences and conflicts between various groups. This prevents proper co-operation and co-ordination among individuals or groups. Thus, what should have been achieved at a community level remains unfulfilled, preventing community empowerment.

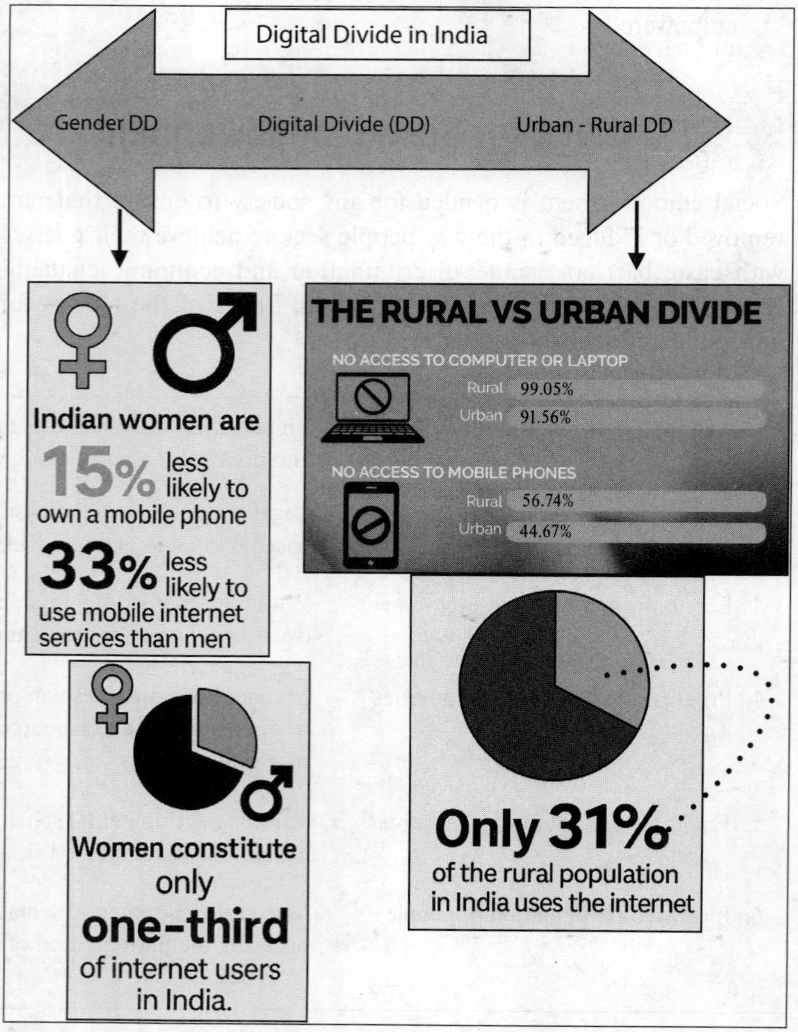

Source: India Inequality Report 2022: Digital Divide by Oxfam India

5 Vulnerable Groups and Government Initiatives

A vulnerable group is a section of the population that is potentially at higher risk of experiencing poverty, discrimination and exclusion if they are not provided socio-economic assistance.

5.1 Women

The Ministry of Women and Child Development (MWCD) has taken various steps to bring women into the mainstream of all the sectors in the country with the aim of empowering them. A few initiatives are:

1. *Beti Bachao Beti Padhao (BBBP)*: It was launched in 2015 to address the issue of declining Child Sex Ratio (CSR), ensure survival and protection of the girl child, and also promote education and participation of the girl child.
2. *Ujjwala Scheme*: It is a centrally sponsored scheme. The objective of this scheme is to prevent the trafficking of women and to Rescue, Rehabilitation, Reintegrate and Repatriate victims of trafficking for commercial sexual exploitation.

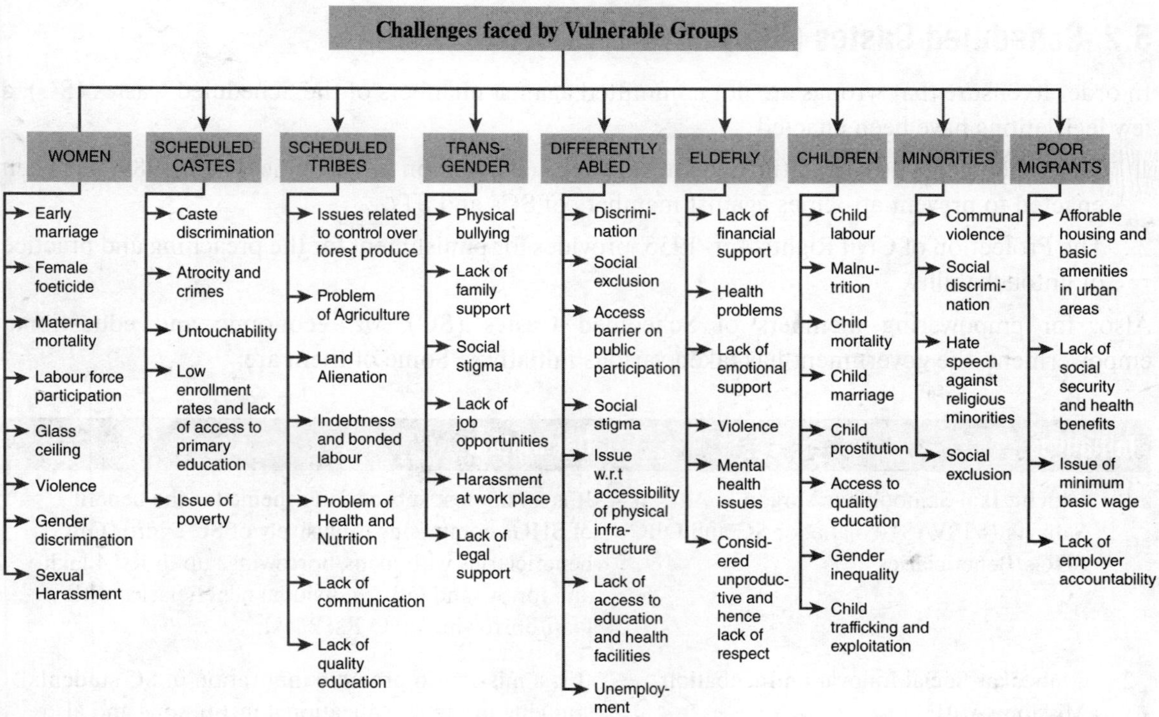

3. *Swadhar Greh Scheme*: It is also a Centrally Sponsored Scheme (CSS). It is being implemented for those women who are victims of difficult circumstances. Such women are given institutional support for rehabilitation so that they can live with dignity.
4. *Pradhan Mantri Matru Vandana Yojana (PMMVY)*: It is a Centrally Sponsored Conditional Cash Transfer Scheme. It is available to all Pregnant Women & Lactating Mothers (PW&LM), except those who are in regular employment with the Central Government or the State Governments or Public Sector Undertakings (PSUs) or those receiving similar benefits under any other law, for the first living child.
5. *One Stop Centre and Universalisation of Women Helplines*: The One Stop Centre, also known as Sakhi Centres, aims to facilitate women affected by violence through services such as legal aid, police facilitation and medical aid.

   Women Helpline (WHL) provides 24-hour emergency and non-emergency response to women affected by violence by connecting them to Police, One Stop Centre, Hospital, Legal Services etc.
6. *Mission Shakti*: It is an integrated programme for the safety, security and empowerment of women. It aims to reduce the care burden on women and increase female labour force participation by promoting skill development, capacity building, financial literacy, access to micro-credit, etc.

5.2 Scheduled Castes (SCs)

In order to ensure that wrongs are not committed against members of the Scheduled Castes (SC), a few legislations have been enacted.

1. The Scheduled Castes and the Scheduled Tribes (Prevention of Atrocities) Act, 1989, has been enacted to prevent atrocities against members of SCs and STs.
2. The Protection of Civil Rights Act, 1955, provides for punishment for the preaching and practice of untouchability.

Also, for empowering members of Scheduled Castes (SC), *viz.* economic and educational empowerment, the government has taken various initiatives. Some of them are:

Initiatives	Description
1. Vanchit Ikai Samooh aur Vargon ki Aarthik Sahayta (VISVAS) Yojana for SC and OBC SHGs/Beneficiaries	It is an interest subvention scheme for the benefit of SHGs comprising exclusively of SC and/or OBC beneficiaries with loans/borrowings up to Rs. 4 lakh and for SC and OBC individual beneficiaries with loan/borrowing up to Rs. 2 lakh.
2. Ambedkar Social Innovation Incubation Mission (ASIIM)	It is a mission to promote innovation in SC students studying in higher educational institutions and also to support innovators and entrepreneurs. It will help the SC students become job-givers rather than job-seekers.

Initiatives	Description
3. Post-Matric Scholarship for Scheduled Caste Students (PMS-SC)	The objective of this initiative is to increase the Gross Enrolment Ratio (GER) of SC students in higher education with a focus on those from the poorest households.
4. Pre-Matric Scholarship Scheme	Provides financial assistance for pre-metric education, i.e. classes I–X. The idea is to minimise the incidence of drop-outs and to improve participation of SC students in the classes.
5. National Fellowships for SC Students	Provides fellowships in the form of financial assistance to SC students to pursue M.Phil/ Ph.D. in Indian universities.
6. Pradhan Mantri Anusuchit Jaati Abhyuday Yojana (PM-AJAY)	It aims to reduce poverty through skill development and income-generating activities.

5.3 Schedules Tribes (STs)

The Constitution of India provides for special provisions for the development of tribals, along with protecting their culture. In this regard, there are provisions related to the conservation of their language and script. Apart from this, the Constitution also provides for the reservation of seats for Scheduled Tribes in Panchayats, Houses of the People and Legislative Assemblies of the States, thus ensuring political empowerment for them.

In addition to this, a separate *Ministry of Tribal Affairs* has also been set up so that special focus can be given on the development of STs. To provide legislative support, the **Scheduled Tribes and Other Traditional Forest Dwellers (Recognition of Forest Rights) Act, 2006**, was also enacted to look after the forest rights of the STs.

For the empowerment of tribal communities in various other domains, such as education, economic and infrastructure, the government has placed special emphasis and adopted various measures:

Domains	Initiatives	Description
Educational Empowerment	1. Eklavya Model Residential Schools (EMRS)	To provide quality education to ST students (Class VI–XII) in remote areas through residential schooling facilities.
Economic Empowerment	2. Pradhan Mantri Vanbandhu Vikas Yojana	Under this, a venture capital fund has been set up to promote entrepreneurship/start-up projects by ST youth.

Domains	Initiatives	Description
Improved Infrastructure and Livelihood Opportunities	3. Pradhan Mantri Jan Jatiya Vikas Mission	To provide marketing support for tribal products by way of procuring Minor Forest Produce under the Minimum Support Price (MSP) with the objective of promoting livelihood opportunities for the tribal population.
	4. Pradhan Mantri Adi Adarsh Gram Yojana (PMAAGY)	To provide basic infrastructure in villages with a significant tribal population - 36,428 villages having 50% tribal population and 500 Scheduled Tribes (STs) have been identified to provide basic infrastructure facilities.

Apart from the above initiatives, other measures such as Pradhan Mantri Awas Yojana, financial empowerment through Jan Dhan accounts, formation of Self Help Groups (SHGs), etc., have helped in empowering the tribals.

5.4 Transgender Persons

A transgender person, as per **the Transgender Persons (Protection of Rights) Act,** *2019*, is defined as a person whose gender does not match with the gender assigned to that person at birth and includes trans-man or trans-woman, people with intersex variations, genderqueer and people having such socio-cultural identities as *kinner, hijra, aravani and jogta.* As per the 2011 Census, there were 487,803 individuals who identified themselves as 'others' and not male or female.

Landmark Judgements

National Legal Services Authority (NALSA) v. Union of India (2014)

Issue: Rights of transgender persons

Judgment: Recognized transgenders as a 'third gender' and declared that they are entitled to fundamental rights. Directed the government to treat transgender people as Socially and Educationally Backward Classes (SEBCs) for the purpose of reservation in education and jobs. This was a major step toward gender and social empowerment and since then, the government has been making serious efforts to make India a trans-inclusive society.

One of the steps for empowering the transgender persons is the enactment of **The Transgender Persons (Protection of Rights) Act, 2019**.

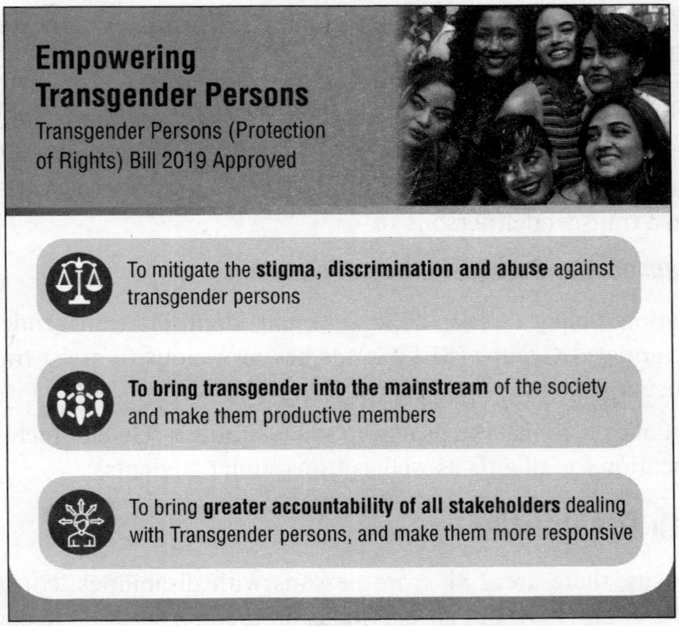

Some of the key provisions of the Act include:

1. There should be *no-discrimination* against transgender persons in educational institutions, employment, healthcare services, etc.
2. *Identity* of the transgender persons to be recognised by conferring upon them the right to self-perceived gender identity.
3. Transgender persons are to be provided with the *Right of Residence* with their parents and immediate family members.
4. *Welfare schemes* and programmes to be formulated for transgender persons in the field of eduction, social security and health.
5. The Act provides for the *National Council of Transgender Persons* to advise, monitor and evaluate the measures for the protection of the rights of transgender persons.

Support for Marginalised Individuals for Livelihood and Enterprise (SMILE) Scheme

It was launched by the Ministry of Social Justice and Empowerment in 2022. It is an umbrella scheme that focusses on the welfare of the transgender community and on persons who are engaged in the act of begging. The scheme includes the following welfare measures for transgender persons:

1. *Financial assistance* in the form of scholarships is to be provided to transgender students studying in classes ninth until post-graduation.
2. Training for *skill-development* and livelihood opportunities.

3. *Healthcare facilities* are to be provided for gender reaffirmation surgeries and pre and post-operative procedures.
4. *Garima Grehs* are to be set up in each state in order to provide shelter facility for abandoned and orphaned transgender persons.
5. Transgender Protection Cells to be set up in the entire country to provide redressal of offences and crimes against transgender persons

Empowerment of Transgender Persons through Education

The National Education Policy (NEP) 2020 of India identifies transgender children as Socio-Economically Disadvantaged Groups (SEDGs). It has provisions to assist transgender children in gaining access to education.

Apart from this, the Policy also has the provision to constitute a **'Gender-Inclusion Fund'** to provide equitable quality education for all girls as well as transgender students.

5.5 Persons with Disabilities

As per the 2011 Census, there are 2.81 crore persons with disabilities, constituting 2.21% of the total population of the country. To put special focus on them, a separate department has also been set up for them - Department of Empowerment of Persons with Disabilities (DEPWD) - within the Ministry of Social Justice and Empowerment. The department aims to create an inclusive society with equal opportunities for the 'Divyangjan', so that they can lead productive and dignified lives.

To provide legislative support, the government enacted the **Rights of Persons with Disabilities Act, 2016**. The Act, apart from other rights, provides for a 4% reservation for them in government establishment. Also, not less than 5% of seats are to be reserved for them in all government and government-aided higher educational institutions. There are a few other important provisions of the Act:

1. The Act focusses on improving the accessibility of PwDs in built-up environment, transportation system and Information & Communication (ICT) ecosystem.
2. It also has provision for promoting participation of PwDs in skill development, sports and recreation.
3. To protect the rights of PwDs, punishment for various offences and violations of provisions of the Act was introduced.
4. There is provision for a special Court as well in order to adjudicate the cases under this Act in a speedy manner.

Accelerating Accessibility: Accessible India Campaign (AIC)

It was launched in 2015 by the Central Government for enhancing accessibility, creating awareness and sensitising people to create a universal barrier-free environment. Its three main pillars are as follows:

- Built-Up Environment
- Transportation System
- Information & Communication (ICT) ecosystems

National Policy for Persons with Disabilities, 2006

The policy recognises that PwDs are valuable resources for the country and seeks to create an environment that provides equality of opportunities for them, protects their rights and ensures their full participation in society.

Salient features of the policy:

1. *Physical rehabilitation*: includes counselling, medical support and the provision of aids and appliances;
2. *Educational rehabilitation*: includes vocational training;
3. *Economic rehabilitation*: to ensure a dignified life in society

The Ministry of Social Justice and Empowerment runs various schemes for the rehabilitation and empowerment of people with disabilities. A few schemes are as follows:

Schemes	Description
1. Scheme of Assistance to Disabled Persons for the Purchase/Fitting of Aids/Appliances (ADIP)	To physically rehabilitate PwDs through the provision of assistive aids and appliances.
2. Deendayal Disabled Rehabilitation Scheme (DDRS)	Address all aspects of rehabilitation, includes projects covering various services ranging from programmes for pre-school and early intervention to the rehabilitation of leprosy-cured persons.
3. Scheme for Implementation of the Persons with Disabilities Act	Funds are provided to projects in order to make buildings barrier-free; support institutions that provide services to PwDs.
4. Scheme of Incentives to Employers in the Private Sector for Providing Employment to PwDs	In this case, payment is made by the government towards the employer's contribution to the Employees Provident Fund and Employees State Insurance for the first three years.

Last but not least, the **National Handicapped Finance and Development Corporation** is working to promote economic development activities and self-employment ventures for PwDs, to extend loans through authorised agencies and to assist the self-employed PwDs in marketing their produce.

5.6 Elderly Population

As per Census 2011, there are approximately 10.38 crore senior citizens, amounting to 8.6% of the total population in the country.

National Policy on Older Persons, 1999

The goal of the Policy is the well-being of older people. The Policy recognises that the concerns of older persons are national concerns and they need to be protected. Keeping this in mind, the Policy envisages state support for financial security, health care, shelter, welfare, protection against abuse and exploitation, and making available opportunities for the development of potential of older persons so that they can improve their quality of life. Special attention is to be given to the elderly females in order to protect them from triple neglect and discrimination on account of gender, widowhood and age.

Schemes for Senior Citizens: In order to ensure that senior citizens live a happy, healthy, dignified and empowered lives, the Department of Social Justice and Empowerment is implementing the Umbrella Scheme of **Atal Vayo Abhyuday Yojana**. Under this scheme, the following welfare schemes are being run for them.

Schemes	Description
1. Integrated Programme for Senior Citizens (IPSrC)	Grants in aid are given for running and maintenance of Senior Citizens Homes/ Continuous Care Homes, Mobile Medicare Units etc. to the Implementing Agencies such as Panchayati Raj Institutions (PRIs), NGOs.
2. Rashtriya Vayoshri Yojana (RVY)	Aids and assistive living devices are provided to senior citizens belonging to the BPL category or those earning less than Rs. 15,000 per month and suffering from age-related disabilities such as low vision, hearing impairment, loss of teeth and loco-motor disabilities.
3. Livelihood and Skilling Initiatives for Senior Citizens	Supplements the efforts of senior citizens by providing them opportunities to enhance their earnings and sense of self-respect; also encourages them to form Self Help Groups and engage in activities that may result in marketable products.
4. Promoting Silver Economy	The objective is to encourage entrepreneurs to think about the problems faced by the elderly and develop some innovative solutions.

5.7 Children

As per Census 2011, India has 472 million children under the age of 0–18 years, comprising 39% of the country's total population.

Legislations for Children

The Protection of Children from Sexual Offences Act, 2012

It has been enacted to protect children from sexual assault, sexual harassment and pornography. A few important provisions are:

1. The Act provides for severe punishments that are graded in nature as per the gravity of the offence.
2. Special Court to be set-up for the trial of offences. The Special Court is to complete the trial within one year, as far as possible.
3. The Act places huge importance on child-friendly process with respect to reporting, recoding evidence, investigation and trial.
4. Media houses are restricted from disclosing the identity of the child without the permission of the Special Court.
5. The Special Juvenile Protection Unit (SJPU) or local police need to inform the Child Welfare Committee (CWC) within 24 hours of recording the complaint.
6. The National Commission for the Protection of Child Rights (NCPCR) and State Commissions for the Protection of Child Rights (SCPCRs) are required to look after the implementation of the Act.

The Juvenile Justice (Care and Protection of Children) Act, 2015

It addresses the concerns of both 'children in conflict with law' and 'children in need of care and protection'. Some of the important provisions of the Act are:

1. The Act provides for constituting the Juvenile Justice Board (JJB) and Child Welfare Committees (CWC) in every district.
2. The Act provides that all children below the age of 18 are to be treated equally, except for heinous crimes. A minor in the age group of 16–18 years, accused of committing a heinous crime, can be tried as an adult. In order to do this, the JJB needs to assess the mental and physical capacities of the child, his/her ability to understand the consequences of the crime, etc., before determining whether the child can be tried as an adult.

   After preliminary assessment, if the JJB finds that there is a need for trial of the said child as an adult, JJB may transfer the case to the concerned Children's Court.
3. The Act also emphasises the mandatory registration of Child Care Institutions, whether run by the state government or by voluntary or non-governmental organisations.

4. It also has provisions for the adoption of children. The *Central Adoption Resource Agency* (CARA) has been given the authority to frame rules and regulations for adoption of orphaned children.
5. The NCPCR and SCPCR are given the responsibility of monitoring the implementation of the provisions of the Act.

   Other legislation passed by the Indian Parliament for protecting and promoting the rights of children include the Commission for Protection of Child Rights Act, 2005, Prohibition of Child Marriage Act, 2006 and Right to Education Act, 2009.

National Policy for Children, 2013

The Policy recognises that a multi-dimensional approach is needed in order to secure the rights of children. The policy has identified four key focus areas for focussed attention. They are:

- Survival;
- Health and nutrition;
- Education and development;
- Protection and participation

Some of the key provisions of the Policy include:

1. Right to life, survival and development goes beyond physical existence and encompasses the right to identity and nationality as well;
2. No child shall be discriminated against on the grounds of religion, race, caste, sex, place of birth, class, language, disability, social, economic or any other status;
3. The family environment is most conducive to the development of children, and they should not be separated from their parents, except when separation is in the best interest of the child;
4. It is necessary that children are to be protected from all forms of abuse, neglect, violence, maltreatment and exploitation;
5. Children's views, especially those of girls, children from disadvantaged groups, marginalised groups need to be heard in all matters affecting them;

Some of the initiatives for the development of children are:

Schemes	Description
1. Integrated Child Development Services (ICDS) Scheme	Holistic development of children up to 6 years of age; services include: • supplementary nutrition • immunisation • health check-up • referral services • pre-school non-formal education • Nutrition and health education

Schemes	Description
2. Misssion Vatsalya	Aims to support and sustain children in difficult circumstances. It promotes family-based non-institutional care of children in difficult circumstances.
3. Saksham Anganwadi and Poshan 2.0	Aims to address the challenges of malnutrition in children, adolescent girls, among others. One of the key objectives is to ensure children's right to survival, development, protection and participation.

5.8 Minorities

In India, there are six centrally notified minority communities, namely, Christians, Sikhs, Buddhists, Muslims, Parsis and Jains. The Ministry of Minority Affairs is implementing the **Prime Minister's 15 Point Programme** for the welfare of Minority Communities. This umbrella programme covers various schemes with the goal of ensuring that the underprivileged among the minority communities would get equal opportunities for availing the welfare schemes run by the government. The programme has the following objectives:

1. Enhancing opportunities for education for minorities
2. Ensuring that minorities get an equitable share in economic activities and employment; credit support for self-employment and recruitment to State and Central Government jobs;
3. Appropriate share for the minorities in the infrastructure development schemes in order to improve their conditions of living;
4. Prevention and control of communal disharmony and violence

Some of the schemes under the programme are:

Domains	Schemes	Description
Educational Empowerment	1. a. Pre-Matric Scholarship Scheme b. Post-Matric Scholarship Scheme c. Merit-cum-Means based Scholarship Scheme	a. Scholarship is given to minority students from class I to X; b. Class XI to PhD; c. Professional and Technical courses, at Under Graduate and Post Graduate level; In each case, 30% of the scholarship are earmarked for girls.
	2. Naya Savera	Free coaching to minority students for qualifying in entrance exams of technical/medical courses and other competitive exams
	3. Padho Pardesh	Interest subsidy on educational loans for overseas higher study

Domains	Schemes	Description
Economic Empowerment	4. Seekho Aur Kamao	Skill development scheme for youth of 14–35 years age group; aims to promote employment, employment opportunities, improve employability of workers, school drop-outs etc.
	5. USTTAD (Upgrading the Skills and Training in Traditional Arts/Crafts for Development)	Provide self-employment, market and opportunity to traditional artisans and craftpersons; organisation of 'Hunar Haats' to provide employment opportunities and markets to artisans/craftsmen
	6. Nai Manzil	Formal school education and skilling of school dropouts or educated in community educational institutions like Madrasas.
Infrastructure Development Programme	7. Pradhan Mantri Jan Vikas Karyakram (PMJVK)	To provide basic infrastructure such as Schools, Colleges, ITIs, Skill Development Centres, hospitals etc in backward areas of the country; it is implemented in the identified areas having a minimum of 25% minority population and whose backwardness parameters is below the national average in respect of socio economic or basic amenities or both.

5.9 Poor Migrants

The number of migrants in India as per the 2011 Census was around 45 crores, i.e. 37% of the total population. The issue of migrants is not new. However, during the COVID-19 pandemic, their poor condition got highlighted as they were the ones to have been worst affected. During the Covid-19 pandemic and immediately after that, various state governments and central government took concrete steps to improve their conditions.

Some of the measures undertaken by the Government for the welfare of migrant workers are:

1. *PM Street Vendor's AtmaNirbhar Nidhi (PM SVANidhi) scheme*: It was launched to provide collateral-free loan of up to Rs. 10,000 for a period of one year to approximately 50 lakh street vendors to resume their business.
2. *Pradhan Mantri Garib Kalyan Rojgar Abhiyan*: It was launched to facilitate employment of migrant workers who had gone back to their Home State, by involving these migrant worker in building rural infrastructure.
3. *Affordable Rental Housing Complexes (ARHC)*: It was launched to address the accommodation needs of migrant workers.
4. *One Nation One Ration Card Scheme*: To facilitate nationwide portability of ration cards. It will greatly benefit migrant workers and their families as they can avail PDS benefits from anywhere in the country.

Apart from these, it would be better if the government adopts sustainable and long-term measures so that the social and economic security of the migrants workers can be ensured. For instance, the recommendation of the **Report of the Working Group on Migration** to frame a comprehensive law for migrant workers can be implemented so that their rights can be protected.

Additional Readings

1. A. Beteille, Empowerment. *Economic and Political Weekly* 34 (1999).
2. M. Mohanty, On the Concept of 'Empowerment'. *Economic and Political Weekly* 30 (1995).
3. Schemes for Empowerment of Rural Women, Press Release (21 July 2023).
4. *Detailed Guidelines for 'Mission Shakti' aimed at Strengthening Interventions for Women Safety, Security and Empowerment, Press Release, dated 14 July 2022.*
5. Initiatives for SC Welfare by Ministry of Social Justice & Empowerment.
6. Empowering Tribals, Transforming India.
7. PIB: Welfare of Transgender Persons in India: Slew of Measures by Central Governement in Last Three Years.
8. Government Initiatives for Redressal of Disability in India.
9. National Policy on Older Persons.
10. Schemes for Senior Citizens.
11. POCSO Act.
12. The Juvenile Justice (Care and Protection of Children) Act, 2015.
13. National Policy for Children
14. Ministry of Women and Child Development issues Guidelines of 'Saksham Anganwadi and Poshan 2.0' - an Integrated Nutrition Support Programme.
15. Mission Vatsalya.
16. Schemes for Upliftment of Minorities.
17. Prime Minister's 15 Point Programme for Minorities.
18. Measures taken by Government to support migrant workers.
19. Social Security And Welfare Schemes For Migrant Labourers.

Previous Years' Question

1. Examine the role of 'Gig Economy' in the process of empowerment of women in India. (2021)

UPSC CSE 2024

1. Despite comprehensive policies for equity and social justice, underprivileged sections are not yet getting the full benefits of affirmative action envisaged by the Constitution. Comment.

(250 words | 15 Marks)

Model Answer

The Constitution of India promotes social justice through affirmative action in education, employment, and political representation (Articles 15(4), 16(4), 46). However, structural and implementation barriers prevent many marginalised groups from fully benefiting.

Comprehensive Policies for Equity and Social Justice:

- **SC/ST (Prevention of Atrocities) Act** ensures protection from caste-based violence.
- **Affirmative action** seeks to ensure adequate representation in education and jobs for SCs, STs and OBCs.
- **Measures** like Stand-*Up India, Pradhan Mantri Adarsh Gram Yojana* and *Eklavya Model Residential* Schools aim to empower backward sections.

Challenges in Realising Full Benefits:

- **Awareness Deficit:** Many tribal and rural communities, especially in the Northeast, remain unaware of their rights and entitlements.
- **Weak Educational Foundations:** Poor school infrastructure, learning outcomes and skilling in rural areas reduce the effectiveness of quotas.
- **Administrative Hurdles:** Delays in caste certificates, scholarships and loans exclude many beneficiaries.
- **Poverty and Social Exclusion:** Economic hardship and caste-based discrimination, especially among Dalits and Adivasis, lead to high dropout rates (UDISE+ 2021–22).

Category	Primary Level	Upper Priary Level	Secondary Level
SC	1.46	3.56	12.55
ST	2.83	6.03	16.62

Source: Unified District Information System for Education (UDISE) 2021-22

- **Exclusion of Nomadic & De-notified Tribes:** These groups lack documentation, barring them from accessing welfare schemes.

Way Ahead:

- Legal Awareness Campaigns via NGOs, especially in remote areas.
- Time-bound trials under special courts for atrocity cases.
- Sub-categorisation of SCs/STs to prioritise the most deprived.
- Strengthening school systems via RTE Act, PM-POSHAN and hostels under PM-JANMAN.

Positive Development: As per AISHE 2021–22, SC student enrolment rose by 44% and ST enrolment by 65% since 2014–15, reflecting improved access to higher education.

In conclusion, while policies exist, targeted and inclusive implementation is key to realising the constitutional vision of social justice.

Source: 1. Ministry of Education releases All India Survey on Higher Education (AISHE) 2021-2022 (PIB: Jan 24)

8 Communalism

1 Communalism: Meaning and Definition

The term 'communalism' has its roots in the word 'commune' or 'community'. It meant a group of people whose allegiance is more to one's own religion, ethnic group or community as compared to society at large. It is to be understood that the nature of society plays an important role in the genesis of communalism.

Historian Bipan Chandra in his book *'Communalism in Modern India'* defines communalism as the belief that because a group of people follow a particular religion, they have, as a result, common social, political and economic interests. Thus, it is the belief in India that since Hindus, Muslims, Sikhs and Christians form different religious communities, they not only share similar religious interests but also common secular interests.

In a multi-religious and multi-ethnic society, scholars opine that when various communities live together amicably in a given territory, communal harmony flourishes. However, whenever there is a dispute among these communities for their exclusiveness, group identity and group interests, even at the cost of national interests, there is communal disharmony. This can also be understood as *communalism*. In such cases, communities try to impose their way of life on other groups. Thus, a lack of understanding and mutual co-operation between religious communities can be a basic reason for the birth of communalism.

2 Characteristics of Communalism

Some of the important characteristics of communalism include:

1. It is an ideological concept with a basic focus on the unity of one's own community against other communities. It promotes the principle of intolerance towards others and, thus, plays a role in the division of society.
2. It is important to understand that communalism is manifested not only in religious activities; rather, it encompasses secular interests, viz. socio-economic and political aspects too.
3. It often results in violence among people from different communities. This is mainly because of the inherent mistrust and lack of faith between communities.
4. The leaders of communal factions promote the idea that the interests of their community are completely incompatible with those of others.
5. People with communal thought processes believe that their own communal interests are superior to those of the national interest. Thus, they focus only on the interests of their own communities.
6. It is also used by political groups to promote their specific interests. Sometimes, even political parties are formed on religious lines.
7. In their extreme form, communal beliefs may lead to a secessionist tendency among communities.
8. It derails the progress of secularism in a society and also attempts to weaken democratic principles.

3 Factors Behind the Rise of Communalism in India

Many factors can be attributed to the rise of communalism and its continuation in India in modern times. Some of them are:

1. *Colonial policies*: The British policies of Divide and Rule, Partition of Bengal in 1905, separate electorate under the Government of India Act, 1909, the communal award in 1932 contributed to the growth of communalism in India.
2. *Socio-economic cause*: Factors such as unemployment, poverty and relative deprivation often result in communal tensions. In such a society, there is always competition between various communities to get a share of the available resources. Thus, secular issues, such as land disputes, often turn into communal incidents.
3. *Political factor*: Power struggle and competitive politics, without any ideological basis, often result in communal politics. Political groups appease various ethnic, religious and cultural groups to gain their votes. Even various political groups are formed on religious lines. These groups promise to provide various opportunities to particular communities against others.

4. *Spread of rumours and distorted news*: Especially in the recent times when most news gets circulated on social media, there is a huge scope for the spread of fake news, which may result in communal violence. Before it can be understood and brought under control by the appropriate authority, the news spreads and people get violent.
5. *Fundamentalist tendencies*: Religious leaders from various communities attempt to propagate their religious beliefs in a way that can potentially fuel communal tensions. Apart from this, based on the above teachings, people indulge in religious-based conversions, further leading to communal issues.

4 Consequences of Communalism

Communalism has the potential to promote enmity and hatred between communities. Many external agents are responsible for the same in order to fulfil their personal interests. Some of the direct and indirect consequences of communalism are pointed out below:

1. *Communal violence*: One of the most direct consequences of communalism is communal violence. India has been witness to various communal riots, beginning with the Partition of India in 1947. Apart from this, there were other communal riots too, including the Babri Masjid demolition of 1992 and Assam communal violence of 2012.
2. *Law and order issue*: Due to communal issues, breakdown of law and order occurs not only at the point of incident, but it spreads to other parts of the country as well. There are losses of human lives as well as damage to public property.

   Moreover, there is a mass exodus from the region of communal violence, which also disturbs the normal lives of people.
3. *Setback to constitutional goals*: As communal incidents occur, there is further setbacks to the progress of the constitutional goals of secularism and religious freedom.
4. *Threat to unity and integrity*: Communal groups sometimes attempt to play with the integrity of the nation as they fight for secession from the mainland. Apart from this, communalism causes hatred and division among various communities, thus impacting the unity among the people of the nation.
5. *Economic loss*: The damage to economic infrastructure causes huge economic loss to the particular region. Moreover, investors may shy away from investing in such disturbed and communally-sensitive regions, further causing economic backwardness.

   As per a report by the *Institute for Economics and Peace (IEP)*, in 2017, India had to suffer an economic loss of around \$800 billion or ~9% of GDP due to violence.
6. *Communalisation of politics*: There have been various reports about political groups seeking votes on communal lines. In this regard, the Honourable Supreme Court in *Abhiram Singh case, 2017,* held that appeals to voters cannot be made on the grounds of religion, caste, race, community or language.

Landmark Judgements

In the Abhiram Singh v. C.D. Commachen case (2017), the Honourable Supreme Court held that electoral appeals made on the basis of religion, caste, race, community, or language violate Section 123(3) of the Representation of the People Act, 1951. The Court clarified that such appeals constitute a "corrupt practice" and are therefore prohibited. This landmark 4:3 majority judgment reaffirmed the secular character of Indian elections and emphasized that the relationship between the voter and the candidate should be free from identity-based appeals.

5 Transformation: Religiosity to Communalism

Religiosity means the degree to which individuals commit themselves to religious beliefs, values, principles, and activities. Sociologists often use the term 'religiosity' to understand the importance people attach to religion and how far their behaviour gets influenced by religion. Many people satisfy their spiritual requirements by involving themselves in religious activities. Also, for many people, religion provides a sense of identity.

Communalism, on the other hand, has a negative connotation. It is an ideology that promotes the principle of superiority of one religion over another and considers people from other religions as antagonists. It generates social disharmony among various communities and often turns into violence. Communalism is promoted by groups to fulfil their personal interests or ambitions by creating division between communities.

Post-independence, there have been instances when religiosity has transformed into communalism. Independent India witnessed uneven development, poverty and unemployment in the initial years. Some communities could get more share than others. This could potentially create rivalries between communities. Those communities, which felt relatively deprived, encouraged communal feelings in order to gain political support from their respective community members. With economic backwardness, people were vulnerable to political manipulation. In some cases, India witnessed communal polarisation and, ultimately, communal riots.

Communal Incidents in India

1. Partition of India-1947
2. Anti-Sikh Riots-1984
3. Babri Masjid Demolition-1992
4. Godhra Riots-2002
5. Assam Violence-2012
6. Muzaffarnagar Riots-2013

6 Combating Communalism and Promoting Harmony

Communalism is one of the major threats to the integrity and internal security of India. It is essential that active steps be taken to combat communal mindset and communalism.

First among such steps is the use of education to reduce orthodoxy and obscurantism in society. Quality education helps promote rationality and humanism in individuals. It is no one's argument that educated individuals do not harbour a communal mindset. Yet, morally sound education helps individuals develop their own moral compass and makes them less susceptible to any absolutist religious notions.

Secondly, as discussed above, socio-economic inequality and a relative feeling of deprivation may promote feelings of communal hatred and jealousy. Equitable development and fair resource allocation are essential in multi-cultural and multi-ethnic societies like India. To achieve such goals, the **Prime Minister's New 15 Point Programme** for the Welfare of Minority Communities is very relevant as it has measures to promote the overall empowerment of minority communities.

For the educational empowerment of minority communities, scholarship schemes, the Maulana Azad National Fellowship scheme for promoting higher education, and the Naya Savera scheme to encourage public sector employment among minority communities are run by the Ministry of Minority Affairs, Government of India.

Under the 15-Point Programme, there is also special emphasis on skill development and economic empowerment of minority communities. The *Seekho aur Kamao* (Earn and Learn) scheme aims to suitably skill minority communities for self-employment. *Upgrading the Skill and Training in Traditional Arts/Crafts for Development (USTTAD)* scheme has been launched to create market linkages for minority community craftsmen and culinary experts through various exhibitions and *hunar haats*. The scheme also helps such craftsmen adapt their product/skill for demands of the modern consumer. The scheme provides livelihoods to traditional arts and craftsmen while keeping India's rich heritage alive. In addition, the *Garib Nawaz Employment Training Programme* is specifically targeted towards up-skilling and re-skilling minority community youth.

Apart from these schemes, there is an institutional mechanism for addressing minority community grievances in the form of the **National Commission for Minorities.** The Commission has been constituted under the National Commission for Minorities Act, 1992. The Act recognises Muslim, Buddhist, Sikh, Parsis and Jains as minority communities. There are also State Minority Commissions that safeguard and protect the interests of minority communities as stipulated in the Constitution. Aggrieved individuals can approach the Commission with their pleas and representation.

Recent experiences suggest that social media can have a very negative impact on social harmony. Social media posts and content are circulated without much fact-checking. The communal violence in Haryana (Nuh district) is a case in point where the State Administration and the National Commission for Minorities have acknowledged the role of social media in inciting communal clashes. Rumour mongering, threats and religious incitement were in circulation days before violence erupted during a religious procession. A meaningful check on social media in keeping with government guidelines is essential for maintaining communal harmony in the current day and age.

The Ministry of Home Affairs (MHA) *Guidelines on Communal Harmony* provides detailed preventive, administrative and rehabilitative steps to be taken to maintain communal harmony. As per the Seventh Schedule of the Indian Constitution, Public Order and Police are state subjects so these guidelines provide a valuable framework for the states. Following are the main steps to be taken to promote communal harmony and contain damage in the event of communal clashes:

- District administration to maintain the demographic profile of the district and a database of communally sensitive locations, institutions and religious events/processions. Administration should maintain good contact with civilians and community leaders in such areas and visit such locations even during periods of normalcy.
- Proper enforcement of the Places of Worship Act, 1991 and the Religious Institutions (Prevention of Misuse) Act, 1988 so that sanctity of religious institutions is maintained.
- Regular gathering of intelligence regarding local conditions.
- Maintaining a watch on communally oriented organisations that have a vested interest in disturbing communal harmony.
- Formation of Peace committees and such other informal groups so as to maintain good communication among communities.
- Preparation of SoPs, Crisis Management Plans in hyper communal sensitive areas.
- Effective law enforcement and prosecution of miscreants in cases of communal violence.
- Media and social media management so that factually accurate and unbiased news is circulated among the communities.
- Meaningful relief and rehabilitation of communal violence victims, if any, is absolutely essential for promoting healing and recovery among the impacted communities. In this regard, The Communal Violence (Prevention, Control and Rehabilitation of Victims) Bill, 2005 may be considered after building adequate political consensus.

With such long-term and short-term measures, communal harmony can be encouraged and nourished in the Indian society.

6.1 Secularism as an Antidote to Communalism

As highlighted in the Preamble, India has embraced secularism as one of its stated goals. Indian secularism is different from the Western model in the sense that India follows the principle of equidistance from all religions instead of complete state-religion separation. Practice of secularism and balanced socio-economic growth is essential for building cooperation and understanding among all communities so that national interests take precedence over any group interests or identities. As envisaged by the Indian model of secularism, respect for the cultural traditions and ways of life of all religions is essential. These practices must coexist within the wider framework of national integrity and positive patriotism. This is not just essential for internal security but also to maintain India's soft power as the world's largest multi-religious, multi-ethnic democracy.

Additional Readings

1. B. Chandra, Communalism in Modern India. Har-Anand Publication Pvt Ltd, Third Revised Edition 2009.
2. Unit 11: Communalism, IGNOU Publication.
3. UNIT 12: Communalism, IGNOU Publication.
4. M. Parthasarathy, What has the SC said about caste and communal appeals in elections?
5. J.C. Mathew, Study puts economic impact of violence in India at $1.19 trillion, *Business Today*.
6. Babri Masjid Demolition: A Timeline of The Ram Janmabhoomi Dispute Case, *Outlook*.

Previous Years' Questions

1. Distinguish between religiousness/religiosity and communalism giving one example of how the former has got transformed into the latter in independent India. (2017)
2. 'Communalism arises either due to power struggle or relative deprivation'. Argue by giving suitable illustrations. (2018)
3. Discuss the impact of post-liberal economy on ethnic identity and communalism. (2023)

9 Regionalism

1 Concept of Region and Regionalism

A region can be described as a geographical area with common features such as soil, vegetation, natural resources, agriculture, etc. As a result of these common geographical features, the inhabitants of the region lead a similar life with common culture, economic, political and social values. In the long term, they develop a sense of oneness among themselves as they share common life conditions. While regionalism can be understood as an ideology or feeling among the local populace residing in a particular geographical area characterised by a unique language, culture, etc. They believe that they are the 'sons of the soil', and hence, they have the first right over the resources and opportunities that exist on their land. Such feelings arise mainly due to the continuous neglect of a particular region or because the people of the region have become politically aware and seek to fight against the perceived discrimination. In most cases, such issues are raised in order to achieve some political gains, but not necessarily.

Insight Box

'Sons of the Soil' Doctrine

The 'Sons of the Soil', also known as *Bhumiputra Movement*, doctrine holds that the state primarily belongs to the local and main linguistic group that inhabits it. They are the original children of the land. Hence, they have the first right over any benefits or opportunities available on their land. In other words, people who have migrated or even who have lived in the city for a longer period of time must not receive the 'Sons of the Soil' benefits. Thus, 'sons of the Soil' want preferential treatment in opportunities *vis-a-vis* employment, educational quotas, government services or natural resources.

2 Forms of Regionalism in India

India is a heterogenous society with people belonging to diverse religions, regions, languages, castes and races. This has led to the rise of various political alliances supporting one or more groups. Sometimes, the activity of these groups results in a virulent form of regionalism in India.

In India, it has assumed various forms, and its manifestation can be seen in more than one way. On the political front, it has assumed the following four forms:

1. Secession from the Indian Union
2. Demand for separate statehood
3. Demand for full-fledged statehood, and
4. Inter-State disputes

Secession from the Indian Union is the most extreme form of regionalism. One of the most serious issues with which India had to contend was the Tamil separatist movement. Led by the *Dravida Munnetra Kazagham* (DMK), the movement advocated the secession of Tamil Nadu from the Indian Union and the creation of an independent and sovereign Dravidasthan. Apart from this, there had been instances when the Akali Dal in Punjab, Mizos and Nagas in northeast India, and the supporters of Khalistan movements had been demanding secession from India.

Demand for separate statehood has also been a part and parcel of Indian politics. For instance, there had been a demand for separate Harit Pradesh to be carved out of Uttar Pradesh (UP). Earlier, in the 1950s, India witnessed successful mass mobilisation for the creation of the state of Andhra Pradesh.

Apart from this, India has also witnessed demand for the creation of a separate state of Bodoland. Bodos believe that without the creation of a separate state, the protection of land, identity, the development of the economy, culture and language would not be possible. Well, there have been various other demands too regarding a separate state.

In the category of full-fledged statehood, there has been continuous demand from Delhi and Puducherry. These are currently union territories. Whether giving them full-statehood status will be good for our polity or not is a matter that requires elaborate discussions.

Inter-state disputes have been a perennial phenomenon in India. Be it due to water sharing or land boundary issue, disputes between states have even reached the doors of the judiciary for adjudication. Some of the inter-state disputes include:

a. Inter-state disputes over Cauvery water between Karnataka and Tamil Nadu.
b. Distribution of water of Krishna River among Maharashtra, Andhra Pradesh and Karnataka.
c. Land boundary dispute between Maharashtra and Karnataka
d. Dispute between Haryana and Punjab with respect to Chandigarh
e. Dispute among the States of Punjab, Haryana, Jammu & Kashmir, Rajasthan and Himachal Pradesh over construction and ownership of dams for the generation of electricity.

Insight Box

Regional Movements in India

1. Creation of Andhra Pradesh in 1953: It was the demand of Potti Sriramulu, a freedom fighter. He died in 1952 after not eating for 52 days in support of a Telugu-speaking state. His death forced Jawahar Lal Nehru to agree to the various demands from other parts of the country with similar demands.
2. Creation of new states- Manipur, Tripura and Meghalaya - as per North-eastern States Reorganisation Act, 1971.
3. Movements for the creation of three new states (created in 2000)-Chhattisgarh out of Madhya Pradesh, Jharkhand out of Bihar and Uttarakhand out of Uttar Pradesh.
4. Creation of Telangana state out of Andhra Pradesh in 2014.

Insight Box

Dimensions of Regionalism in India

After independence, regionalism has assumed three important forms in India, namely, supra-state regionalism, inter-state regionalism and intra-state regionalism.

Supra-state regionalism is an expression of group identity of several states (federation units) which join hands to take a unified stand on issue of mutual interest *vis-a-vis* another group of States or even the Union of India. The best example is provided by the case of the *South versus North* on the language issue.

The second form of regionalism is co-terminous with state boundaries and involves juxtaposing of one or more states' identities against another in certain issues that clash with the interest of one another. For example, border disputes, disputes over sharing of river waters and over the location of 'central projects'.

In case of intra-state regionalism, a part of a state develops the quest for self-identity and self-development positively, and negatively, it reflects a psyche of deprivation or exploitation in relation to the other parts of the same state. This phenomenon, also called sub-regionalism, is directed against the state governments rather than the Union of India. Such demands as the creation of new and separate political and administrative units within the existing federal structure and of some regions within a state for equitable treatment come under this category.

3 Factors Responsible for Regionalism in India

In India, several factors are responsible for generating and strengthening the feeling of regionalism among various sections of people. Some of them are:

1. Firstly, India is a vast country with uneven progress. Different regions of the nation are at different stages of economic and political development. It is argued that continuous neglect of an area or region by the central political leadership and concentration of authority has given rise to demand for decentralisation of authority and even bifurcation of states. It is also associated with the promotion of 'sons of soil' theory' to advance the interests of the neglected.
2. With time, there has been increased awareness among the people of backward regions. It may be due to the spread of better transport systems and Information & Communication Technology (ICT). Today, people realise the status of their relative deprivation. They compare the progress of their regions with that of the developed ones. They raise their voice if they are neglected by the government in any respect, be it the allocation of grants or funds.

   For example, the Gorkha Nationalist Liberation Forum (GNLF) started its movement in the Darjeeling. In the view of the GNLF, Darjeeling was the most underdeveloped region in comparison to the southern part of West Bengal. Such feelings are then translated into actions by the community leaders within the region according to their interests and ideological inclinations.
3. Political experts believe that India also witnessed a situation in her political journey in which the central leadership became relatively weaker. This gave the regional leaders opportunity to fulfil their political aspirations by encouraging regional tendencies. As a result, one can see the emergence of several regional parties in various states with specific interests.
4. The idea of 'nation-state' is yet to penetrate deeply into the minds of the people of India. There is lack of feeling of oneness among people. People identify themselves mainly with their language, caste and region. There is a feeling that their interests differ from others, and sometimes, even antagonistic to others. Not surprisingly, India has witnessed several demands for the creation of separate states based on language. This further reinforces the feeling of regionalism.
5. In the North-East regions, the tribal factor gave rise to regionalism. In these regions, several tribes inhabit, each having their own language, culture and tradition. For a long time, they have been isolated from mainstream society and national life. They have been making efforts to maintain their sub-culture and aspire for a greater degree of self-government.
6. In the North-West, religious factors were responsible for the rise of regionalism. Before independence, it resulted in the creation of two nation-states. While, after independence, the region witnessed demand for Sikh home land, to be called Khalistan.
7. Geography-related factors, in combination with political tussles, have also been responsible for the rise of regionalism in India. There have also been instances of inter-states disputes regarding sharing of resources such as land and water. Such issues could be witnessed among Maharashtra-Karnataka, Tamil Nadu-Kerala, etc.

8. Last but not least, subject experts say that increasing interference by the central government in the affairs of the state has also resulted in the growth of regionalism. Earlier, there have been instances when states protested against the misuse of Article 356 of the Constitution of India.

   Well, whatever the cause of regionalism, it must be curbed if it threatens the national unity of integrity of a nation. On the other hand, regionalism can also a positive impact if people with regional feelings are able to balance their regional interests without affecting the interests of other regions or nations.

3.1 Role of Regional Political Parties

Over the years, the Indian political system has witnessed the rise of a large number of regional political groups. The regional groups operate mainly in a limited geographical region and aspire to fulfil mainly the local interests of the particular region. Some states where regional parties are active include Assam, Tamil Nadu, Telangana and Maharashtra, among others.

Even though the regional parties operate in a limited geographical region, they have played an influential role in the national political arena as well. The representatives of regional parties raise their local issues in Parliament. They also try to influence the policies of the national government to promote their own interests.

Insight Box

Reasons for the Rise of Regional Political Parties

1. Indian society is known for its diversity of culture, way of life and also each region has unique issues. It might be difficult for a national party to give adequate recognition to the problems of all regions. As a result, it becomes necessity for the people to form regional parties to look after the needs of specific groups.
2. Some regions are economically backward compared to others. People there feel that they have not been given enough attention in terms of allocation of resources. Thus, they develop ill-feelings towards the centre. This also encourages rise of regional parties.
3. Some regions feel that there has been undue increase in central power. In order to protest against this, some regions have formed their own regional parties.
4. Certain regions in India, for their historical reasons, aspire to preserve their specific traditional culture, practices and identity. In order to maintain such identity, regional parties have come up. This is most relevant in case of North-East India.

In fact, many regional parties could form governments on their own at the state level and execute their own policies and programmes. Some of the important regional parties to have formed governments are Assam Gana Parishad in Assam, DMK and AIDMK in Tamil Nadu, Indian National Lok Dal (INLD) in Haryana, and the National Conference in Jammu and Kashmir, among others.

Apart from this, the regional parties have also contributed to imparting political knowledge to the people of their regions by shifting their attention to various issues of national importance.

Some of the regional parties were partners in the coalition governments formed in several states, particularly after the general elections in 1967 in India. In recent times, one has seen such a situation in Bihar and Maharashtra, among others. At the centre too, the regional parties have played a critical role in forming governments.

The above discussions show how regional parties could play a positive role in strengthening and deepening democratic roots in India. However, when some of them, in order to provide support to the local groups, act antagonistic to the interests of 'outsiders', it results in a breakdown of constitutional principles.

Insight Box

Formation of Jharkhand

The call for the creation of the independent state of Jharkhand illustrates the complexities of regional politics in India. This demand was made by the Jharkhand Mukti Morcha and spanned a period of nearly fifteen years. Various political parties actively participated in this struggle. The region in question is abundant in valuable minerals such as iron ore, coal, copper ore, mica, bauxite, graphite, limestone, and uranium. Jharkhand officially became a state on 15 November 2000, coinciding with the birth anniversary of Birsa Munda, a tribal hero highly respected in the area. Initially comprising 18 districts of Bihar, the state currently consists of 24 districts.

The inspiration behind the demand for a separate state stemmed from the strong identity of being a Jharkhandi, as exemplified by Birsa Munda. The people of Jharkhand argued that they belonged to socially disadvantaged groups and were deprived of essential resources. This disparity arose because political leaders in Bihar allocated the resources to particular areas, leaving other regions marginalised. The creation of Jharkhand as a state was also motivated by the desire to preserve and celebrate its unique tribal cultural heritage.

4 Consequences of Regionalism in India

It is important to note that regionalism should not always be seen from one perspective. In general, one tends to perceive regionalism in a negative light. However, it is not so. There are both the positive and negative aspects of regionalism in India. Let's highlight the positive aspects first.

4.1 Positive Consequences of Regionalism

1. As we have discussed above, important regional economic and political matters are taken by the local leaders to the highest political level for consideration. This results in increased *political awareness* among the local people. It also helps in *nation-building* if the demands of the regions are accommodated by the political system of the country.
2. In a diverse set-up like India, the central authority may not be able to promote the local language, culture, religious practice, etc., on an equal basis. There is scope for imbalanced progress in these aspects. Here, regional leaders play a crucial role in promoting local practices. This also instills confidence among local people as they appreciate their historical belonging. It also provides *psychological satisfaction* for them.
3. It is also true that promoting regional identity has not necessarily led to opposition from others. Regional identity and national identity can go hand in hand. Focussing on the region has resulted in a deepening of the democratic roots in India's governance. In India, we can see how democracy has penetrated to the grassroots level through the panchayati raj system. In other words, it has resulted in *democratic decentralisation*.
4. Apart from this, a significant chunk of the population in India belongs to the *Adivasi community*. The community members still live in a traditional way and follow unique practices with respect to land management, marriage process and political participation, among others. The common laws of the land might not accommodate their interests. Hence, regional leaders have made an effort to provide them with a different administrative set-up. In this regard, one can see the constitution of the Tribal Autonomous District Council (TADC), the Tribal Advisory Council (TAC) and similar such institutions.
5. If the demand for statehood or regional autonomy is granted, it gives *self-determination* to the people of the region and they feel empowered and satisfied. It is to be noted that internal self-determination of community, whether linguistic, regional, religious, or any combination, has remained the predominant form in which regionalism has expressed itself in India.

4.2 Negative Consequences of Regionalism

1. Firstly, virulent forms of regionalism are seen as going against the unity and integrity of the nation. Sometimes, regionalistic and insurgent groups propagate the feelings of regionalism against the mainstream politico-administrative setup of the country. It can also pose internal security challenges for the country.
2. It has also been observed that regional leaders engage in vote bank politics in order to fulfil their personal ambitions. This has the potential to affect healthy democratic principles. In order to gain votes, caste and religious equations are employed. As a result, it causes friction in society among various members.

3. Moreover, regionalistic jingoism creates a law and order problem too. There have been instances when people from a state have been targeted in Tamil Nadu, Assam, etc. Apart from this, such steps by regional leaders also violate the constitutional rights of citizens to move freely across any part of the country.
4. Regionalism has also affected the international diplomacy of India. For instance, the Tamil Nadu regional leaders protested against the Prime Minister of India's decision to attend the Commonwealth Heads of Government Meeting (CHOGM) in Sri Lanka. This had the potential to adversely affect India's relations with Sri Lanka. Similarly, West Bengal did not agree to the Land Boundary Agreement (LBA) between India and Bangladesh.
5. Last but not least, regionalism reaches its extreme form when there is a demand for a separate nation. India has witnessed such a situation when there have been demands for a separate nation to be called Dravida Nadu, *Nagalim*.

5 Regionalism and Nationalism

As we have already discussed above, 'regionalism' is a feeling or ideology among the local population residing in a particular geographical space characterised by a unique language, culture, etc. They believe that being 'sons of the soil', every opportunity in their land must be given to them first and not to the outsiders. Thus, in regionalism, the focus is on the local level.

While 'nationalism' is the feeling of oneness among citizens residing in a geographical territory, it is a belief or political ideology in which an individual identifies himself with the nation. Also, there is an unsaid understanding and emotional attachment among the citizens and they agree to live under one political system. Benedict Anderson defines 'A nation as an imagined political community and imagined as both inherently limited and sovereign. It is imagined because the members of even the smallest nations will never know most of their fellow members, meet them, or even hear of them, yet in the minds of each lives on image of their community'.

It is understood that until there is a regional imbalance in terms of development and interference from the central political set-up, the feeling of regionalism will remain alive. This is because regionalism is the manifestation of those neglected socio-political elements that fail to find expression in mainstream politics and culture. However, it must be made clear at the beginning that regionalism and nationalism are *not necessarily contradictory*.

If regionalism is understood as people taking pride in their language and culture, it does not affect our national unity and sense of nationalism. Also, if people in a particular region aspire for greater focus from central authorities in terms of, say, devolution of funds, political self-determination, economic development of

Debate Corner

Does the rise of regionalism in India reinforce cooperative federalism by empowering states, or does it undermine national unity by promoting parochial interests?

their region, promotion of their language, etc., it can ultimately lead to overall national development as well.

The issue with respect to regionalism arises when it takes a militant and aggressive turn. In such cases, people in the region are made to feel that their interests are not in consonance with the interests of other regions or even the nation. They develop an ill-feeling towards people from other regions.

In its mild form, there is an anti-migrant tendency among people in the particular region. This violates the fundamental rights of migrants as provided by the Constitution of India. In its extreme form, as discussed above, there is a demand for secession from the Indian nation. This goes against the idea of national unity and sense of nationalism.

6 Measures to Promote National Unity and Integrity

As we discussed above, regionalism in itself might not be threatening to national unity and integrity. Considering the diversity of India, some scholars argue that regionalism is a natural consequence. This is because every region is so unique that any central intervention might not be enough for equitable development. Hence, regional leaders may have to put forth their case.

Nonetheless, India has been witness to the fact that in the name of regionalism, several activities have taken place that go against the principle of nationalism. Thus, time and again, it is necessary that India adopt steps that can promote national unity and that fissiparous tendencies are nipped in the bud.

1. First, as far as possible, it is of utmost importance to develop all regions equally. Regional imbalance is an important cause of ill-feeling. People from neglected and less developed regions must be made to feel that they are part of the national mainstream.
2. Central leadership needs to avoid intervention in state and regional matters unless it threatens national interests. As far as possible, regional and state leaders need to be given space so that they can run administration on their own. In other words, democratic decentralisation needs to be promoted in its true sense.
3. Time and again, it is necessary that constitutional principles are adhered to and not misused or violated. The constitutional principles are to be followed in true letter and spirit by both the regional and central leaders. The regional leaders need to follow this whenever there is a question of migrants. While the central leaders need to consider this whenever there is a question over the resolution of inter-state disputes and imposition of the president's rule, etc.
4. In order to ensure that regionalistic activities do not cross constitutional boundaries, law and order enforcement machinery needs to be strengthened.
5. A national policy can be thought of in matters of creating new states or changing names of places. In the absence of any concrete policy, it often becomes a political question rather than an administrative necessity. To satisfy the political interests of a region or a section of people, such decisions are made in haste. A policy in this regard would act as a source of guidance to deal with such matters.

6. Political education and the political empowerment of common citizens can go a long way towards promoting unity and integrity. Having the right political education would make sure that common people do not fall into the trap of 'vote-bank politics' in the name of caste and/or religion. They would know that vote-bank politics have a short-shelf life and might not be in the interest of the nation in the long term. The right mission and vision for development and pure intention towards people's welfare are necessary for political goals.
7. It is also important to have timely and periodic meetings of the National Integration Council (NIC). It was established in 1962 with the purpose of addressing the issues of communalism, casteism, regionalism, linguism, and narrow-mindedness. The objective was to explore methods to combat these problems and formulate clear conclusions to guide the country forward.

   NIC members include cabinet ministers and chief ministers of states, among others. Thus, it can be an effective platform to discuss and promote national integration.
8. Last but not least, developmental activities need to be in consultation and co-ordination with the local people. At the end of the day, development is for the people. It cannot be done at the expense of people. Specifically whenever there is a question of land acquisition in the tribal regions, the authority should act with more sensitivity.

Insight Box

National Integration under *Ek Bharat Shreshtha Bharat*

The Government of India has introduced a program called *Ek Bharat Shreshtha Bharat* (EBSB) with the aim of promoting national integration. This initiative encourages coordinated mutual engagement among States, Union Territories, Central Ministries, Educational Institutions, and the general public through various channels such as linguistic, literary, cultural, sports, tourism, and other forms of people-to-people exchanges. A Group of Ministers headed by Minister of Human Resource Development periodically reviews the steps taken by the States/UTs and concerned Ministries/Departments to bridge the cultural gap in the country and enhance interaction between people living in different States.

Additional Readings

1. Salma Abdul Sattar, Regionalism: A Great Threat to National Unity of India. *The Indian Journal of Political Science*.
2. R.L. Hardgrave, Jr., *The DMK and the Politics of Tamil Nationalism.* (Pacific Affairs, University of British Columbia).

3. P. Amrutkar, *The Backwardness and Demand for a Statehood of Vidarbha.* (Indian Political Science Association).
4. S. Kumar, *Regionalism vs Nationalism – In India.* (Alva's College, Moodbidri, Karnataka).
5. HRD Ministry has taken several initiatives to promote National Integration under Ek Bharat Shrestha Bharat, PIB, dated 31 December 2018.
6. S.C. Hazary, *Politics of Regionalism: Implications for Political Development in India* (Indian Political Science Association).

Previous Years' Questions

1. 'Growing feeling of regionalism is an important factor in generation of demand for a separate State.' Discuss. (2013)
2. What is the basis of regionalism? Is it that unequal distribution of benefits of development on regional basis eventually promotes regionalism? Substantiate your answer. (2016)
3. Do you agree that regionalism in India appears to be a consequence of rising cultural assertiveness? Argue. (2020)

UPSC CSE 2024

1. What is regional disparity? How does it differ from diversity? How serious is the issue of regional disparity in India? (250 words | 15 Marks)

Model Answer

Regional disparity refers to the unequal distribution of resources, economic opportunities and development outcomes across different geographical regions. For example: Development in Maharashtra and Gujarat compared to the relatively underdeveloped regions of Eastern India.

In contrast, *regional diversity* reflects natural variations in language, culture and traditions, geography, which enrich a nation's pluralism. For example: Diversity in terms of language, food habits, marriage rituals among the North Eastern states.

Difference between Regional Disparity and Diversity:

Aspect	Regional Disparity	Regional Diversity
Nature	Unequal development	Natural, social and cultural variation
Effect	Causes imbalance and exclusion	Strengthens pluralism and identity
Policy Approach	Needs redressal and redistribution	Needs recognition and preservation

Impact of Regional Disparities in India : A Serious Concern

1. **Socio-Economic Inequities:** Persistent disparity widens the gap in living standards, access to education, healthcare and employment, undermining the goals of inclusive growth.
2. **Out-Migration and Urban Pressure:** Economic migration from underdeveloped regions like Bihar and eastern UP to industrial hubs like Delhi and Mumbai strains urban infrastructure and leads to informal settlements.
3. **Social Unrest and Identity Movements:** Regional imbalances fuel alienation and identity-based demands for autonomy or statehood (e.g., Gorkhaland), sometimes triggering violent agitations.
4. **Governance Challenges:** Disparities undermine cooperative federalism, creating tensions in resource sharing, fiscal transfers and centre-state relations. Eg Inter-state water disputes.
5. **National Security Concerns:**
   Backward and neglected regions - such as parts of central India and North-East - often become breeding grounds for extremism (e.g, Left-Wing Extremism).

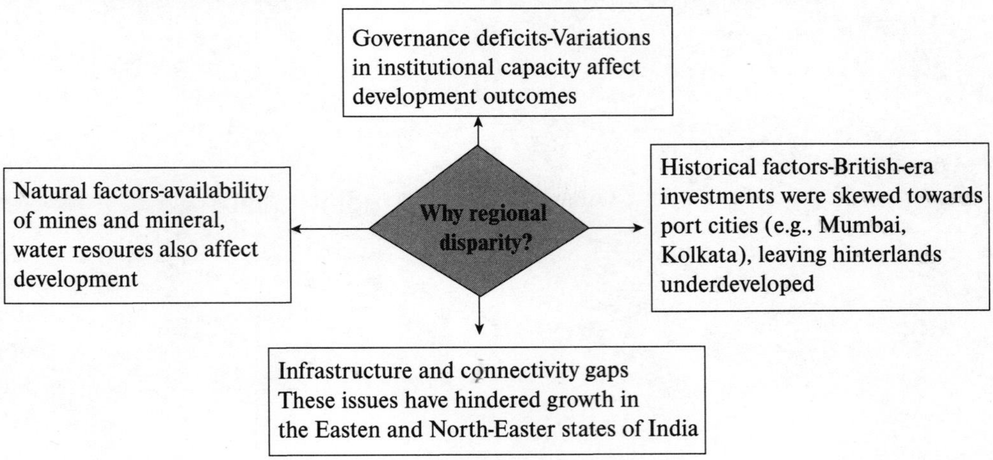

How can we bridge the disparity?

1. **Balanced Regional Planning:** Strengthen institutions like NITI Aayog to drive region-specific development tailored to local needs.
2. **Revamping Fiscal Transfers:** Ensure greater equity in resource allocation through performance-based grants and enhanced devolution to backward regions under the Finance Commission.
3. **Boosting Infrastructure and Connectivity:** Prioritise roads, rail and digital infrastructure in lagging areas to spur private investment and connectivity.

4. **Skill Development and Employment Generation:** Align Skill India with local industry to create jobs and curb out-migration.
5. **Strengthening Local Governance:** Provide financial and functional autonomy to PRIs and urban local bodies for grassroots development.
6. **Leveraging Technology and Innovation:** Use GIS mapping, remote sensing, and data analytics to track regional gaps and monitor policy implementation.

Bridging regional disparity is essential for national unity, economic stability, and the realisation of constitutional goal as highlighted in Article 38 (2) - the state shall strive to minimise inequalities in income, status, facilities and opportunities.

10 Secularism

1 Concept of Secularism

Secularism is understood as a political and legal system whose basic function is to establish a certain distance between state and religion, though there are disagreements about defining the term more precisely.

Secularism rests on two major principles, namely, *equality of respect and freedom of conscience*. A democratic state provides equal respect and dignity to all its citizens. Scholars believe that in order to realise this, there should be a *separation of religion and state* and the *state's neutrality towards religious and secular movements of thought*. This is because fusion between the state and religious conceptions of the world would make others, who do not espouse the state's official doctrine, as second-class citizens.

The other principle is with respect to protecting the freedom of conscience of its citizens. The state need not dictate individuals with respect to the conception of good. Rather, the secular state shall protect and respect their freedom of conscience or moral autonomy, that is, their right to conduct their lives in light of their own choices.

Insight Box

A secular state is one that ensures the freedom of religion for both individuals and organisations. It treats every individual as a citizen regardless of their religious beliefs, without any constitutional affiliation to a specific religion. Additionally, a secular state does not aim to promote or interfere with any religion.

Upon closer analysis, it becomes apparent that the concept of a secular state encompasses three distinct yet interconnected sets of relationships involving the state, religion, and the individual. These three sets of relations are:

1. religion and the individual (freedom of religion),
2. the state and the individual (citizenship), and
3. the state and religion (separation of state and religion).

One way to conceptualise this idea is to visualise a triangle, where the two angles at the base symbolise religion and the state, and the apex represents the individual. The sides and base of the triangle symbolise the three sets of relationships involving the state, religion, and the individual.

In the Indian context, the term 'secular' is mentioned in the Constitution. However, critics argue that there are certain principles in the Constitution itself that go against the idea of secularism. Here, we need to analyse it properly to answer the following question:

How far can we be called a 'secular state'?

Let's analyse the Indian Constitution in relation to the three components of this conception of secular state: freedom of religion, citizenship, and the separation of state and religion.

1.1 Freedom of Religion

The Constitution of India declares that every person enjoys the fundamental right to not only hold their personal religious beliefs (freedom of conscience) but also manifest his beliefs through actions as prescribed by his religion and also to propagate its tenets among others (right to profess, practise and propagate religion).

However, it is important to note that this right is not absolute in nature. The exercise of this right is, however, 'subject to public order, morality and health'. Thus, if one believes that human sacrifices are an integral part of their religious worship, the government has a right to ban such practices.

Article 25(2) of the Indian Constitution imposes certain restrictions by granting the State the authority to regulate secular activities related to religion. It also allows the State to legislate social reforms and compel Hindu religious institutions of public nature to be accessible to all classes and sections of Hindus.

1.2 Citizenship

This is the second component of being a secular state. It considers a citizen, i.e. an individual, as a basic unit. The state assigns duties and responsibilities to individuals, and in return, it ensures rights and privileges for them. The combination of these individual-state relationships defines the concept of citizenship.

The Indian Constitution does not have any religious considerations in defining the rights and duties of citizens. It provides equal treatment to all citizens without any consideration for their religion. Article 15(1) specifically says that 'The state shall not discriminate against any citizen on grounds only of religion, race, caste, sex, place of birth or any of them.'

Scholars, however, argue that the existence of different personal laws contradicts the principle of non-discrimination by the State contained in Article 15(1). They believe that only when there is a Uniform Civil Code (UCC), one can say that India fulfils the fundamental principle of the secular state.

1.3 Separation of State and Religion

This principle preserves the integrity of the other two relationships, i.e. freedom of religion and citizenship. If this principle is not followed in the true spirit, it opens the door for the state to interfere in an individual's religious liberty. It can also result in state discrimination if the individual happens to dissent from the official creed.

It is clear that India does not have a very concrete and compartmentalised separation of state and religion. There are many areas in which state intervention in religious matters is permitted by the Constitution itself, e.g. the financial administration of temples and *maths*.

The chief reason for the intervention is that religions in India cover various aspects of the life of its adherents from birth to death. In this scenario, there is an urge for effective social and religious reform in present-day India and it can only be satisfied by state action.

Having discussed this, it is also important to note that there are, however, other aspects of the principle of separation of state and religion that are supported by the Indian Constitution:

1. There is no provision regarding an official state religion; also, no official recognition is given to the religion of the majority, unlike some nations across the world.
2. There can be no religious instruction in state schools.
3. There can be no taxes to support any particular religion.

It is to be noted here that the separation of religion and state is a necessary but not sufficient ingredient of a secular state. A secular state should adhere to principles and objectives that are derived, at least in part, from non-religious sources. These objectives should encompass peace, religious freedom, and protection from religious-based oppression, discrimination, and exclusion. Additionally, they should promote inter-religious and intra-religious equality.

1.4 Brief Evaluation

If one evaluates the Indian Constitution strictly based on the above three relationships, there will be much to criticise considering the limitations and exceptions enshrined in the Constitution. However, if one does this, one is sure to miss the dynamics of the Indian situation. All aspects of contemporary Indian life – political, economic, social, and religious – are in a process of rapid change. India needs several social changes associated with religion to provide its citizens with the constitutional necessity of the right to equality.

Insight Box

Characteristics of a Secular State

1. Principle of Liberty: This principle mandates that the State allows the practice of any religion within the boundaries defined by certain fundamental rights that the State is obligated to safeguard.
2. Principle of Equality: This principle dictates that the State should not favor one religion over another. It ensures equal treatment of all religions without any bias.
3. Principle of Neutrality: This principle emphasises that the State should not show favoritism towards religious beliefs or non-religious perspectives. It implies that the State refrains from involvement in religious affairs or organisations, maintaining a neutral stance.

Insight Box

Secularism and Indian Constitution

The word 'secular' was not placed in the Indian Constitution when it was promulgated on 1 January 1950. The word was introduced in the Preamble to the Indian Constitution by the 42nd Amendment which came into effect on 3 January 1977. Before the Amendment, India was described in the Preamble to the Constitution as a 'Sovereign Democratic Republic'. After the Amendment, it was described as a 'Sovereign Socialist Secular Democratic Republic'. No Article of the Constitution, however, was required to be amended because of the amendment in the Preamble. This was because, as observed by Justice Ahmadi in the case of *S.R. Bommai vs Union of India*, the Amendment merely made explicit what was already implicit in the provisions of the Constitution.

2 Western Model of Secularism

The Western model of secularism is best exemplified by the American model. Whenever it is to be decided if any state is truly secular or not, it is generally done by comparing the prevailing practices in the specific state with those in the American state. However, it is to be understood that what is 'truly and absolute secular' is a matter of debate and discussion.

In the western part of the world, separation of state and religion is generally understood as '*mutual exclusion*' of these two institutions. In other words, the State will not interfere in the affairs of religion; religion will not do so in the affairs of the State.

Apart from this, the State cannot provide any kind of aid to a religious institution, even if any secular activity is to be carried out by the religious institution. For instance, the State cannot provide financial support to educational institutions run by religious communities.

In fact, the State is not allowed to obstruct any activities of religious communities, as long as these activities abide by the legal limits set by the country's laws. For example, if a religious institution prohibits women from becoming priests, the State has no choice but to refrain from interference in this matter. Similarly, if the religious organisation decides against allowing some of its members in the sanctum of its temple, the State can do little about it. Thus, in the Western scheme of things, religion is considered to be entirely a private matter, not a matter of state policy or law.

Also, there is no scope for providing community-based rights or minority rights. This model considers freedom and equality in an individualist manner. Liberty is the liberty of individuals. Equality is equality between individuals. Hence, there is minimal or no opportunity for the notion that a community has the freedom to adhere to practices of its own preference. This might be due to the fact that most Western societies are marked by a great deal of religious homogeneity.

Most importantly, the Western model does not believe in the idea of state-supported religious reform. It follows directly from the fact that the State and church share a relationship of mutual exclusion.

3 Indian Model *versus* Western Model of Secularism

Many subject experts emphasise the point that Indian secularism is an imitation of western secularism. However, if we carefully read and understand the Indian model of secularism, we would come to know that it is fundamentally different from the Western model. India has developed its own model in light of the practical realities of Indian society and the level of societal development.

Indian secularism goes beyond mere church-state separation; it places significant emphasis on the concept of inter-religious equality. The Indian interpretation of secularism is unique because it developed within the backdrop of profound religious diversity that existed prior to the introduction of Western modern ideas and nationalism.

Indian secularism holds the view that separation does not necessarily imply strict non-interference, mutual exclusion, or equidistance between the state and religions. Instead, it advocates for a 'policy of principled distance', which involves a flexible approach regarding intervention or abstention. The decision to intervene or abstain depends on the specific context, nature, or current state of religion.

Therefore, Indian secularism vehemently opposes the oppression of Dalits and women within Hinduism, discrimination against women within Indian Islam or Christianity, and potential threats posed by the majority community to the rights of minority religious communities. This fundamental stance marks a significant departure from mainstream Western secularism.

Additionally, Indian secularism emphasises not only the religious freedom of individuals but also the religious freedom of minority communities. Consequently, every individual possesses the right to practice, profess, and propagate the religion of their choice. Along with this, religious minorities also have the right to maintain their own culture and educational institutions. *This is also an important difference.*

Another *important point of difference* is that the Indian model of secularism supports and encourages state-led religious reforms. Thus, the practice of untouchability has been banned by the Indian Constitution. Also, reforming laws were enacted to ban child marriage and promote inter-caste marriage, to name a few.

Debate Corner

Is the Indian model of secularism–where the state maintains principled engagement with all religions–better suited to a diverse society than the Western model of strict separation between religion and state?

3.1 Brief Conclusion

The key feature of Indian secularism is that it is neither theocratic nor has given preference to any majority religion. It engages and disengages as per the requirements of reform. Thus, it engaged with religion negatively when religion sanctioned untouchability. Similarly, religiously sanctioned caste hierarchies were not accepted within Indian secularism. It engaged positively when it felt the need to provide religious minorities the right to establish and maintain their own educational institutions. Through this strategy, the state is trying to promote the values of peace, freedom, and equality.

Many social scientists underline that this unique model of secularism has helped India thrive as the only successful multi-religious democracy in South Asia. All over the world, India is recognised and respected for its successful experiment with secularism.

Points of Distinction	Western Secularism	Indian Secularism
1. Interaction between State and religion	No interaction between the state and religion.	The state interacts with religion to encourage equality, gender justice and social equity.

Points of Distinction	Western Secularism	Indian Secularism
2. Level of State's intervention	The state maintains arm's length distance from all religions, which is the same for all religions. The State does not intervene in religious matters.	The state maintains a 'principled distance' from religions – implying that state intervention varies across various religions. State may intervene in religious matters for the sake of social reforms, e.g. ban on untouchability, sati.
3. Display of religious value in public	Religion and the display of religious values in public are discouraged. Religion is seen as a private matter, e.g. the Burka ban in France.	Recognises the reality of the Indian sub-continent that religion is woven into the fabric of life. Hence, religion is present in public life, e.g. Sikh soldiers are allowed to wear a turban.
4. Suitability	Suited to a mostly homogeneous population in the West.	Suited to the multi-cultural and multi-religious society of Indian sub-continent.

4 Criticisms of Indian Secularism

Indian secularism is not without criticism, though. Some of them are as follows:

1. *Anti-religious*: One of the arguments is that India's secularism is anti-religious. It is also argued that our secularism threatens religious identity. However, this criticism seems to be invalid.

   As we have already seen, Indian secularism promotes religious freedom and equality and protects religious identity rather than threatening it. The Indian Constitution itself promotes such values.

2. *Western import*: Another criticism is that secularism is a Western concept and not suited to Indian conditions. However, this criticism seems shallow in its reasoning. In India, the need for secularism as a practice has been discussed and debated over the years. India has developed its own variant of secularism, considering the presence of various religious communities.

   It is also important to note that secularism has both Western and non-Western origins. In the West, secularism was primarily church-state separation. In countries such as India, the idea of peaceful coexistence among different religious communities has been important.

3. *Minoritism*: Another criticism is that Indian secularism advocates minority rights. Here, it is important to understand that India is a multi-religious society. In a multi-religious society,

some minority community members may lag behind in availing the benefits of development if a helping hand is not provided by the State.

Therefore, establishing separate arrangements for minorities does not entail granting them special treatment. Instead, it signifies treating them with the same respect and dignity that all others receive.

4. *Interventionist*: Some criticise that Indian secularism interferes excessively with the religious freedom of communities. However, this criticism might also not stand the test of time. It is true that Indian secularism rejects non-interference in religion.

   However, Indian secularism intervenes only when some religious practices go against the morality and health of society. Otherwise, Indian secularism follows the concept of principled distance which also allows for non-interference.

5. *Vote bank politics*: Last but not least, critics argue that Indian secularism promotes vote bank politics. Supporters of Indian secularism argue that there is nothing wrong with this if such an act promotes the welfare of minority communities, along with other communities. However, they caution that such a practice should not undermine the interest of the majority communities. Otherwise, this has the potential to create another form of injustice.

5 Challenges to Secularism in India

1. *Communalism*: Undoubtedly, one of the most serious challenges faced by Indian secularism is that of communalism. Sometimes, extreme loyalty to one's religious community easily leads to communal rivalries. Communal rivalries are endemic in India and easily erupt into violent conflict.
2. *Religion and politics*: It has often been seen that political groups represent the interest of a particular religious group as they are organised on communal lines. In order to achieve and safeguard their political interests, few indulge in communal politics.
3. *Customs and traditions*: No doubt, following and adhering to one's customs and traditions should be encouraged. However, issues arise when people follow traditions that might not be compatible with modern practices. They are rigid in their thinking. It often results in unequal treatment of women across various religions. Thus, it hampers the progress of secularism in India.

Debate Corner

Is the blending of religion and politics in India a challenge to the secular character of the State, or does it reflect the democratic accommodation of its religious diversity?

6 Secularism and the Indian Judiciary

Landmark Judgements

The use of the term 'secularism' by the Indian judiciary predates its inclusion in the Constitution. The Supreme Court's first recognition of secularism was in 1962, in the *Sardar Taheruddin Syedna Saheb vs State of Bombay* case, wherein it was explained that Article 25 and Article 26 of the Constitution 'embody the principle of religious toleration... besides, they serve to emphasise the secular nature of Indian democracy, which the founding fathers considered to be the very basis of the Constitution'.

The Indian judiciary, over the years, has played a key role in promoting the secular vision of India. Starting from the *Kesavananda Bharati vs State of Kerala, 1973* case, which has since become 'the bedrock of constitutional interpretation in India', the court actively played an important part in shaping India's secular sensibility. The Supreme Court remarked that the 'Secular character of the Constitution' was one of the features that formed part of the basic structure of the Constitution. It was also reiterated that 'India is a secular State in which there is no State religion. Special provisions have been made in the Constitution guaranteeing the freedom of conscience and free profession, practice and propagation of religion and the freedom to manage religious affairs as also the protection of interests of minorities...'.

Again, in the landmark judgement of *S.R. Bommai vs Union of India 1994* case, the Court held in clear terms that secularism is a part of the basic structure of the Constitution. The judgement made it clear that encroachment of religion into secular activities of the State is prohibited. It further added, 'We have accepted the said goal (of secularism) not only because it is our historical legacy and a need of our national unity and integrity but also as a creed of universal brotherhood and humanism. It is our cardinal faith. Any profession and action which go counter to the aforesaid creed are a prima facie proof of the conduct in defiance of the provisions of our Constitution...'. Justice B. P. Jeevan Reddy, in this case, argued that in the matter of state, religion was irrelevant.

Well, there has been some criticism too with respect to how the court decides on the matter of secularism in India. Some argue that there is a lack of consistency in interpreting the matter of secularism. They say that in some cases, the court has strongly supported the viewpoint that secularism is a non-amendable feature of the Indian Constitution. In others, it defines secularism, which seems to be more in consonance with the interests of the majority community; while in others, it privileges the interests of minorities. Well, this situation arises because the Indian Constitution has not defined the meaning of secularism in clear terms.

Another issue connected with this subject is with respect to the fact that it is the judiciary in India that determines what constitutes a religion. The Supreme Court is of the view that the problem with secularism in India is the demarcation between 'what are matters of religion and what are not...Religion is not defined in the Constitution and it is a term that is hardly susceptible of any rigid definition'. It has also been seen that courts have been deciding what constitutes the 'essential practices' of a religion. Subject experts argue that this increases the interference by the State in the matter of religion. However, supporting arguments are also presented. These groups believe that in order to achieve necessary social reforms, judicial intervention is needed.

7 Uniform Civil Code and Secularism

The Uniform Civil Code (UCC) aims to establish a consistent legal framework for all citizens, regardless of their religion, concerning matters related to marriage, divorce, and succession. As of now, these issues are governed by religion-based personal laws. UCC finds mention in Article 44 under the Directive Principles of State Policy (DPSP). It states that 'The State shall endeavour to secure for the citizens a UCC throughout the territory of India'.

Insight Box

Constituent Assembly debates on UCC

During the Constituent Assembly debates when the Constitution was being drafted, the discussion on the implementation of a UCC was noteworthy due to the arguments presented both in favor and against it. Congress leaders following the ideals of Jawaharlal Nehru believed that a UCC was integral to India's identity as a secular state. In contrast, certain Muslim opponents argued that their personal laws were a fundamental aspect of their religion, and thus, the State should not interfere in such matters. Some Muslims contended that their personal laws related to divorce, marriage, and inheritance were derived from the Quran and, therefore, should remain unalterable. However, there were others who acknowledged the eventual need for a uniform code but believed that the consent of the Muslim community had to be gradually obtained and that the time for its implementation had not yet arrived. In the end, the objective of a UCC for India was left in the status of a 'directive principle' included in the Indian Constitution, which said that 'the State shall endeavour to secure for the citizens a UCC throughout the territory of India' (Article 35 in the Draft Constitution; Article 44 in the present Constitution).

We may, thus, say that since Independence and after the adoption of the Indian Constitution, the matter of continuation of 'personal laws' has not been fully clarified.

The issue of UCC has been in discussion since the time of independence. Various debates and discussions took place on this subject in the Constituent Assembly. The practice of following personal laws results in different treatment of citizens across religious groups. For instance, in some religious and customary personal laws, the legal marriageable age for Muslim women differs from that of others. Certain religious and customary practices permit polygamy and polyandry, while others do not. Likewise, the criteria for divorce and alimony vary across different religious laws.

The issue of enacting a UCC gained momentum, particularly during the famous *Shah Bano* case of 1985. In this case, the Supreme Court ruled that Shah Bano, a Muslim woman who was divorced by her husband, should be given financial support for maintenance. However, this was against Muslim personal laws. Subsequently, this decision was overturned by the incumbent government.

On the one hand, religion-based personal laws (laws concerning marriage, inheritance, and other family matters) can be seen as manifestations of community-specific rights that are protected by the Constitution.

On the other hand, some individuals perceive these laws as contrary to the fundamental tenets of secularism because they result in unequal and unjust treatment of women. It is anachronistic to see that different religions in India, all citizens of the same country, are governed by different inheritance laws.

It is to be understood that such internal conflicts are part and parcel of any complex democracy, especially in India. There is always room for reform. Personal laws can be reformed in a manner that upholds both minority rights and gender equality, ensuring that they reflect principles of fairness and equal treatment between men and women. However, such reforms should be brought only after consultation and the consent of all religious groups, especially minorities. There cannot be coercion in enacting such codes. The state needs to act as a facilitator by supporting liberal and democratic voices within every religion.

Debate Corner

Should personal laws rooted in religion be subject to reform by the State, or would such intervention undermine the constitutional guarantee of religious freedom in a pluralistic society?

Insight Box

Dr B.R. Ambedkar on the relationship of personal laws (Hindu, Muslim, Parsi, etc.) to religion:

The religious conceptions in this country are so vast that they cover every aspect of life from birth to death. There is nothing which is not religion and if personal law is to be saved I am sure about it that in social matters we will come to a standstill....I personally do not understand why religion should be given this vast expansive jurisdiction so as to cover the whole of life and to prevent the legislature from encroaching upon that field.

In Support of UCC	Against UCC
Necessary to promote gender equality and national integration.	UCC could infringe upon religious freedom and might clash with religious practices.
Personal laws based on religion can sometimes lead to discriminatory practices, especially against women.	India is a diverse nation with various cultures; different communities should have the right to maintain their distinct customs and practices.
UCC would reinforce the principles of secularism in India.	Minority communities would be unable to maintain their essential religious practices. Without minority protection, our secularism would turn into majoritarianism.
Implementation of the UCC will make legislation in terms of succession and divorce easier and will oust a lot of outdated religious personal laws.	UCC is not a fundamental right. It is part of directives only. Thus, there should not be any coercion, and nothing should be done without consent.

Insight Box

Current Status with Respect to UCC

The 22nd Law Commission of India has sought views and ideas of the public and recognised religious institutions about UCC. The Commission has received more than 75 lakh suggestions. The overwhelming response from the stakeholders show the importance and relevance of the subject in the minds of the people. A UCC emerging from such wide consultation and brainstorming is more likely to be accepted and implemented.

Society Today

The Uniform Civil Code, Uttarakhand, 2024

It is an Act to govern and regulate the laws relating to marriage and divorce, succession, live-in relationships, and related matters. This Code applies to all residents of Uttarakhand, even if they reside outside the State, irrespective of their religion. Uttarakhand has become the first State in the country to have enacted such a Code post independence. As of now, State of Goa follows a UCC based on the Portuguese Civil Code of 1867.

Important features of the Code

1. Scheduled Tribes have been exempted from the Code.
2. Marriage: Compulsory registration of all marriages within 60 days of solemnisation. An unregistered marriage will also have legal validity. However, non-registration of marriages may attract fine.

3. Uniform age for marriage: Minimum 18 years for females and 21 years for males for all religions.
4. Prohibition on Bigamy or polygamy: Bigamy and polygamy have been prohibited for all communities under this Code.
5. Prohibited practices: Practices such as halala, iddat, triple talaq, and child marriages have been prohibited across all religious communities.
6. Divorce: Various divorce methods including talaq-us-sunnat, talaq-i-biddat, khula, maba'arat, and zihar, are punishable with imprisonment.

   Any extrajudicial mode of divorce such as customary divorce deeds or panchayat divorces is to be penalised.
7. Live-in relationships: Mandatory registration of all live-in relationships within a month from the date of entering into such a relationship.

   If live-in relationship is not registered, there is provision for imposing fines or even imprisonment. The Code also provides for legal recognition to children born out of such relationships.
8. Property rights: The Code provides for equal property rights for sons and daughters, irrespective of religion.
9. Adoption: Since the Code does not provide for a uniform adoption law, The Hindu Adoption and Maintenance Act (HAMA) and the Juvenile Justice Act (JJ Act) will continue to be applicable.
10. Guardianship and Custody: The Code does not amend the existing law on guardianship and custody of children, meaning the prevailing laws on this matter will continue to be valid. Ordinarily, father is considered the guardian, while the mother is the custodian.
11. The Code does not include the members of the LGBTQIA+ community in its ambit.

Marriage Mandatory registration within six months; ban on polygamy and child marriage (minimum marriageable age of 18 for women and 21 for men)	**Live-in relationships Mandates** registration to provide legal recognition, thus ensuring rights of partners and children. But penal provisions raise questions over the right to privacy	**Applicability** It applies not only to state residents but also its natives living elsewhere
Divorce Uniform divorce grounds across communities; practices such as triple talaq, iddat and halala criminalised	**Inheritance** Equal property rights for sons and daughters; children born out of live-in relationships, surrogacy and adoption are treated as legitimate heirs	**Exemption** Scheduled Tribes are exempted, allowing them to continue following their customs

Table 10.1: Key provisions of Uttarakhand UCC

Critical analysis:

1. The code seeks to promote *gender equality* across communities by having a common law and eliminating the discriminatory practices with respect to marriage, divorce and inheritance.
2. The Code respects different religious beliefs and cultural practices by allowing marriages to be conducted as per the individual's religious custom and ceremonies such as "Saptapadi," "Ashirvad," "Nikah," "Holy Union," etc.
3. The Code aims to simplify complex legal procedures related to divorce, inheritance, maintenance.
4. Regarding live-in relationships, the Code ensures better legal clarity by making its registration mandatory. If women in such relationship are deserted, they can seek maintenance. Thus, there is financial support and safeguard for women in case of abandonment.
5. Some experts also believe that giving legal sanction to live-in relationship can prevent false cases.

The Code, however, is not without its share of criticisms. Some of them are discussed below:

1. One of the criticisms is regarding violation of the right to privacy of live-in partners under Article 21 of the Indian Constitution. The registration process can be seen as an intrusion on the privacy of adult individuals.
   - In fact, the Code provides for imprisonment as punishment in case of non-registration of such relationships.
   - This provision has the potential to promote *moral policing* in the State.
2. In the case of live-in relationships, if either partner is between 18 to 21 years of age, the authorities would intimate their parents.

   In India, when an adult couple - 18 years or more - can marry without parental consent, questions arise as to why they cannot be in live-in relationship without parental knowledge. It tends to undermine the autonomy of adult individuals.
3. On this issue of maintenance in live-in relationships, only the women can claim maintenance on the ground of desertion. Thus, there is *gender bias* in this provision.
4. The code does not address the issue of LGBTQIA+ community. It may invite discrimination against them in the State.
5. Critics also argue that this Code goes against Art 25 and 26 of the Indian Constitution, which provides for religious freedom and allow the religious communities to manage their own affairs.

Despite its limitations, the Code provides for a more gender-just and uniform civil framework with respect to issues of marriage, divorce, maintenance, inheritance. It also fulfils the goal as mandated in the Directive Principles of State Policy (DPSP) of the Indian Constitution. Its effective implementation can provide much-needed guidelines for other States who are also in the process of enacting similar Code.

8 Future and Way Ahead

If one considers the issues of communalism, religion-based politics, corruption and value-free politics, poverty, and unemployment, then secularism seems to be under threat. These are the forces that have the potential to thwart the progress of secular forces in India. Apart from this, the issue of growing fundamentalist tendency, in which certain religious factions consider only their religion to be true, can create further impediments to the growth of secularism in India.

Thus, it is important that the nation divert its attention to some of the immediate and long-term needs so that such prohibitive forces can be tackled. A few aspects to focus on are as follows:

1. First, it is well understood that unemployed youth can easily be induced to think and act on communal lines. Thus, the chances of deep-rooted secularism will certainly brighten with more economic progress and reduced levels of unemployment.
2. Value and ideology-based political strategies need to be promoted. Citizens need to be made more aware of the fall-outs of divisive politics and how they impact overall national progress and development.
3. Efforts may also be made to create a situation in which women and children across religious groups enjoy similar rights in terms of marriage, inheritance, and property rights. Whether this solution can be achieved through the Uniform Civil Code or reform of personal laws is a question of public debate.
4. Also, in the present times, the forces of social media have become stronger in spreading polarising content. Such content can cause friction among various social and religious groups. These narratives need to be countered effectively.

Insight Box

Sabarimala Temple Issue

This case study is a classic example where religious beliefs seemed to be in direct confrontation with the principle of gender equality. Located in the Periyar Tiger Reserve (Pathanamthitta District, Kerala), the Sabarimala Temple is considered to be the abode of celibate deity Lord Ayappa. As the presiding deity is believed to be 'Brahmachari', women of menstruating age were customarily not allowed entry in the temple.

Travancore Devaswom Board, the autonomous body managing the temple had argued that exclusion of menstruating age women was an 'essential practice' for the religion. It further argued that the Board had right to manage internal affairs under Article 26 of the Indian Constitution.

But others pointed out that such exclusion was discriminatory and violated women's right to equality guaranteed by the Constitution. The question of women's entry went up to a Constitution Bench of the Supreme Court. In September 2018, it was held that such exclusion was unconstitutional. It held that such social exclusion of women was violative of Right against Untouchability and the Board could not maintain customs that violate the principle of gender equality.

This is just an example of how the state and, more so, the judiciary has intervened in religious matters in India. Such intervention has sometimes been seen as judicial activism and at other times as judicial over reach.

Insight Box

Jiyo Parso Scheme: A Case Study

The Indian Model of Secularism allows the State to make positive interventions in religious matters. One example of this is the Jiyo Parso scheme run by the Ministry of Minority Affairs. Launched in 2013-14, the goal of the scheme is to arrest population decline of this already small community and thus help it thrive as an equal member of this multi religious country. This is perhaps one of its kind example where state is encouraging specific religious community so as to save it from extinction.

Additional Readings

1. R. Bhargava, *Secularism and its Critics* (Oxford University Press, 1999).
2. Secularism. *Political Theory Class 11 NCERT*, Chap..
3. V.M. Tarkunde, *Secularism and the Indian Constitution* (India International Centre, 1995).
4. S.Y. Quraishi, A walk through the several decades of Indian secularism. *Outlook* (dated on 9 Nov 2022).
5. S. Padhy, Secularism and justice: A review of Indian Supreme Court judgments. *Economic and Political Weekly* (2004).
6. P. Benu, BL Explainer: What is the Uniform Civil Code all about? *Businessline* (July 2023).
7. P. Joshi, The case against Uniform Civil Code. *Business Line* (June 2023).

8. S. Mishra, UCC: Law Commission gets over 75 lakh responses as deadline for suggestions ends. *The Week*
9. D.E. Smith, *India as a Secular State* (Princeton University Press, 1963).
10. Uttarakhand first state to bring UCC into force (Hindustan Times: Feb 2025)
11. Decoding the Uniform Civil Code: A Critical Analysis of Uttarakhand's Landmark Legislation (Manupatra: May 2024)
12. Uttarakhand Uniform Civil Code | Making a beginning (India Today: Feb 2025)

Previous Years' Questions

1. How do the Indian debates on secularism differ from the debates in the West? (2014)
2. How the Indian concept of secularism is different from the western model of secularism? Discuss. (2018)
3. What are the challenges to our cultural practices in the name of Secularism? (2019)
4. Are tolerance, assimilation and pluralism the key elements in the making of an Indian form of secularism? Justify your answer (2022)